Portraits of "Primitives"

Portraits of "Primitives"

Ordering Human Kinds in the Chinese Nation

Susan D. Blum

ROWMAN & LITTLEFIELD PUBLISHERS, INC.
Lanham • Boulder • New York • Oxford

ROWMAN & LITTLEFIELD PUBLISHERS, INC.

Published in the United States of America
by Rowman & Littlefield Publishers, Inc.
4720 Boston Way, Lanham, Maryland 20706
http://www.rowmanlittlefield.com

12 Hid's Copse Road
Cumnor Hill, Oxford OX2 9JJ, England

Copyright © 2001 by Rowman & Littlefield Publishers, Inc.

British Cataloging in Publication Information Available

Library of Congress Cataloging-in-Publication Data
Blum, Susan Debra.
  Portraits of "primitives" : ordering human kinds in the Chinese nation / Susan D. Blum.
    p.   cm.
  Includes bibliographical references and index.
  ISBN 0-7425-0091-8 (alk. paper) — ISBN 0-7425-0092-6 (pbk. : alk. paper)
    1. Ethnicity—China. 2. China—Ethnic relations. I. Title.
GN495.6 .B57 2001
305.8'00951—dc21

00-036923

Printed in the United States of America

♾™ The paper used in this publication meets the minimum requirements of American
National Standard for Information Sciences—Permanence of Paper for Printed Library
Materials, ANSI/NISO Z.39.48-1992.

For my parents,
A long-awaited and much-overdue public tribute

In all Indian cultures "the Whiteman" serves as a conspicuous vehicle for conceptions that define and characterize what "the Indian" is not. . . . "The Whiteman" comes in different versions because "the Indian" does, and it is just for this reason—that conceptions of the former constitute negative expressions of conceptions of the latter (and vice versa)—that in rendering Whitemen meaningful, "the Whiteman" renders Indians meaningful as well.

Keith H. Basso, *Portraits of "the Whiteman"*

C ONTENTS

ILLUSTRATIONS

FIGURES

MAPS

TABLES

PREFACE

Most countries in the contemporary world are far from homogeneous; some, such as Japan, have small foreign populations; some, such as Italy, have collected people from adjacent regions and attempted to unify them; some, such as the United States, are composed of people from all corners of the earth; some, such as India, are diverse in virtually every way. This book is about China's diversity. In proportion to some nations, China is not especially heterogeneous. Only 8 percent of its population is officially considered to belong to ethnic minority groups. Yet, in a nation of 1.3 billion, that small percentage translates into 104 million people—the size of Mexico's entire population. The minorities live on all of China's borders with other nations, and they occupy lands last incorporated into the modern nation of China.

How does a huge, not entirely industrialized nation cope with this challenge? The world provides an assortment of lessons, of which the Chinese case is one example. If you were the czar of China's ethnic policies, what would you do? Emphasize commonalities? Eradicate differences? Celebrate differences?

This book concerns ethnic minorities in China, but from the perspective of the majority group. The Han, officially counted at 92 percent of the population of the People's Republic of China, are also heterogeneous. Yet their differences are glossed over in many contexts when the topic is ethnicity. In some ways, then, a focus on ethnic difference is useful for emphasizing the unity of the Han and, by extension, the unity of the nation-state of which they constitute a majority. Much work has been done by the government to encourage unity of the Han nationality.

At the same time, appreciation of the quaint aspects of the lives of ethnic minorities has been fostered, especially in the 1980s and 1990s, usually in the context of discussions of Han modernization. In contrast to the Han, most minorities are clearly "primitive." In many ways, the differences between the Han and minorities serve to celebrate the Han, and thus China's, twentieth-century achievements.

This book is an exploration of how successful such work has been. It looks at how "human kinds"—the categories by which humans are sorted into an orderly framework—pattern in a variety of contexts. I argue that much information as it filters into ordinary people's consciousness is sketchy, but it nonetheless demonstrates a kind of order. This order has some resemblance to that proposed by official conversations about human kinds but is not identical to official ordering. *Portraits of "Primitives"* is concerned with representing the models of the human kinds that people in the city of Kunming, the capital of Yunnan province in southwest China, may convey in various ways.

The tasks confronting people who wish to provide some order to the messiness of human kinds is certainly not unique to China. People everywhere (including anthropologists and other social scientists) attempt to create such order. What are the human categories of each society? The salient ordering principles may differ. In some places, social "race" may predominate; in others, religious differences are most noticeable. In some places, differences are celebrated, in some tolerated, in some forbidden. In some places, fine distinctions of class constitute the main concern of members of society; in others, the primary concern may be physical strength. But in all societies, people distinguish groups from other groups. All humans have models of human kinds, whether physical, cultural, linguistic, or personal attributes make up the relevant features. An understanding of the salient features of human kinds in China can contribute to our understanding of how ordinary humans analyze their world and of how many diverse ways there are to bring order to the complexity of the human universe.

ACKNOWLEDGMENTS

In the course of writing this book, I have benefited from a wealth of assistance. As any anthropologist knows, bonds of obligation increase along with integration into society. I must now be fully bound and weighted in the world. My fear is of missing the mark and inadvertently forgetting someone.

My first expressions of gratitude must be to individuals and institutions that helped me in my fieldwork. My first research was supported by a dissertation grant from the Committee on Scholarly Communication with the People's Republic of China (now the Committee on Scholarly Communication with China) of the National Academy of Sciences. My host departments were history and Chinese at Yunnan University, where my two advisors were Professor Lin Chaomin and Professor Li Zhaotong. Assistants included Ma Jing and Xue Caide. A second trip came along with a teaching obligation, when I took eleven students from Colorado to Kunming. A third trip, funded by the American Philosophical Society for a different project, permitted me to update and confirm my earlier accounts. Though I was not yet an anthropologist, I enjoyed the time I spent teaching English in 1982 at the Jiangsu Educational Institute in Nanjing. I have profited from conversations and friendship with Deng Lan, Ding Yuanren, Jiansheng Guo, Li Gen, Li Ping, Ma Ruoyu, Pu Fengying, Angela Tang, Tao Naikan, Yang Guosheng, Yang Ping, Zhao Zhengmin, and Zhong Ming. Other friends in China have been Jeff and Carol Book, Margaret and Colin Dennis, Lucien and Bonnie Miller, and Gerry and Molly Schwartz.

I wish to single out Susan McEachern of Rowman & Littlefield Publishing Group, whose enthusiasm and professional guidance in bringing this book to light have been invaluable. Dru Gladney made extremely helpful suggestions about improving the manuscript, and copy editor Shana Harrington contributed greatly to the final version. Cindy Tursman stepped in to oversee the final production.

My next debt is to the Department of Asian Languages and Cultures and the Center for Chinese Studies at the University of Michigan. My teachers there—William Baxter, James Crump, Kenneth DeWoskin, Robert Eno, Shuen-fu Lin, Harriet Mills, Donald Munro—made sure that I could read texts in classical and modern Chinese and situate them within the sweep of Chinese civilization. In the department of anthropology, my teachers were Alton Becker, Paul Dresch, Sergei Kan, Conrad Kottak, Bruce Mannheim, Sherry Ortner, the late Roy Rappaport, Aram Yengoyan, and especially Norma Diamond. Norma guided me through the thinking and practical arranging that are needed for any research with an astonishing grasp of the China field. At the end, Rob Burling agreed to join Norma, Bruce, and Bill Baxter on my committee.

At the University of Pennsylvania, Sandra Barnes, Mel Hammarberg, Webb Keane, Igor (and Barbara) Kopytoff, John Lucy, Victor Mair, Julia Paley, Greg Possehl, Peggy Sanday, Brian Spooner, and Greg Urban were brilliantly supportive colleagues. John Lucy has continued to be especially helpful.

Over the years, I've benefited from conversations about China, ethnicity, anthropology, and writing with Emily Chao, Nicole Constable, Sara Davis, Dru Gladney, Chas McKhann, Lucien Miller, Beth Notar, Louisa Schein, Shih Chuan-kang, Peggy Swain, Sydney White, Ken Wissoker, and Steve Harrell, who read three versions of this book. Others who read a draft include Lorri Hagmann and Naomi Quinn. David Kempf—a kind and as-yet-unmet colleague—responded to my Internet appeal and helped valiantly to track down the photograph of Zhon Enlai that appears in chapter 4.

At the University of Colorado at Denver, my colleagues in anthropology have been extremely cordial and encouraging. Tammy Stone and Myra Rich (of History) both kindly read the manuscript. John Brett, Robert Carlsen, Brenda Chalfin, Kitty Corbett, Antonio Curet, Linda Curran, Craig Janes, Steve Koester, Gene Mendonsa, Lorna Moore, Duane Quiatt, Jean Scandlyn, Mark Spencer, Tammy Stone, David Tracer, and Stacy Zamudio have read, listened, and been buddies and friends. Mike Ducey, Carl Pletsch, Jim Wolf, and Myra Rich in History have been friends and colleagues. Connie Turner held up more than her half of our sky.

Local Asianist colleagues in Denver and Colorado include Vicky Cass, Tim Cheek, Howard Goldblatt, Ginni Ishimatsu, Sylvia Lin, Dennis McGilvray, Sarah Nelson, Tim Oakes, Nancy Park, Alice Renouf, Julie Seagraves, Tim Weston, Marcia Yonemoto, Susan Cherniack Wei, William Wei, and members of the Colorado Asian Studies Salon, who have offered much-needed intellectual support and friendship in the sunshine and shadows of the Rocky Mountains.

My new academic home at the University of Notre Dame promises intellectual camaraderie and inspiration across and within departments. Its Institute for Scholarship in the Liberal Arts, under the direction of Julia Douthwaite, kindly assisted with the costs of reproduction rights.

For all-around friendship, which sometimes includes asking incisive intellectual questions and sometimes just sharing thoughts over wine or coffee, I must mention Hal and Risa Aqua, Christine Baier, Nikki Beach, Diane and Larry Blum, Nancy and Roy Crawford, Ted Duncombe and Marian Ullman, Jennifer Ethridge and Jianmin Fan, Micha'el Fahy and Jan Leigh, Brewster Fitz and Carol Moder, Marc Fitzerman and Alice Blue, Peter and Ketl Freedman-Doan, Rita and John Gasbarro, Tammy Hertz, Vicki and Konrad Howitz, Barbara Inwald and Mike Harris, Leslie King, Mariya and Yuzik Kotliar, John Lucy and Suzanne Gaskins, Lonnie Graham, Nora Kyger and Jack Szarapka, Lam Tong, Huei-min Lu, Susan Luerssen, Lori Lowenthal Marcus and Jerome Marcus, Kevin Martin, Robert Mayer and Elizabeth Williams, Maggie Miller and Doug Gertner, Tami Moore, Liane Morrison, Justine Nathanson, Sharalyn Orbaugh and Fadi Samaha, Jana Paschal, Vicki Phillips, Barbara Ritchen, Rebecca Archer Ritter and Tim Ritter, John Sackett and Elaine Lee, Bob and Betsy Sharf, Ann Sherif, Don Siegel, Jonathan and Yoko Silk, Craig Sloan, George Steinitz, Cathy Summer, John and Judith Temple, Camden Toy, Leslie Schaeffer Trento and Sal Trento, Marjory and Michael Ulm, Leslie Wright, Galit Zolkower and Bruce Kutz, and the Cory Elementary School community in Denver.

My husband's family—his sister, Anne Marie Jensen, and his parents, Gloria and Millard Jensen—have been loyal and helpful supporters, and their love has enriched my life more than I ever expected. Thanks for the *lagniappe*.

My own family includes an assortment of siblings among whom I first struggled to comprehend the problem of identity. Kathi Moss, Bobby Blum, Linda Long, and Barbara Blum made fun of me and distracted me and taught me about communal identity despite myself. Now we enjoy one another and our respective families, including David Moss, Tracye Valasco, and Ken Long, plus their eight progeny: Leah Elizabeth Moss, Henry Evan Moss, Natalie Mara Blum, Madeleine Ilana Blum, Cameron Vincent Blum, Weston Benedict Blum, Veronica Megan Long, and Sara Louise Long.

My parents, George Blum and Joyce Zuieback Blum, deserve much more than a mere book dedication. Their enthusiasm for travel and for understanding, their belief in my capabilities, and their own very firmly established identities have mixed with my variations on all those themes to propel me to carry on with this and other projects. They will be embarrassed (especially Dad!) but I wish to proclaim publicly how much I love and appreciate them. *Wan sui!*

My daughters, Hannah Neora Blum Jensen and Elena Oriana Blum Jensen, are the sun and moon of my life (don't ask which is which!). They care about my writing and my work, but they also make sure that I remember to have fun and laugh. Without them there would be no point in doing anything.

Lionel Jensen has once again been my anchor and my mirror, my sounding board and my chef, my cheerleader and my critic, my true friend. There are no words to explain what a mensch Lionel is in public and private, always working for justice and kindness—along with flawless bibliographies and spelling. His sense of perspective on what matters has always kept me on track; we take turns keeping each other optimistic. Let us move forward to celebrate the bounty that we have sown together.

PART I

ETHNICITY
IN CONTEXT

AGAINST AUTHENTICITY: SELF, IDENTITY, AND NATION-BUILDING

I sat on a bus winding through the lush mountains of subtropical western Yunnan, going from Ruidian to Mangshi on the Burma Road in the Dehong Dai and Jingpo Autonomous Prefecture. The stones of the road's surface had been placed by hand decades earlier to smooth the travel of goods from India through Burma and into China, supporting U.S. efforts to assist the Nationalists in defending China against further incursion by the Japanese. India and China, even the provincial capital (Kunming), to say nothing of the United States, felt infinitely distant from here. Burma seemed closest.

There was nothing drab about the landscape. Banyan trees shaded areas for resting; fields of greens patched together, terraced, testified to the land's fertility. Socialist architecture had not quite taken over; buildings were of bamboo, and temples were of white and gold. Roads were marked with distance from Beijing in impossibly huge numbers: 3,400 km, 3,401 km. . . . How could decisions in such a far-off place influence the texture of life here? The region did not even switch to daylight saving time in the summer; people called it "Beijing time." What could a person born and raised in these mountains possibly have in common with a Shanghai native, a cadre from Tianjin, an entrepreneur from Guangzhou? All nominally Zhongguoren (Chinese), the people's differences appeared much greater than the similarities. The area appeared almost to be a timeless, untouched part of Asia, where authentic, colorful ethnic people could be found living traditional lives. It was hard to imagine that behind this dreamlike world lies a high-stakes game concerning the very definitions and connections of the Chinese nation.

Before me was a woman of the Dai ethnic group, clearly identifiable as Dai by her headgear: a piece of pastel cloth wound impeccably around her head, above a high forehead. Yet sitting just a foot or two away, I could see that in fact this ever-so-traditional-looking turban was a machine-made, department-store-bought terrycloth towel (see figure I.1). Like the fierce-looking New Guinean photographed on the cover of a recent issue of *Time* magazine (Sept. 23, 1991), a plastic drinking straw piercing his cheek, this was a case where found objects served unintended purposes, by which minorities established their separateness. The meaning "difference" came across clearly.[1]

This book discusses what "difference" means in the context of Chinese nation-building. Difference is critical to definitions of unity; how difference is regarded, how much is tolerated, and what difference contrasts with are all matters explored here. I look especially at how those considered "the same"— that is, the so-called Han majority—regard ethnic minorities, and at the relationship between the political economy of China and the psychological construction of images of others. I do so by close examination of language used in speaking about ethnicity and identity and of responses to psychologically

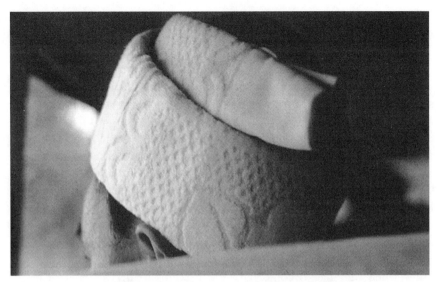

Figure I.1   A Dai woman's head covering

oriented tasks. The aim is to discover patterns in presuppositions, in models held of identity, both self-identity and identification of others.

I unpack, for instance, the meanings of moments like the following:

In January 1997 at the Minority Village just outside Kunming, a young Lahu woman told me and my friend, whom I'll call Li Kun, how she came to Kunming at age thirteen because her grandparents and parents wanted her to get to know and marry a Han. She said she has met nineteen or twenty *xiao huozi* (guys) and may be ready to marry one, now that she's nineteen years old. Then, we asked, what would your children be? Lahu. Where would you live? Kunming—though she would take her groom home to meet her family. Would she teach her child the Lahu language? No. Then why have the child be Lahu? Because you get special treatment, she's heard.

We both shook our heads and walked away, talking in Kunming's perfect light, shaded by the blossoming cherry trees. We didn't quite know how to comprehend this: a young woman hired to represent her ethnicity to the world, crassly—was it crassly?—planning to marry up, to get "superior" opportunities, pushed away from home when American girls are just leaving Girl Scouts behind. And my friend, who is Han and whose husband and son are Bai, told me that this special treatment—not needed in her husband's case because he scored second in the province this year in the college entrance exam—did not apply to all minorities. Special treatment (*youdai*, or *zhaogu*) was the common association with being minority in Yunnan but was often misunderstood. She and her husband let their son choose his nationality, which he could do as the child of parents of "mixed" ethnicity. Their son chose to be Bai—but at the time he was only seven years old!

The day before, I had also been with this family. Little Yongyong heard someone say, in a different context, that Han weren't *laoshi,* honest, unlike some minorities, and he said, *"Dan wo mama shi Hanzu, wo mama shi laoshi"* (My mother is Han, and she's honest [emphatic *shi*].). He is a great defender of the Han, to whom he is closest kin. He accepted his identity as Bai, in contrast to his mother's, but was nonetheless attentive to what was said of the Han.

And Li Kun went on to say that when she met her husband, she didn't know he was Bai. (It was an arranged marriage, by the way, of two college-educated city people in their twenties.) When she found out, she didn't know what it meant *(bu zhidao shi shenme yisi),* because according to their family history they are from Nanjing, where there are no Bai; she didn't know when they had become Bai. And it seems to her to be *kong, jia*—empty, false, with no content—Bai in name only. They don't speak Bai; their home, clothes, food—everything is exactly the same as among Han.

Li Kun criticized those who rely on ethnicity for its alleged social advantages. She emphasized her husband's capability and the fact that he didn't have to get extra points on the college entrance examination. (Bai in Kunming don't get extra points anyway for provincial-level exams because they are not disadvantaged educationally with respect to the rest of the province.) Her very young son's choice of ethnicity had to be sentimental rather than practical and calculating, since he couldn't possibly grasp the ramifications of his choice. And her saying several times that her husband's family's Bainess did not set them apart from the Han she knew suggests that for her, as for most Han, a *zhen* (real) as opposed to a *jia* (false) minority is one whose cultural identity is *shi* (full) as opposed to *kong* (empty). This identity should be full of visible differences, the kinds displayed at minority villages and museums. Li Kun's comments suggest too that there might have been cultural conflicts, and perhaps difficulty, if the Bai person she married had carried a real, full life of Bainess.

Or it could be that she thought I would believe that minority identity involves a kind of visible cultural content and form, knowing as she did that I am an anthropologist. She is an English teacher, has taught Chinese to foreigners, and is very interested in getting along with foreigners. So perhaps her story about her family's ethnic connections was intended to share what she thought were my assumptions about ethnicity. And if this is the better explanation, she thought I assumed ethnicity was about authenticity.

The purpose of including such stories is to show that the quest for authenticity, like that for the Holy Grail, ends in failure, though the search itself turns up unimagined treasures. Discussion is often of what is "really" a property of this or that minority. What one finds are rather more like the emblems of minority identity, to use Michael Moerman's characterization, borrowed in turn from Meyer Fortes (Moerman 1965:1218). The fashion-show-like performances of minority dances, in which all minorities are played by a few actors, homogenized by bland music and sameness of fabric, consist principally of parades of purported minority costumes. Purists might prefer retaining minority people in a more authentic drab mode, arguing that in the past, the colors were not so bright and that this is inauthentic. But the minority people themselves like the chance to be more flashy and smooth. In this book I discuss what desires are fulfilled by such demonstrations, why the state sponsors them, and why ordinary people flock to witness the displays.

The Chinese state and the intelligentsia who lead it have been involved for over a century in defining China's character, *guocui* (national quintessence), as a previously dynastic empire sought to transform itself into a nation-state. Dynastic empires are much less concerned with the subjective identities of their subjects than are nation-states with those of their citizens. Nation-states attempt to govern through compliance, not only threat of force; in order to gain the cooperation of those citizens, the citizens must feel that they have a stake in the nation's fate. For such voluntary identifications to form, the state itself must orchestrate a daunting array of activities designed to create a united polity, eventually from the inside out.

The larger issue considered here concerns contemporary Chinese nationalism and self-identification. Nationalism is very much an idea still undergoing realization in China. It is not clear that the idea of nationalism has been internalized among classes other than the intelligentsia. Peasants' primary loyalties are to their villages or regions, and minority groups who have been welcomed with a vengeance into the greater Han nation are often thoroughly uninterested in such hospitality (see, for example, Dreyer 1976:130–31).

In the West, many scholars argue that the age of nationalism is at an end (Hobsbawm 1990, Anderson 1991, Appadurai 1996; but also see Duara 1995), that the world has tried it out and witnessed a period of success but that it is now failing. The unit of a nation, they argue, is the wrong size to achieve a stable identity. At most, by mustering symbols—especially that of a common language—of this "community" that can only be imagined, a nation can gel for a while. How much diversity may be contained within the boundaries of a single state is unclear; fragmentation along ethnonational and ethnolinguistic lines has been the common fate of plural nations in places like Yugoslavia, Czechoslovakia, and the Soviet Union, as each group attempts to bring about the self-determination that nationalism promises. Nationalism as an idea is often fostered by an elite or ruling class that works hard to inculcate an imagined community in every citizen's mind.

In China, the largest of all nation-states, leaders have continued their work in attempting to create just such a community. The task is daunting. The people of inland and coastal China, the educated and illiterate, urban people and rural, plains dwellers and inhabitants of mountains, northerners and southerners, Han and ethnic others: the goal is to make them all Zhongguoren, people of China, who can speak a common language of identity, if not a literally common language. In China the language of identity tries to use the language of difference to strengthen itself. Whether it will succeed is unclear.

The Chinese state declares itself a "multinational unified country," with a fixed number of identifiable ethnic groups guided by the more advanced Han, yet its approach to the issue of national minorities has been mixed. On the one hand, it does not accept the idea of separatism, so these disparate peoples must somehow be contained within the nation, fostering a tendency toward assimilation and unity. On the other hand, it does accept the idea of some degree of cultural self-determination (as in the autonomous areas), respecting people's customs and practices (to some degree), especially in recent years, and fostering a tendency toward dissolution and division. Similarly, the state professes admiration for the differentness of its ethnic others, while pushing for the eradication of that difference through the "inevitable" modernization of the nation, even at its periphery. The theoretical claim is that all nationalities will eventually wither and die. Meanwhile, nationalities' differences remain and are in some ways supported.

One aspect of the modernization project has been to develop a sense of pride in China's achievements. One explanation for the state's engagement in the issue of ethnicity is that it hopes for benevolence and cohesiveness on the part of the Han, especially by contrast with the minorities. The Han are by far the majority—about 92 percent of the population—and have generally higher educational levels. They are thus in positions of relative advantage and have a corresponding obligation to serve as leaders. By contrast with the "backward" and "primitive" and "less cultivated" and "illiterate" nationalities, the Han may indeed feel that they have attained the modern world of progressing nation-states. This book argues that the specific aspects of ideas of ethnic identity cannot be understood except in conjunction with the nation-building project that has occupied China's governments since the beginning of the twentieth century.

This book examines some of the ways distinctions, boundaries, and contrasts are drawn among various groups. Just as the state's policies are inconsistent, attitudes toward China's ethnic others are likewise multiple. The seven portraits in part 2 show how wide a range of attitudes there may be.

I suggest that those differences that fit within the cognitive frameworks already existing are those that are salient, understandable, and likely to endure. The state—like individuals—emphasizes those differences and identities that make categories clearer, and the examples that are selected (song-and-dance performances, photographs of costumed young women in rural settings) are repeated and repeated and repeated, until the "made-ness" of these images has been replaced with the naturalness of the categories. I describe the organizing principles of this system, one among many possible ways of conceptualizing identity in China.

SITUATING DIFFERENCE

Western scholars who focus on ethnicity in China have been reaching a kind of consensus on the nature of the ethnic group in China: from an outside (objective?) observer's point of view, it appears as if ethnicity is constructed, created by the state and often perpetuated by the groups themselves, grouping together people with few common characteristics and separating groups that perhaps have something in common (see, for example, Harrell 1990, Mackerras 1994, 1995, Keyes 1995, McKhann 1995, Brown 1996). We tend to agree that Chinese policy has vacillated, that it is employed to further the aims of the state with regard to various foreign-policy and domestic-policy considerations, that it was modeled on the policy of the former Soviet Union and the very imperfectly imported ideas of self-determination. We agree as well that policy often bears little resemblance to application, and that notions like autonomy (*zizhi;* lit. "self-rule") are not necessarily what the words would lead one to believe (see Dreyer 1976). We also know that the state celebrates ethnic diversity while urging ethnic minorities to evolve toward greater "civilization" (see Harrell 1995a).

Many scholars also agree that ethnic identity may involve *belief* in shared descent, *whatever the actual facts.* That is, an old (several decades old) question about whether ethnicity was primordial (descended from some ancient common ancestors) or circumstantial (chosen freely for the benefits accruing in given circumstances) has pretty much been shown to be a question of viewpoint: from the participants' viewpoint, ethnicity is primordial, while from outside observers' viewpoints, it is often demonstrably circumstantial. The observer cannot fruitfully focus on one without at least glancing at the other.

A further consensus is developing in postcolonial studies as well as in psychology and several other disciplines: one cannot define a self without having an other with which to reflect the self. *Alterity,* the study of otherness, has become a major field of investigation, studying the practices of (to use a verb I find displeasing to the ear, if useful) "othering" in various societies: how societies create "others," often inferior others, to serve as scapegoats or subalterns ("sub" = inferior; "alterns" = others) to bear the brunt of social criticism. In American society, we have ethnic groups, women, people of minority sexual preference, people with disabilities, elderly people, children, and so forth to fill this role. Such a list, of course, raises the suspicion that, in some way, most of us are others, even subalterns, and that the notion of an overarching "self" that contrasts with those "others" is actually a minority fiction. Why then is this ideological notion of "minority" status maintained? Analysis of class in a capitalist system provides some answers.

In China, however, the background for such identity is different. China is not entirely a capitalist system, nor is it a socialist system (Watson 1994). China's subalterns are perhaps fewer and perhaps more numerous (it depends on how one defines this category in that society); perhaps all but the highest-level cadres are subalterns. China claims to have a good deal of ethnic/"racial" homogeneity. Yet ethnicity is in many ways flourishing in contemporary China; groups classified as ethnic minorities are increasing in population and increasing in proportion to the rest of the population. So how do we fruitfully regard the issue?[2]

I have chosen to approach the understanding of popular notions of ethnic identity in contemporary China by looking at how a third group (the "majority"?) regards ethnicity—not the participants, the ethnic groups themselves, and not only the state, but rather those who hold the ethnic minorities to be "other" to themselves in China. Like Charlotte Linde in *Life Stories* (1993), I look at some of the forces that converge in shaping these viewpoints. These forces include state attempts to instill a sense of fraternity between the so-called Han majority and their ethnic brethren; the pervasive state discourse about modernity and its assumption of a single evolutionary direction; what Linde calls "expert systems" and their transformation into nonexpert "explanatory systems"; a sense of economic scarcity combined with policies favoring the ethnic minorities; a history of extolling the virtues of high Chinese literate culture; the recent promotion of a standard Chinese spoken language as superior to all other forms of speech; long-standing local and regional loyalties; suspicion of religious activity; urban prejudice toward country folk and lowland prejudice toward mountain dwellers; and the power of long-heard ideologically charged phrases to reappear in certain contexts but not in others.

As this list of factors suggests, there is not one single direction of influence. Chinese people are not parrots of the party line—or not only parrots. They are not active "resisters" who see through the fallacies of teleology—or most people are not. They do not all share a pure sense of Han nationalism—but some do, sometimes. These factors push and pull, making people open-minded and closed-minded, making them tolerant and affectionate toward ethnic minorities at the same time that they are dismissive and intolerant. People talk for themselves and think for themselves, but they and their language are not created anew with each individual birth; they use words and thought patterns that precede their own existence. They are agents, and they have some control over their own actions, but they live within loose structures that anthropologists used to call "culture."

This book attempts to complicate the discourse about ethnicity in China. At the same time, it seeks to suggest methodological issues that could be applicable to other complex societies as well. The similarity with Mexico is startling, for instance, in the way the state sponsors ethnological museums and folklore/ethnic festivals, though there are also numerous and instructive differences between the two situations. The Chinese case is unique yet also has implications for some other social settings. The focus is on cognitive prototypes, but these cannot be understood apart from the many contexts, including political and historic, in which they are shaped. Unlike many works on psychological anthropology, this book is set in an unfamiliar setting, requiring that some of these contexts be spelled out. Unlike many works on ethnicity in China, it does not take focus on politics and policy as its ultimate aim.

So far I have been saying "Chinese society," but what I really mean is the local context in which I did my research: the city of Kunming, in the far (from Beijing) province of Yunnan. All experience is local, and one generalizes from that only with trepidation. But in a nation-state like China, a local orientation exaggerates boundaries that are actually quite permeable. What we see is one particular constellation of local, regional, and national factors (see Augé 1995). I think there are lessons to be learned about China in general from my conclusions, but I would not be surprised by flat-out disagreement from researchers in other Chinese settings.

I also expect readers to ask themselves a question with each portrait: "But what do the Naxi think?" "What do the Yi believe?" I agree that knowing how people regard themselves is more central than knowing how others regard them. But for four reasons I have chosen to restrict this book to the latter: (1) Our sources on Yunnan's minorities' self-conceptions are still sketchy. Fieldwork has only begun to be permitted, and the young scholars of my cohort have just begun to publish their results. (2) I did not want to do a study of a single group. Such studies are extremely valuable, but I wanted to explore the entire ethnic universe of Kunming. (3) The attitudes of the dominant group toward the dominated (to grossly oversimplify relations) are extremely significant for understanding relations between groups and even the cultural bases of policy. (4) The Han as a group have not been discussed in the literature on ethnicity. I wanted to examine their self-conception as it contrasts with their views of others. But if the portraits send the reader off in search of more native portrayals, I will consider my efforts well rewarded.

I generalize in the portraits that follow about how "Han in Kunming" regard ethnic minorities. This is not to say I believe all Han think with one mind. In fact I regard the category "Han" with great suspicion. It has been used only in this century to describe the citizens of a nation-state, and only in contrast to minorities. With each occurrence, the reader should include a "so-called." A question that demands to be researched is the following: How psychologically real is the category "Han"? When I began to conceptualize this research, I thought I would find an answer. But I don't think I have, at least not a sufficient one. I believe that this lack of an answer is largely but not completely because the category "Han" has very little importance except contrastively, rhetorically.

So "Han in Kunming" is an artificial generalization. But without the ability to generalize, anthropologists can write only verbatim transcriptions of single conversations (cf. Crapanzano 1980). While these transcriptions have a place, I believe our methods should be more diverse than unitary. I have tried to include (representations of) the voices of people speaking, but I have also synthesized from the many verbal and nonverbal interactions I have had in Chinese society over the course of a twenty-year career (so far) studying China.

Since I first read Keith Basso's *Portraits of "the Whiteman"* (1979), in which he showed how some Apaches joked by imitating "Whitemen," I have been intrigued by the idea that identities may in many ways be observed contrastively in terms of unconscious models and prototypes that are often not directly articulated. Like many who write about identity for example, Mc-Farlane [1981], Wetherell and Potter [1992], I too am concerned about economic and political argumentation over rights, privileges, and interests, sometimes in the form of ethnic differentiation and squabbles such as the ones that have reached their logical conclusion in Bosnia, where religious and class differences have emerged as "ancient ethnic hatred." In Burundi, former schoolmates now act as Hutus and Tutsis who hate one another. Identity is, in this view, more about boundaries than about contents.

In one way, then, this book explores what some would regard as the components of racism as it is defined in such studies as *Mapping the Language of Racism* (Wetherell and Potter 1992) and *Communicating Racism* (van Dijk 1987). But this term contains a condemnation that I do not intend. This work is concerned simply with the categories and components of identity in southwest China and as such is concerned more with psychological structure than political consequence. In this way, its affinity is more with *Reading National Geographic*, where Lutz and Collins (1993) examine the way the popular magazine functions in American life, reading Americans' readings as evidence of what American culture had to be like in order to support such views of others. Political considerations are always important too, of course, but there are psychological forces just as strong that operate in politically saturated environments.

Portraits of "Primitives" looks at "portraits"—the images of ethnic groups held in general in Yunnan by people who are not experts or policy makers. It includes the kinds of knowledge one would need to have a conversation about ethnicity in southwest China, the background meanings and definitions that provide a baseline in everyday life. I use the term "portraits" deliberately. Like the portraits painters produce, trying to represent their subject's nature through a version of the "face" they present to the world (Brilliant 1991, Walker 1983), these portraits are selective representations of their subjects. Incomplete, tendentious, momentary. . . . I offer representative representations of groups often not personally known to the persons doing the representation.

In some ways, most people familiar with Kunming should not learn very much. They should recognize the everyday nature of the portraits; if I'm successful they will say "I never thought of it that way, but that is what people think about XYZ," or what Deborah Tannen calls "the aha factor" (1981:146). I have attempted to capture the common sense views of identity upon which political and intellectual action or transformation can occur. But one person's common sense is not necessarily another's (Geertz 1983, Gramsci 1957:58–75). Subalterns come in all different flavors, and the Chinese subalterns in southwest China have a particular bouquet of flavors, not knowable merely by projecting from a Western experience. Nor do evaluations necessarily proceed the way one might expect. For instance, McFarlane's study (1981) of the way Shetlanders regarded themselves and "Incomers" is very similar to mine in many ways. (It's also very different from mine because of the multiplicity of "others" in southwest China.) In McFarlane's study, the incomers are believed to have certain qualities such as conspicuous consumption. That sort of quality as a characteristic of minorities is never mentioned in southwest China (though it exists!), but honesty is—with honesty not necessarily valued in and for itself. This book contributes to anthropology in offering a view of the way common sense works in one corner of the world.

You will find here a preliminary sketch of the kinds of identities that people in Kunming construct for people they consider to be different from themselves. The topic is in service to a broader question: How do people in this large nation-state, where identity has both an official, political valence and a more personal dimension, view the human world they inhabit? This question has implications for the study of prejudice, of ethnic relations, of nation-building, and of cognition in general. These are the aspects that will be considered here.

As this book's title suggests, many Han view many minorities as "primitives" *(luohou)*. I use the term loosely: not *all* ethnic minorities are considered primitive, but by far the majority of them are. I hope I am not engaging in the usual blasting of China for not adhering to Western anthropologists' disdain for "outdated" theories of cultural evolution. Stocking (1982), Todorov (1984); Torgovnik (1990), Lutz and Collins (1993), and others talk about the way Westerners have looked with condescension on groups that were merely different from those observing them. Buoyed by firm faith in cultural relativism, we look at China and see our own discarded theories everywhere.

I see my job rather as one of describing, of seeking patterns. Some of Chinese ethnic policy can be explained by the Chinese reliance on theories that come from Morgan, Engels, Marx, Stalin, Darwin. I might wish it were otherwise, but it isn't. So I spend my time here chronicling the consequences of this presupposition. Sure, I dislike the Chinese government. But we all have presuppositions, and it has been fairly persuasive. This is not to say that a single system exists in China, just as it does not exist in "the West." Explanatory systems can coexist; worldviews can be fragmentary and inconsistent.

Chapter 1 introduces the setting for the research I conducted in Kunming, describing the city, the national and historical context, and my own research situation and methods. Chapter 2 presents the conceptual models I employ in pursuing questions about cognitive models of identity, drawing on ideas from cognitive anthropology (especially the idea of cognitive prototypes), social psychology, and Charlotte Linde's notion of explanatory models (1987, 1993). Chapter 3 introduces some prototypical aspects of minority identity, which are discussed in greater length in the chapters that follow. I discuss briefly the topic of Han identity and compare it to the study of "whiteness" in the United States. Also in chapter 3, I begin to introduce the idea of *salience*. It is the need to explain the relative salience of the various ethnic groups that motivates the core chapters of the book.

Part 2 consists of four chapters that present portraits of seven commonly invoked ethnic groups (Dai, Wa, Tibetan, Hui, Naxi, Yi, and Bai) and the prototypes surrounding them. With each portrait, I add one significant component of the popular cognitive model of ethnicity. Finally, in the conclusion, I discuss the significance of these schemata for Chinese identity in general, for Chinese nation-building in modern times, and for the cross-cultural study of identity.

CHAPTER ONE

FIELDWORK IN KUNMING: COGNITIVE AND LINGUISTIC ANTHROPOLOGICAL APPROACHES

China declares itself a multinational state in the first line of its constitution and spends much money and labor in matters related to its ethnic groups. Inheriting some practices from the dynastic leaders who preceded them, borrowing some from the USSR, and inventing others, leaders of the People's Republic of China (PRC) have established many policies and theories about nationality. These include categorizing and identifying distinctive groups (currently numbering fifty-five minorities plus the Han), locating them on a scale of "primitive" to "advanced" on the basis of their economic and social practices, demonstrating "respect" through preservation of their "customs," fostering harmonious relations among them, establishing "autonomous areas," and controlling or eradicating undesirable practices.[1] The state sponsors academic research on ethnic groups, supports publishing efforts in minority languages, and establishes educational policies as they pertain to ethnic minorities. Some areas have bilingual schools, while in others the speakers of minority languages are expected to learn the Han language.

These policies are detailed in many recent works. I list them here because they form part of the backdrop for my study. Policies fluctuate, at times favoring "autonomy" while at others favoring "assimilation," to use Thomas Heberer's terms (1989). What Stevan Harrell calls the "civilizing project" (1995a, 1995c) occurs within a broader cultural context, shared by bureaucrats and ordinary people alike, of categories and prototypes that resonate with other aspects of identity.

To see how these categories were instantiated, at official and popular levels, I conducted fieldwork in Kunming, in Yunnan province. My focus was on ordinary representations in order to sketch cognitive models for identity.

KUNMING, YUNNAN:
COSMOPOLITAN LOCALE ON THE BURMA ROAD

I chose Kunming for this research for several reasons: it is known for its ethnic complexity, is touted in tourist information, and is located far from the more usual places in which research on contemporary China is conducted. Kunming is also far from centers of power—political, economic, cultural—and so has something of a marginal position even while it is indisputably and solidly within the Chinese nation-state.[2] I was interested in seeing how official ideas bubbled out into sites far from their origin.

Yunnan province in China's southwest is bordered by Burma, Laos, and Vietnam on its south, Tibet, Sichuan and Guizhou provinces, and the Guangxi Zhuang Autonomous Region on its west, north, and east

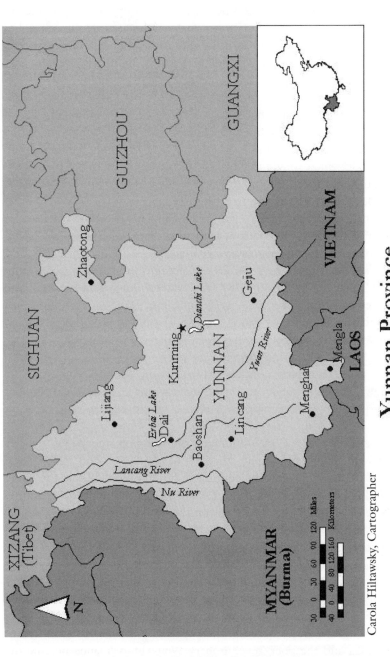

Yunnan Province

Map 1.1   Yunnan and Kunming

Carola Hiltawsky, Cartographer

(see map 1.1). Yunnan is ethnically and linguistically extremely complex, claiming to have the greatest number of ethnic groups of any province in China, with a third of its population non-Han. Its capital, Kunming, lies on the Yunnan-Guizhou Plateau at an elevation of about 1,900 meters. The proportion of its non-Han population is just slightly higher than that of China as a whole, at about 10 percent.

Despite its remote location from the perspective of "China proper," Kunming is an oddly cosmopolitan city as a result of its location on the old southern Silk Road (Xu, Wang, and Duan 1987) and the modern Burma Road and of successive migrations over several centuries and continuing until the present; it is increasingly the locus of inland southeast Asian trade from Burma and Thailand—including drug trade. Goods flow in from southeast Asia and out through Kunming to Hong Kong.

The name "Kunming" is that of an old ethnic group, known in Chinese sources for nearly two millennia, at least since Sima Qian (145–89 B.C.E.) mentioned it in his *Shiji* (Historical Records), "Treatise on Southwest Barbarians" (see Yu 1986, Liu 1991:25); it became the name of the city in 1276 (Xu, Wang, and Duan 1987:31). Marco Polo went through the major cities of Yunnan (contemporary Kunming, Dali, Baoshan; he called them "Yachi," "Kara-jang," and "Vochan") on his way out of China through Burma.[3] The province has been under continuous Chinese control only since 1253, during the Yuan dynasty, when soldiers of the Mongol court came to extend political control of the Mongol empire in the west. Many Mongols stayed, marrying local women. There are a number of Mongol enclaves remaining in Yunnan, where people claim descent from the soldiers who arrived in the Yuan.

The greatest wave of Han immigration came in the Ming dynasty (1368–1644), encouraged by the Ming founder Zhu Yuanzhang (1328–1398) and followed by continued immigration during the Qing (1644–1911) (Liu 1991:244–66). A further influx of outsiders—mostly from the east, with a large number from the Nationalist capital Nanjing— came to flee the ravages of the anti-Japanese and Civil Wars during World War II between 1937 and 1945, driven south and west by bombings, starvation, and a desperate quest for safety. Making a virtue of necessity, during the war an ad hoc constellation of professors "exiled" in Kunming from Beijing, Qinghua, and Nankai universities formed the Southwest Associated University (Xinan Lianhe Daxue, abbreviated Lianda) (He 1993:34, Israel 1998). Among this group were the anthropologists Fei Xiaotong and Francis L. K. Hsu and the poet/revolutionary Wen Yiduo. Lianda became the kernel of Yunnan Teachers' University (Yunnan Shifan Daxue), one of Kunming's many institutes of higher education.

Since 1949, a further wave of internal migration has brought people from every part of China, especially from contiguous and populous Sichuan province, to Kunming. Yunnan is one of the least densely populated provinces of China: Yunnan had an average of eighty-three people per square kilometer in 1982, compared with, for example, 175 in Sichuan, 265 in Hunan, 289 in Guangdong, 485 in Shandong, and 590 in Jiangsu (Banister 1987:298–99). Though Yunnan is often viewed as "backward," especially by the more privileged people from China's major cities, it is also seen as presenting possibilities for earning a livelihood precisely because it has not yet been "developed."

All of these influxes of people have left their mark on Kunming, as have the sinicized minorities drawn to the provincial capital. The metropolitan population is around four million, yet Kunming until the early 1990s had the character of a sleepy, backward town.[4] Horse carts still provide a great deal of the transportation in town, though in recent years they have been restricted to the ring road that circles the city and to smaller streets. Building is proceeding with furor, as elsewhere in China, and old, charming (though reportedly unsanitary and clearly land-consumptive) neighborhoods of wooden houses built around courtyards are being destroyed as soon as the cities can afford to make way for ostensibly more efficient and certainly more capacious new concrete and brick apartment complexes, usually of six to eight stories. After its chalk outline is drawn in the dirt, a new building can be completed in a matter of months—sometimes in just weeks (see figure 1.1).

The remaining old neighborhoods have uneven pavement winding along narrow alleys, often with lovely traditional murals painted on specially provided plaster squares, interspersed with the inevitable blackboards reporting on the latest political, social, or public health campaign. In 1991, campaigns were announced for fighting drugs, catching mice and rats, increasing adherence to the one-child policy, respecting the land-management laws, and encouraging the celebration of the seventieth anniversary of the founding of the Communist Party in 1921. The focus changed quickly; in 1994, people were urged to take better care of themselves by, for example, relaxing and eating better food. The state reaches out into every alleyway, but its reception cannot be determined by the officials who prepare the slogans from their central place nor from the mere presence of such written slogans. Weary after decades of changing political winds, people seemed completely uninterested in these expressions of political correctness. There were new con-

Figure 1.1a

Fig. 1.1b   A building constructed quickly

cerns blowing through China, mostly about economics and building. While, in 1991, people grumbled about the state, by 1994 it was largely irrelevant. Progress, modernization, development, making, building, planning, and starting were the common terms I heard. Even Kunming was seen as eligible for transformation, though it is one of China's slower capital cities to join the modernization train.

Most of the old houses have no indoor plumbing, so people rely primarily on public toilets, which have a familiar odor. Kunming's ubiquitous banks of open, blue garbage cans are emptied regularly but filled just as frequently. On the hottest summer days, the stench can be powerful.

A few traditional teahouses endure, where mostly old men but sometimes old women congregate to smoke, drink an often-refilled cup of tea, read the paper, play chess, and tell stories. Near Cuihu (Green Lake) Park in the northwest quadrant of the city, retired people play croquet on the sand; inside, old men play traditional instruments and sing opera during the day. This park is also the location of regular gatherings involving "ethnic" singing and dancing, especially Yi (see Thrasher 1990). On Sundays the parks fill with parents and children, and with students taking breaks. Many people wear fine clothes in celebration of what is their sole day of rest, posing for photographs at particularly presentable spots. (Since 1996, the weekend officially includes two days of rest, Saturday and Sunday, so even students go to school only five days a week now.)

Kunming's weather has earned it the nickname "Chuncheng" (spring city), and the phrase most often offered to describe Kunming is "siji ru chun" (four seasons [that is, year-round] like spring), just as New York might reflexively be called "the Big Apple" or Denver "the Mile-High City." Street life is consequently evident all year, with open-air markets, repair persons, snack suppliers, newspaper vendors and, near the glitzy hotels appropriate for foreigners, minority people—mostly Sani women—selling handicrafts (see Swain 1991) or offering to change money for a rate higher than the official one (on the so-called black market). Peasants come in from the nearby peri-urban areas to sell vegetables and fruits; most people agree that the fruit sellers are much more unscrupulous than the vegetable sellers, because the former buy fruit at wholesale prices and sell at a huge profit, while the latter merely sell produce that they or their fellow villagers themselves grew.

The markets are a miracle of abundance and color, and with each visit to China I find more variety available. Whereas, in 1982, the only fresh produce I could find in Nanjing in the winter were a few spotty apples, by 1994 in Kunming there were four kinds of apples, along with oranges, bananas, plums, peaches, litchis, longyan, melons, pineapples, and more. And this when fruit is peripheral to the Chinese diet, with the vegetables and other foods regarded as the main focus of the markets.[5]

Kunming's physical environment is quite pleasant, with many carefully tended flower collections, including perennial poppies, hollyhocks, and geranium bushes, maintained by both individuals and institutions. There are palm trees and evergreens, and even eucalyptus. Kunming's many parks, such as Cuihu (Green Lake; mentioned above) and Daguan (Broad Vista) parks, are quite lavish and popular, and the city's zoo is one of the more humane and lovely ones in China.

Several of the large Buddhist temples, notably Yuantong Temple, have been recently, and garishly, refurbished, as have several of the mosques, with vivid primary colors contrasting with those in the older, faded temples or as-yet-unrestored portions of temples. Indeed, Islam and Christianity, both Protestant and Catholic, have many adherents, including people of minority nationalities, and Kunming's Hui (Chinese-speaking Muslim) residents are an important segment of the population, large enough to support several mosques (see Song 1985 on Kunming's religious activities, especially pages 138–43 on the Hui). All is not smooth sailing, however. One of the mosques most active in 1991 had burned just before my visit in 1994. A poor, angry Hui woman who lived nearby took me to her ramshackle house to confide that the fire had been set with the acquiescence of officials because the department store adjacent to the mosque wanted to expand into its area. She claimed that the fire department was deliberate in not responding. The official caretaker, herself Hui, told me that it would soon be rebuilt, more beautiful and "authentic"— that is, like in the Middle East—than ever. The woman speaking in the shadows of the destruction said that this was a lie, and that the mosque would never be rebuilt. But in late 1996 I was told that it was indeed being constructed—but it was inaccessible to outsiders.

Indigenous religious activities flourish as well; on the street one can buy spirit money and various "spirit goods, " such as paper clothing and cars to burn for ancestors. One can stumble across neighborhood shrines tucked away in corners; some of them were renovated during my stay. Fortune-tellers are increasingly common, often using sticks or other divining tools.

Kunming is home to many colleges and technical institutes, bringing students from throughout the province and even from outside Yunnan. Yunnan University and Yunnan Teachers' University are the most well-known, but there is also the Yunnan Minorities Institute, just a few blocks down the ring road from the other schools. The Yunnan Academy of Social Science does not conduct classes but is a further source of intellectual activity, with at least two branches concerned solely with minority affairs. Kunming also has Kunming Teachers' College, Kunming Metallurgical Institute, Kunming University, and Yunnan Institute of Technology. Other institutes of higher education pop up occasionally, willing to take in students who can pass the entrance examination—and pay tuition.

ETHNIC AND LINGUISTIC VARIETY

Occasionally on the streets one can see people who by their dress and demeanor are obviously from elsewhere: overseas Chinese from Hong Kong or Taiwan in clothes that strike a Westerner as stylish; mainlanders from coastal areas in Kunming for business; foreigners on tours, studying, teaching, or surreptitiously evangelizing; peasants in town for the first time; and ethnic minorities still in their native clothing (see figure 1.2). In most cases it is women who wear traditional costumes; the exception is Tibetan men, mostly sellers of such (illegal) medical supplies as tiger paws and deer horn, wearing striped cloth draped across one shoulder.

The human diversity of Yunnan, and of Kunming, is promoted in tourist guides prepared for foreigners and natives; even a World Wide Web site for Yunnan speaks mostly of its minorities (1996). Yet the street life is much less evidently plural than such guides suggest. Inquiry into ethnicity in Kunming always provokes the suggestion that one would best "go down" *(xia qu)*—a

Figure 1.2   Ethnic minorities visible in Kunming

symbolic descent—and do investigation *(diaocha)* in a minority area. It is true that the lives of ethnic minorities in their least acculturated form must be investigated in such rural settings, but relations between groups can be explored in sites of great interaction.

Still, the fact that informants frequently acknowledge only rural minorities is significant for the pursuit of the Chinese construction of ethnicity. Ethnic minorities are most often assumed to be peasants by Kunmingers.

ATTITUDES TOWARD LANGUAGE

Language evokes extremely strong responses. Differences in the kind of language spoken—what ordinary people call "dialects" and "languages" and "accents" but linguists and anthropologists simply call "linguistic varieties"—may produce attitudes ranging from indifference to disgust to attributions of mystical power to devotion.[6] These attitudes have everything to do with the political and cultural situations in which the languages are found; attitudes toward linguistic varieties are invariably attitudes toward the speakers of the varieties. Strongest negative feelings are often found toward varieties spoken in places where social conflicts occur. Would Americans so readily say that German is "guttural" if we had not fought Germany twice in world wars and if stereotypes of harsh, cruel military commandants were not prevalent? North Americans often dislike the sound of Cantonese, but Chinese speakers of various dialects overwhelmingly find Cantonese to be pleasing, a consequence at least in part of the contrasting social standing of the Cantonese in the two societies. (My impression is that the large number of tone classes in Cantonese also figures into the dislike English speakers feel for it.) Chinese often say that Japanese sounds like inconsequential chatter and is not pleasant to hear at all—not surprising given the fact that Chinese in general abhor the Japanese.

Attitudes toward languages, and the speakers of languages, are often held subconsciously, especially where there is not a good deal of ideological concern or metalinguistic discourse about such matters. Such attitudes, if discernible, can be fruitful sources of information about relations between groups, between the speakers of varieties of languages and their hearers (Lambert 1972, Gumperz 1982a, 1982b, Woolard 1983, 1989).

One of the principal sources for the views of ethnic differences that I describe in the rest of this book is attitudes expressed about apparent linguistic differences. As I will explain below, I use reports about attitudes toward linguistic varieties to reveal attitudes toward the speakers of those linguistic varieties.[7] Ultimately, I claim, such attitudes reveal how identity and difference are conceptualized and talked of in China. For instance, people in Kunming find others who speak Kunminghua (Kunming dialect) to be likeable at the same time that they admire—from a distance—speakers of standard Mandarin and disdain speakers of minority languages.

The linguistic situation in China is quite complex, with eight major language groups: Sinitic, Altaic, Tibeto-Burman, Mon-Khmer (Austroasiatic), Austronesian, Tai, Hmong-Mien (Miao-Yao in Chinese), and Indo-European. The languages spoken by ethnic minorities belong to all of these language families (see Ramsey 1987). The Sinitic group is further divided into seven or eight "dialects," and each of these includes countless local dialects (topolects, in Victor Mair's helpful translation of *fangyan*; Mair 1991), many of which are mutually unintelligible. While Mandarin *(Putonghua)* is defined as the official, standard language of China, there are many situations in which it is not spoken or is spoken in a "nonstandard" way. Official treatment of linguistic diversity in China has fluctuated, but the predominant goal is that everyone learn Putonghua. It is assumed that in time the other varieties will fade away through disuse, but perhaps this "utopia" lies far in the future. In my fieldwork, I found a tremendous degree of vibrancy of local varieties in Kunming. For convenience I have divided them into five general categories:

1. Putonghua (standard Mandarin),
2. Kunminghua (Kunming dialect),
3. Yunnanhua (Yunnan dialect(s)),
4. other Chinese dialects, and
5. other languages (including minority languages).[8]

In Kunming one hears little standard Mandarin spoken in the course of everyday life. As the provincial capital, Kunming attracts people from throughout China in addition to those from throughout Yunnan. The most common linguistic variety in Kunming is Kunminghua (Kunming-language), a dialect of Mandarin that is phonologically quite distinctive. It has few to no off-glides (Mandarin *sui*, Kunminghua *sei*). Like Mandarin it has four tonal categories, but each is more "flat" than the corresponding category in standard Mandarin. For instance, fourth tone in Mandarin moves from the highest to the lowest levels of the speaking register, while in Kunminghua it moves only from a middle level to a low level. In addition, there are both grammatical constructions and lexical items that set it apart from other Mandarin dialects. A speaker of only standard Mandarin might take a week or two to comprehend even simple Kunminghua with ease—and then only if willing to learn it.

Kunming residents speak Kunminghua at the market, in hospitals, school corridors, post offices, and restaurants, and on the public bus (everybody but the driver, who announces the stops in Putonghua). On private buses, the so-called *mianbaoche* (bread loaf vehicles—named after their shape), even the stops are announced in Kunminghua.

Putonghua is spoken in Kunming mainly by outsiders to the area whose positions permit them to evade the social pressure to learn Kunminghua: teachers, officials, foreigners. People like small-time entrepreneurs must make the effort to learn the local variants; if they do not, they are seen as having unjustifiable attitudes of superiority. Only people from Sichuan can get away with retaining their own dialect; Sichuanhua and Yunnanhua together are considered variants of "southwestern Mandarin," and Sichuan people—Sichuan *haozi,* "Sichuan rats," who scurry everywhere away from their crowded province in search of opportunity—are familiar, comprehensible neighbors. The Yunnanese may dislike them automatically, as I learned when a neighborhood ice cream and yogurt seller (age 13) had his eye blackened by a Sichuanese bicycle repairman working the same alley and commented, "What do you expect from a Sichuanese?" It seems to be the dislike of people nearly alike, competing for what is perceived as a "limited good" (to use George Foster's apt phrase [1967]): an economic niche in an increasingly competitive service sector.

People from the countryside speak their own variants of Yunnanhua and, while understood, are immediately recognized as being from somewhere else, *shanqu* (mountain area) or at best *xiancheng* (county seat). People say that every town in Yunnan has its own dialect, some variant of southwestern Mandarin, and many ethnic groups have their own languages from several different language families. The differences between other varieties of Yunnanhua and Kunminghua lie principally in vocabulary and phonology, including tones, and do not constitute an insurmountable barrier to communication. Still, they are markers of identity; within the context of Yunnan, Kunming is the big, shiny, fast-paced city that sets the standard for a variety of matters. Kunminghua is the dominant linguistic variety in Kunming, at least as measured by frequency of use.

Some people in Kunming speak what is referred to derogatively as "Mapu" or "Majie/Magai Putonghua" (street Putonghua). This term indicates the speakers' failure to succeed in speaking Putonghua despite their desire to do so. It is usually said of people with lower levels of education from the countryside or suburbs of Kunming. Though I have heard people use it humorously to describe their own language, it is usually used derisively of others.[9]

Kunminghua, Yunnanhua, and Putonghua (even Mapu) would seem clearly to be different varieties. Indeed, people never hesitated to identify what they heard, confidently giving it an appellation. Though Kunminghua and Yunnanhua (variants of southwestern Mandarin) are easily intelligible by speakers of the other, so much so that participants in a single conversation will use them with each other, Putonghua is rather more different. Nearly all educated people, especially young people, can understand Putonghua, but they cannot necessarily speak it without effort, practice, and extensive exposure. The same is true for Putonghua speakers who may speak Kunminghua or Yunnanhua, with the difference that they may not be able to understand detailed conversation without practice, and there is no official channel for learning Kunminghua or Yunnanhua. Long-time residents may or may not choose to speak Kunminghua. The two are not merely different varieties of the same language, as, for example, are African American English and Standard American English, but are of different branches of Mandarin. For example, pronouns have different pronunciation, as do the tone categories, and there are regular phonological variants. The sum of these small differences is a considerable barrier to effortless communication. The following two sentences are indicative of the differences between the two varieties (the numbers indicate tones, with 5 being high in the speaker's vocal range):

Kunminghua: T'e^{22} ji^{44} sei^{22} la^{44}?
Putonghua: Ta^{55} ji$^{21(3)}$ suei^{51} le^{0}?
"How old is s/he?"

Kunminghua: xiao^{44} hom^{31}
Putonghua: xiao$^{21(3)}$ hong^{35}
"(my friend) Hong"

People who are willing to learn Kunminghua have to learn correspondences between sound categories, a fairly manageable task and one familiar to Chinese speakers of Chinese dialects. Minority languages in contrast are considered to be unintelligible by Han; with no genetic relationship believed to exist between Chinese and most minority languages, these minority languages are seen as truly "other" (if not foreign).

Minorities are signaled in the popular imagination by their clothing as well as their speech, while Han of various regions are distinguished primarily by speech. Clothing and appearance can certainly be employed as well, especially to assess a person's degree of sophistication or "class" (a term used advisedly in the context of this self-proclaimed classless society). Precise origin,

however, is seen as indexed by varying aspects of speech. Just as in the
United States, a Texan without the accompanying "accent" would be considered remarkable, so it is assumed in China that "accents" (*kouyin,
kouqiang, difang qiang*—different phonological patterns employed within a
given linguistic variety) and "dialects" (*fangyan*—different linguistic varieties) reveal the origins of the speaker.[10] Persons wishing to disguise their
identities must choose carefully the variety of speech used and make an effort to speak without the telltale accent. Emily Honig writes of Subei speakers in a stigmatized area north of Shanghai avoiding Subei dialect when away
from home to escape the disdain automatically directed toward Subei people
(Honig 1992:117).

Use of minority languages is legally permitted, at least in certain contexts
such as signs on government buildings in autonomous areas. Uneducated
minority nationality people in Kunming are likely to speak their minority language in small, private groups of conationals, but outside such settings they
speak either the local "Hanhua" (Han language—a term not used by academic students of language elsewhere in China) of their region (whatever
version of Yunnanhua is the local lingua franca) or Kunminghua. Putonghua
would be used only if an interlocutor initiated a conversation in Putonghua;
otherwise, a minority person using it would be seen as putting on airs.

One might expect the minorities institutes to be full of talk in minority
languages, but such is not the case: many of the minorities at the Minorities Institute are minority by classification, but in fact only one parent is of
that minority, the other usually being Han. And many of them cannot speak
their "own" language. Some can understand it, since their grandparents
spoke it, but a number of the students are urban minorities who are minority in name only. (This applies as well to minorities at Yunda and the other
colleges and universities in Kunming.) When I told a Chinese friend that I
had done some research on China's minorities and that I had particular interest in the Miao, he brought a Miao student to see me. We talked for a
while; I asked him about his parents, his hometown, his language. It turned
out that he had been raised in Kunming, that he did not speak Miao, and
that he had been to his ancestral village in Wuding county only once or
twice, finding it very dirty. His parents, he said, could speak Miao but not
as well as his grandparents.

Of course, in order to do well on the college entrance examination, the
student had to have been fairly well educated, even taking into consideration
the extra points given to most minorities and the fact that he was paying for
his education himself. The minorities that have received the "best" education
are in general those living in urban settings, usually dominated by Han; they

often come from the regional county seat. Many speak the Han language even at home.

In the linguistic marketplace in Kunming, languages have greatly differing amounts of power. In a national sense, Putonghua is powerful and desirable and is known to be a sine qua non for economic and occupational advancement in the state political system. Minority languages are permitted in all-minority regions, but monolingual speakers of minority languages tend to be confined to the obscurity of border areas. Regional and local languages remain the language of everyday life in about 30 percent of China.

Like the recent studies by Susan Greenhalgh of de facto and de jure family planning and the relative strengths of state and society in determining policy (Greenhalgh 1993, 1994), language use demonstrates a disjunction between state and society. The actual consequence of China's policy with regard to education of its ethnic minorities is considerably different from what the policy would suggest. While the numbers of minorities in higher education may be cited, we must recall that a good number of them—in Kunming, at least—are thoroughly sinicized, that is, they accept almost completely the practices of the greater Han culture, speak its language, and are virtually indistinguishable from the Han. Often they are the children of "mixed marriages," which in China means an ethnic minority and another minority or, more usually, a Han. ("Mixed-blood" marriages with foreigners is another issue, one that elicits great interest on the rare occasions on which it occurs [cf. Cen 1988].) This form of gentle assimilation promises to eradicate differences between minority and Han to a far greater extent than the more violent forms attempted during periods of political radicalism.[11]

Colored by the ideals of language standardization, responses to questions about what linguistic varieties are in actual use show some disagreement. People responsible for setting standards and acting as models may emphasize the successes of the promulgation of the standard. (A linguistics professor who was also an assistant dean at a university told me that 70 percent of the classes were conducted in Kunminghua.) Officials tend to present optimistic pictures of the work for which they are responsible.

I was able to get another view of language diversity through a group of students studying Western-style linguistics with a foreign teacher. During their unit on codeswitching and multilingualism, I asked the foreign teacher to ask what varieties of language were actually used by the students' teachers when they were in school. The responses—though not entirely reliable because they depended on memory and because they might have been shaped in the direction of increasing the reported diversity to please the foreign teacher—were quite revealing: only four out of twelve students responded that all of their primary school teachers used Putonghua. Of those four, two mentioned that there was a regulation about language use, and one qualified her response by saying that there was codeswitching even though the primary variety was Putonghua. Three of the twelve mentioned that their Chinese (language) teachers used Putonghua, while teachers of all other subjects used local dialect.

For middle school, three students recalled that all of their teachers used Putonghua, two said that most of their teachers spoke in Putonghua, and seven said that their middle school teachers spoke local varieties. One student commented that no teachers at her middle school spoke Putonghua outside class, but all spoke Kunminghua.

In describing the language use of their university teachers, interestingly only five of the twelve responded at all; one explanation is that they did not want to state frankly information that contradicted policy for identifiable individuals. (The students were currently in college; everyone knew who their teachers were.) Of the five who did respond, two said that all their professors spoke Putonghua, two said that most did, and one said that almost all did—in class. This distinction indicated that outside class, no matter what the ostensible regulations about teachers living exemplary lives in all aspects, teachers speak the varieties they feel comfortable with, which are often something other than Putonghua.

I conducted a more detailed survey of the linguistic division of labor among eighty-five people in Kunming, asking about the respondents' own language use in various contexts. Even assuming self-reports to be biased in favor of the prestige variety, these responses reveal enormous variation (see table 1.1). Of eighty-three usable responses (thirty-eight males, thirty-eight females, and seven who did not specify gender), only seven people, or 8.4 percent, claimed to use only one variety (and of those seven, three were from a factory, for which there was a total of thirteen responses). The impression one has from these responses is of a cacophony of dialects spoken in various settings, such as in the dormitory, where people claim to speak their preferred variety.

Dividing up the responses according to the institutional affiliation of the respondent (Yunnan University, the Kunming Metallurgical Institute [now the Kunming Metallurgical College], and the Kunming Metal Factory), then according to the hometown of each (Kunming, elsewhere in Yunnan, another province), we find some revealing patterns.

Most people use the local variety, which is named after the place, especially at home and in the dormitory. Travel reduces the number of varieties reported to be spoken, presumably because speakers attempt to find a lingua franca.

One can see that the language of instruction varies even at the most prestigious institution in the province. In fact there is more variation at Yunnan

Table 1.1: Language Varieties Used in Various Settings as Reported by Survey Respondents

Language Usually Spoken:		In dormitory	On street	In class	Traveling	Other
In general	*At home*					

YUNNAN UNIVERSITY

Students from Kunming

In general	At home	In dormitory	On street	In class	Traveling	Other
KMH (8)	KMH (8)	KMH (6)	KMH (7)	PTH (9)	PTH (9)	KMH (1)
PTH (1)	Han (1)	PTH (2)	PTH (2)	PTH (9)	KMH (1)	PTH (1)
		dialect (1)				depends (3)

Students from Yunnan

In general	At home	In dormitory	On street	In class	Traveling	Other
dialect (7)	dialect (5)	dialect (10)	dialect (7)	PTH (14)	PTH (20)	dialect (5)
YNH (4)	YNH (3)	YNH (3)	YNH (3)	dialect (7)	dialect (5)	depends (5)
Han (4)	Han (5)	Han (3)	PTH (5)	YNH (2)	Wuding (1)	PTH with PTH speakers (5)
PTH (4)	Bai (3)	PTH (2)	KMH (4)	Han (2)	Han (1)	Dong chuan (1)
Bai (3)	Dongchuan (2)	KMH (2)	Han (3)	Wuding (1)	Simao (1)	Wuding (1)
Dongchuan (2)	PTH (1)	Dongchuan (1)	Dongchuan (1)	Lincang (1)	depends (1)	Yuxi (1)
Tuodian (1)	Tuodian (1)	Baoshan (1)	Baoshan (1)	Gejiu (1)		
Baoshan (1)	Wuding (1)	Wuding (1)	Wuding (1)			
Wuding (1)	Jianshui (1)	Jianshui (1)	Jianshui (1)			
Jianshui (1)	Baoshan (1)	Chuxiong (1)	Lincang (1)			
Yuxi (1)	Xuanwei (1)	Lincang (1)	Gejiu (1)			
Lincang (1)	Yuxi (1)	Longchuan (1)				
Longchuan (1)	Zhaotong (1)	Gejiu (1)				
Simao (1)	Lincang (1)	all kinds of dialects (1)				
Gejiu (1)	Longchuan (1)					
	Simao (1)					
	Naxi (1)					
	Gejiu (1)					

Table 1.1: *Continued*

<u>*Language Usually Spoken:*</u>

In general	At home	In dormitory	On street	In class	Traveling	Other
Students from Elsewhere						
Chinese (1)	Han (1)	dialect (1)	PTH (2)	PTH (2)	PTH (2)	depends (1)
PTH (1)	SW Mand. (1)	PTH (1)	dialect (1)	dialect (1)	dialect (1)	
Hunan (1)	Hunan (1)	YNH (1)				
KUNMING METALLURGICAL INSTITUTE						
Students from Kunming						
KMH (13)	KMH (11)	KMH (11)	KMH (10)	PTH (12)	PTH (12)	KMH (5)
PTH (1)	PTH (4)	PTH (1)	PTH (3)	KMH (4)	depends (2)	PTH (2)
	Sichuan (1)				KMH (1)	
Students from Yunnan						
dialect (5)	dialect (5)	dialect (6)	PTH (10)	PTH (14)	PTH (13)	PTH (4)
PTH (3)	Gejiu (4)	Gejiu (5)	dialect (5)	KMH (1)	dialect (1)	depends (3)
Gejiu (3)	PTH (2)	English (3)	Gejiu (3)	English (1)	English (1)	Gejiu (3)
English (2)	Han (2)	PTH (2)	KMH (1)	Gejiu (1)		dialect (3)
KMH (1)	YNH (1)	KMH (2)	English (1)	dialect (1)		KMH (1)
Yuxi (1)	Jianchuan (1)	Xuanwei (1)				foreign lang.
Jianchuan (1)	Xuanwei (1)					
YNH (1)	Fujian (1)					
Xuanwei (1)						

(continued)

Table 1.1: Continued

Language Usually Spoken:

In general	At home	In dormitory	On street	In class	Traveling	Other
Students from Elsewhere						
PTH (1)	YNH (1)	YNH (1)	YNH (1)	English (2)	PTH (2)	PTH (1)
KMH (1)	PTH (1)	KMH (1)	KMH (1)	PTH (1)		depends (1)
		English (1)				
KUNMING METAL FACTORY						
Workers from Kunming						
KMH (5)	KMH (5)	KMH (5)	KMH (5)	PTH (5)	PTH (5)	KMH (3)
YNH (2)	dialect (2)	YNH (2)	YNH (2)	KMH (2)	KMH (2)	depends (2)
dialect (1)	YNH (2)	dialect (1)	dialect (1)	YNH (1)	YNH (1)	PTH (1)
depends (1)						
Workers from Yunnan						
PTH (1)	dialect (1)	dialect (1)	dialect (3)	PTH (2)	PTH (4)	PTH (2)
local PTH (1)	local PTH (1)	local PTH (1)	local PTH (1)	local PTH (1)		depends (1)
YNH (1)	YNH (1)	PTH (1)	YNH (1)			
Gejiu (1)	Jiangyang (1)		PTH (1)			
	Eshan (1)					

PTH=Putonghua
KMH=Kunminghua
YNH=Yunnanhua

University than at the Kunming Metallurgical Institute, a difference that may be attributed to the equivalent of what Labov termed "linguistic insecurity of the lower middle class" (1972:132): the students at the latter institution are trying hard to succeed, despite the fact that they have not managed to arrive at the best school. For them, using Putonghua in class (reported as 77 percent of the time, versus 62 percent of the time for Yunnan University students) may be perceived as the best route to success. Or, alternatively, they may be reporting such usage because they are aware of the greater prestige of Putonghua. Random observations turned up no instances of classes conducted in Putonghua at the Metallurgical Institute.

This, then, is the context in which I carried out my research: Kunming is a multilingual, multiethnic provincial capital with a fairly clear hierarchy of human categories and linguistic varieties. Official policies encourage assimilation, but in fact one finds a great deal of permitted diversity of practice in the 1990s. Understanding how people conceptualize and order this diversity is the basic goal of this book.

COMMENTS ON RESEARCH METHODS AND CONDITIONS

The fieldwork I conducted in Kunming, like all research in the PRC, was restricted and watched, and it required application for certain types of permission.[12] Yet, since I was working in the city, I avoided many of the bureaucratic battles that plague anthropologists trying to do rural fieldwork. I lived with my husband, a historian of China who taught English during our sojourn, and daughters (one in 1991, two in 1994) in a "foreign guest house" on the campus of Yunnan University, which assumed responsibility for me. This had both positive and negative aspects; without a host "work unit" one can accomplish nothing in China, yet such affiliation also facilitates surveillance. Mail routed through the "foreign affairs office" is read and often intercepted—and of course there is no alternative means of receiving it other than asking people to carry it in from outside China. Phone calls and visitors are monitored, and sometimes one is watched and listened to within one's own apartment.

Outside the university, however, I had great freedom to make acquaintances and pursue friendships. My Chinese friends might also be monitored; too-frequent visits from foreigners might raise eyebrows or provoke questions. If our friends were on poor terms with their neighbors, matters could be made quite uncomfortable. Still, we were frequently invited to dinner in people's homes, and they showed no evidence of nervousness about it. People came to see me, and only a few expressed reservations about having to register at the bottom of the stairway. Some openly expressed disdain for the whole matter of being monitored.

The fact that I was part of a family, with one child and a girl to boot—a curly-haired, fair-skinned, blue-eyed outgoing girl who began to learn Chinese—was extremely helpful in quickening relationships with new acquaintances and defusing suspicion. A summer trip in 1994 included our two daughters, then ages four and one. Many invitations seemed intended to gain closer access to our children, and people were invariably gracious and kind to both girls and to their parents. (See Cassell 1987 for a collection of accounts of taking children into the field.)

I have studied Chinese since 1977 and read and write modern Mandarin; I also read classical Chinese. Almost all of my interactions took place in Mandarin. Exceptions occurred when English students wished to practice English or, in the rarer case, when conversations in Kunminghua or minority languages were translated into Mandarin. I began to understand Kunminghua but could not speak it. I did feel my pronunciation of Mandarin became more like that of Kunmingers over time.

SOURCES OF INFORMATION

The sources of my information are of several sorts. Because some of what I wanted to know involved national-level policies, and because I did not work within a self-contained village, my methods were not limited to interactions with individuals.[13] For convenience, I will break them down into ten types.

Formal Interviews

The most standard source of ethnographic information is a series of interviews I conducted, arranged for the most part by a colleague as part of his responsibility in assisting me. They took place in his dormitory room, and he was present at all of them until he grew tired of them and their repetitiveness. The respondents he introduced were all college students, and I asked a fairly similar battery of questions of all of the students, though the format was more that of a conversation than of an interrogation or even of a questionnaire. My understanding of the issues I was researching evolved over the course of the interviews as did my technique, so the later ones were much more effective than the earlier ones, though they may still be compared and compiled. After asking permission, I taped the majority of the interviews, although I experimented with simply taking notes during some of them (when taping, I also took notes). With shyer students, the presence of the tape recorder combined with that of their teacher induced a bit of reticence. With bolder students, their teacher's presence mattered more than the tape recorder. The interviewees came in groups of two, three, or four, which initially concerned me because I had expected to interview people alone. I came to realize, however, that the fact that others were present made the event less anxiety ridden and less like a political interrogation. The cultural nature of interactions is often not considered by anthropologists doing fieldwork, but we quickly find out that our anticipation of particular kinds of speech events can't be met in fact (see also Briggs 1986).

I also asked several other people to go to my apartment and be interviewed. These people included students of my husband (two of them members of ethnic minorities), women who worked in the guest house, and friends.

Student Essays

I also made use of the fact that my husband and several foreign friends were English teachers at colleges and universities and assigned writing on various topics to their students. We discussed some of my interests, and several of them assigned topics germane to my work. I then typed out a copy of the 155 essays. The assignments included the following:

1. Write about ethnic minorities from the point of view of the Han and about the Han from the point of view of ethnic minorities.
2. Write about an experience that you have had personally with ethnic minorities.
3. What would paradise be like for you?

The mere act of writing, especially within an institutional setting, is likely to evoke a level of formality that exceeds that of everyday talk in most societies. Foreign teachers may elicit further reserve—or they may succeed in encouraging candor and personal revelation, though this would in any case be less than among trusted friends. (As a teacher, however, I can recall moments of shocking confession on the part of scarcely known students, even in the classroom.) So the essays are generally more formal than informal, but the fact that they are written in a foreign language means that the writers have not been able to use all the formality available to them in their own language.

The essays were written in English, for two different foreign teachers of English at two different institutions. This fact may appear to render them problematical, but there are a number of reasons for using them. First, the fact that foreigners were the known audience meant that students may have felt less constrained to produce what might be regarded as the standard version of the minority nationality story. Second, the foreigners were more amenable to addressing slightly unusual topics of their students than Chinese teachers would have been. We designed the topics together, accommodating my research interests while maintaining pedagogical integrity. Third, from comparison with other reports, stories, and so on, it is clear that in many cases the English used by the respondents was a direct translation of Chinese terminology. Fourth, there is a well-established vocabulary for discourse about ethnic others, as evidenced by tourist books, translations of scholarly books, and so on, from which the students were also able to draw. The principal disadvantage of using such essays is that many of the students were limited by their linguistic abilities in a foreign language. One set of fourth-year English majors at a prestigious university, however, demonstrated impressive facility in using what had become a comfortable linguistic variety. Some of the essays are gripping stories; others are full of delicate emotion. I edited only to make the English sound less awkward, without making it correspond to that of a native speaker.

With each batch of essays (beginning with a general one, "What is a minority?," not included here), I was able to refine the questions so that they went from very general to fairly pointed. They became correspondingly more personal and less formulaic, though there were many stereotypical formulations interwoven with other, more individual and idiosyncratic accounts. Novelty and originality are far less emphasized in Chinese education than in American education.

The Press

For a time I read six papers from the local, regional, and national press every day, collecting clippings of articles and pictures, which I then tabulated and compared. This process was especially useful for revealing the official viewpoints on various issues. *Renmin Ribao (People's Daily), Zhongguo Qingnianbao (China Youth News), Guangming Ribao (Illustrious Daily),* and *Yunnan Ribao (Yunnan Daily)* are most representative of official views, having undergone the greatest degree of scrutiny; *Kunming Ribao (Kunming Daily)* is slightly less concerned with national viewpoints; and *Chuncheng Wanbao (Spring City* [Kunming] *Evening News)* is filled with nothing but stories of local interest, which is not to say it is not also cleared through the appropriate channels. I read occasionally in the monthly *Minzhu yu Fazhi (Democracy and Law),* a fascinating compilation of shocking stories of drug smuggling, murder, deceit, and immorality intended to bolster the moral sense of its readers but probably proving more titillating to them than anything else.[14] I also picked up random editions of magazines and other publications to see what was being disseminated in various circles. I discuss the results in chapter 3.

Interviews with Officials

I interviewed two officials: Dai Meifang, director of the Education Commission of Yunnan Province and of the Office of the Yunnan Province Language and Literature Work Committee, and Yang Yingxin, director of the Office of the Yunnan Province Minority Nationalities Language and Literature Work Executive Committee. Both kindly agreed to meet with an inquisitive foreigner, permitted me to ask whatever questions I liked, and allowed me to tape-record the entire interview. I assume that they understood themselves to be giving me the most official views in Yunnan of the issue. Both of them were gracious and showed a great deal of sense and concern for the appropriate administration of current policy. They were critical of past policy but appeared to embrace the recent policy—though in one case one person admitted that the policy embodied a wish for the future rather than an accurate representation of the current state of affairs. They demonstrated detailed knowledge of both policy and practical circumstance. It is also clear that they had had contact with the people among whom their work was to be carried out, and that theirs was not entirely abstract, remote knowledge. My research assistant was present at both interviews, but there were no translators.

I also met and talked with a good number of scholars involved in minorities research, including linguists, historians, and ethnologists.

Classroom Observations

I was allowed to observe classes in a junior high school and an elementary school, which I did to see what the medium of instruction was, how "errors" in Putonghua were corrected (if at all), and what attitudes toward linguistic varieties were being inculcated. Because I was a foreigner, I was taken to observe the teachers with the "best" Putonghua.

Linguistic Identification and Evaluation Task

The most precise data I employ come from my administration of a variant of Wallace Lambert's "matched guise test" (Lambert et al. 1972); I call my test a "linguistic identification and evaluation task." The original test was designed to uncover attitudes toward English and French in Montreal in the 1960s by recording bilingual speakers speaking in English once and French once. The listeners were unaware of the fact that each speaker spoke twice, and they took each speaker as an individual. The listeners were asked to rate the speakers in terms of a number of features. The results showed clearly that bilingual speakers in their French "guise" were overwhelmingly perceived to be nice, poor, religious, and filial, while in their English "guise" were seen as educated, powerful, secular, and tall. Since Lambert first carried out his work, others have applied this methodology (for example, Woolard 1983, 1989, Giles and Saint-Jacques 1979), but always in clearly demarcated bilingual situations. Both French and English speakers can without difficulty identify the two languages in question, and the test was not intended to ask them to do so; such identification was rather a precondition of their ability to respond at all.[15]

My linguistic identification and evaluation task was designed to yield identification of a broad range of linguistic varieties spoken in Kunming as well as to elicit attitudes toward those varieties. Both Kunminghua and (other) Yunnan dialects are varieties of southwestern Mandarin and are known as distinctive to varying degrees. Putonghua is defined with regard to a fixed standard pronunciation, and speakers are judged to speak it with varying degrees of close fit to that single standard.

I recorded eleven speakers speaking sixteen varieties, then scrambled the order to mask the fact that several speakers were used more than once. The varieties included three instances of Kunminghua, two of other Yunnan dialects, five of Putonghua (standard Mandarin) spoken by people from various places, two of minority languages from Yunnan, and four of Chinese languages from other parts of China. Five of the speakers had "matched guises," that is, they spoke in two or, in one case, three different varieties. Each person read a passage—a joke—and some agreed to retell it in their own words. Those who did not speak in a Mandarin variety had to "translate" the passage into their own variety. Table 1.2 gives the identities of the speakers.

Eighty-five respondents from three different institutional settings (Yunnan University, Kunming Metallurgical Institute, and a factory) were asked to identify the variety of language; the degree to which it was *biaozhun* (standard); the place of origin of the speaker; the speaker's level of education, ethnic identity, job category, wealth, and suitability as a friend; and a vague category—*Zheige ren bucuo ma?* (Is this person okay?)—trying to get at the overall decency of the person.

I rely heavily on the results of this test in the following chapters, using them in conjunction with other sources of information. Since the actual identifications were nearly random, having little to do with the variety actually heard, the results yield a sort of free association with regard to ethnic and regional identity, similar to the projective tests used by psychologists. That

Table 1.2: Speakers in Linguistic Identification and Evaluation Task

Speaker no.	Native place	Ethnicity	Gender	Linguistic variety	Years of education	Occupation
1	Kunming	Han	male	Kunminghua	2	repair person
2 (= 12 = 15)	Lijiang	Naxi	female	Putonghua	11	floor attendant
3 (= 11)	Shanghai	Han	male	Shanghaihua	18	college professor
4	Baoshan	Kucong	male	Baoshanhua	5	gatekeeper
5	Kunming	Han	female	Kunminghua	15	administrator
6 (= 14)	Kunming	Hakka (Han)	male	Hakka	13	vocational college student
7	Dongbei	Han	female	Putonghua	18	college professor
8	Sichuan	Han	female	Sichuanhua	8	floor attendant
9	Jiangxi	Han	male	Jiangxihua	17	graduate student
10 (= 16)	Honghe	Yi	female	Yi	8	nanny
11 (= 3)	Shanghai	Han	male	Putonghua	18	college professor
12 (= 2 = 15)	Lijiang	Naxi	female	Lijianghua	11	floor attendant
13	Japan	- -	male	Putonghua	24	college professor
14 (= 6)	Kunming	Hakka (Han)	male	Kunminghua	13	vocational college student
15 (= 2 = 12)	Lijiang	Naxi	female	Naxi	11	floor attendant
16 (= 10)	Honghe	Yi	female	Putonghua	8	nanny

is, a vague stimulus (a Rorschach inkblot, an unknown language, an indistinct picture) is administered, and the response yields information about the concerns or cognitive patterns held by informants. In this case, the groups that came to the respondents' minds showed which groups were salient, and the characteristics they assumed to apply to the speaker reveal what models are held by informants.

Tourism, Museums, and Other Forms of Commoditization

Yunnan's ethnic diversity is evident in several concrete forms, including promotion for tourists, museum displays, photographs and paintings, minority artifacts for sale, a Minority Village *(Minzu Cun)* on Kunming's outskirts, and—probably the most widely known presentation of ethnicity in China—song-and-dance performances. I collected, visited, and observed as many forms of representation as possible.[16] To summarize what I observed, however, I will state only that (1) emphasis for foreign and domestic tourists especially is about Yunnan's ethnic diversity (the foreign tourists reciprocate with eager interest); (2) ethnicity is often equated with sexuality, depicted by lovely young women dressed in exotic costumes and jewelry—and sometimes scantily clad; (3) ethnic groups are often presented serially, as in the song-and-dance shows where all twenty-six of Yunnan's officially recognized ethnic groups must be presented; and (4) stylized representations of ethnic people and their artifacts are sold both by Han and by ethnic minorities themselves (see also Blum 1994, ch. 2).

Policy

Policy toward minorities is brought in as a sometimes-kindred, sometimes-antithetical counterpart of more popular cognitive models of ethnic identity. Many have written on the reach of the Chinese state (see, for example, Shue 1988) and on resistance to the Chinese state (see, for example, Anagnost 1987). Many have also written about policy toward minorities (Wiens 1954, Dreyer 1976, Eberhard 1982, Harrell 1990, 1993, 1995a, 1995b, 1995c, Gladney 1991, Mackerras 1994, 1995). Here my interest is in what policies reflect about views of ethnic others and in popular reception of those views.

Most relevant here are various policies having to do with the following:

1. Classification and recognition of ethnic groups, now officially numbering fifty-five minorities (Fei 1980, Heberer 1989, Gladney 1991, Harrell 1995a, McKhann 1995) and the anomalies—such as the Chinese-speaking Muslims, the Hui—who do not fit with standard definitions and criteria for constituting minority groups.

2. Autonomous *(zizhi)* areas, at the level of *qu* (region), *zhou* (prefecture), and *xian* (county), recognizing groups that *juju* (live [collected] in compact communities) and constitute at least one-third of the population. Of Yunnan's fifteen *zhou*, eight are autonomous *zhou*. There are intriguing disparities here as well in terms of size of population and number of designated autonomous areas. For instance, the Bai, with 1.12 million people, are given one autonomous prefecture and one autonomous county, while the Wa, with only 298,000 people, are named in five autonomous counties (see tables 1.3a and 1.3b).

3. Special treatment *(youdai)* for minorities, ranging from extra points on national and some provincial college entrance examinations and higher stipends for minority students to exemption from the one-child policy (for some rural minorities). These treatments are mentioned frequently by Han.

4. Governance, including the Nationalities Affairs Commission (Minzu Shiwu Weiyuanhui), which was founded in 1950, just a year after the establishment of the PRC, under the direction of the State Council and is now under the Propaganda Department. This includes also the question of mi-

Table 1.3a: Autonomous Prefectures and Counties in Yunnan

Prefecture	Principal Nationalities
Xishuangbanna Dai A. P.	Dai, Hani, Blang (Bulang), Yi, Yao, Va (Wa), Hui, Lahu, Jinuo
Wenshan Zhuang-Miao A. P.	Zhuang, Miao, Yao, Hui, Yi
Honghe Hani-Yi A. P.	Hani, Yi, Miao, Zhuang, Yao, Dai, Hui
Dehong Dai-Jingpo A. P.	Dai, Jingpo, Achang, Lisu, De'ang
Nujiang Lisu A. P.	Lisu, Nu, Bai, Drung, Yi, Tibetan
Chuxiong Yi A. P.	Yi, Miao, Dai, Zhuang, Hui, Lisu, Bai
Diqing (Deqen) Tibetan A. P.	Tibetan, Lisu, Naxi, Yi, Bai, Nu, Pumi
Dali Bai A. P.	Bai, Yi, Hui, Lisu, Miao, Dai

Counties within Prefectures	Nationalities Named
Diqing Tibetan A. P.	
Weixi Lisu A. C.	Lisu
Nujiang Lisu A. P.	
Gongshan Dulong-Nu A. C.	Dulong, Nu
Lanping Bai-Pumi A. C.	Bai, Pumi

(continued)

Table 1.3a: *Continued*

Prefecture	Principal Nationalities
Lincang District	
Gengma Dai-Wa A. C.	Dai, Wa
Cangyuan Wa A. C.	Wa
Simao District	
Nujiang Lahu-Wa-Bulang-Dai A. C.	Lahu, Wa, Bulang, Dai
Ximeng Wa A. C.	Wa
Lancang Lahu A. C.	Lahu
Menglian Dai-Lahu-Wa A. C.	Dai, Lahu, Wa
Jingdong Yi A. C.	Yi
Zhenyuan Yi-Hani-Lahu A. C.	Yi, Hani, Lahu
Mojiang Hani A. C.	Hani
Pu'er Hani-Yi A. C.	Hani, Yi
Jiangcheng Hani-Yi A. C.	Hani, Yi
Honghe Hani-Yi A. P.	
Jinping Miao-Yao-Yi A. C.	Miao, Yao, Yi
Pingbian Miao A. C.	Miao
Hekou Yao A. C.	Yao
Qujing District	
Xundian Hui-Yi A. C.	Hui, Yi
Kunming City	
Luquan Yi-Miao A. C.	Yi, Miao
Lunan Yi A. C.	Yi
Lijiang District	
Ninglang Yi A. C.	Yi
Lijiang Naxi A. C.	Naxi
Dali Bai A. P.	
Weishan Yi-Hui A. C.	Yi, Hui
Nanjian Yi A. C.	Yi
Yuxi District	
Yuanjiang Hani-Yi-Dai A. C.	Hani, Yi, Dai
Xinping Yi-Dai A. C.	Yi, Dai
Eshan Yi A. C.	Yi

A. P. = Autonomous Prefecture

A. C. = Autonomous County

Note: Name does not include all the nationalities found in each autonomous area, only the largest groups. "District" is used for areas that are not designated as autonomous areas, while autonomous areas of the same size are referred to as "autonomous prefectures."

Table 1.3b: Yunnan Autonomous Areas and Population

Nationality	No. of autonomous prefectures	No. of autonomous counties	Population in Yunnan (1982)
Yi	2	14	3,352,000
Bai	1	1	1,120,000
Hani	1	5	1,060,000
Zhuang	1	–	894,000
Dai	2	5	836,000
Miao	1	3	752,000
Lisu	1	1	467,000
Hui	–	2	438,000
Lahu	–	4	300,000
Wa	–	5	298,000
Naxi	–	1	236,000
Yao	–	2	147,000
Tibetans	1	–	96,000
Jingpo	1	–	93,000
Bulang	–	1	58,000
Pumi	–	1	24,000
Nu	–	1	23,000
Dulong	–	1	4,500
Unrepresented by autonomous area			
Achang			20,000
De'ang			12,000
Jinuo			12,000
Mongolian			6,200
Buyi			4,900
Shui			4,000

nority cadres and their increasing numbers (Moseley 1973:110–113, Dreyer 1976:108–114, 233–234, 271–272, Avedon 1984:312, Gladney 1991:161).

5. Language policy, based on a line in China's current constitution: *"Gege minzu dou you yuyan, wenzi de ziyou"* (Every nationality has freedom of speech and writing). (Chinese usage distinguishes lexically between "spoken language" *[yanyu]*, "language in general" (usually assumed to be mostly a written language or a Language *[yuyan]*,[17] and a "writing system" *[wenzi]*.) While the eventual goal is fluency in Standard Mandarin by every-

body in the country, it is understood that intermediate steps are necessary. Aside from the scholarly issue of genetic relationships among vast numbers of languages,[18] attention of the Chinese state is directed toward the more practical matter of fostering communication among people who speak so many different language varieties. Hence, policies toward language diversity and actual attitudes may be compared.

6. Educational policies, including the ten nationalities institutes established for the twin purposes of training minority cadres and providing a setting within which minority culture and history can be studied. Educational policies include fluctuating policies toward bilingual education.

7. Cultural tolerance, including policies that permit minority practices in the realms of marriage, religion, and subsistence. These policies have fluctuated broadly, from the relative repression of the Cultural Revolution period (1966–76), when "superstition" and "feudal practices" were suppressed forcefully, to the relative permissiveness of the 1980s, when minority populations increased dramatically relative to the overall population of China.

8. Cultural classification, modernization, and cultural evolution. The mainstream ideas are based on Morgan, Engels, Marx, and Stalin, who posited that all human activity leads to classification at a certain level of advancement *(fada)* or primitiveness *(luohou)*. Cultural evolution toward a particular set of practices is seen as inevitable, and classification of groups along this single continuum is seen as scientific and useful.

Scholarly Writing

Chinese scholarship, including institutional structures and the place of the minorities institutes, also involves the subject matter of scholarly research and publications (both their topics and approaches). Given that scholars are both part of their culture and more influential on it than other folks, this aspect of minority study also provides evidence for changing or unchanging views about minorities. I have read many scholarly treatments of ethnicity, some published in the early 1980s and others as recently as the late 1990s, and can discern both trends and constants. There have been recent tendencies to train scholars to conduct ethnographic research, as well as the continuation of using surveys to fill in what are essentially taxonomies of ethnic minorities. More and more translation of poetry and folklore from minority languages has been published, and there are increasing numbers of works published in minority languages.

Most scholarship on minorities accepts the "scientific" claims of the classificatory discourse of a cultural evolutionary scale and begins with an assumed placement of these groups. Wa, for instance, are universally placed as *luohou* and Bai as *fada*.

Informal Observation

Finally, the most amorphous source of my understanding of these issues comes from my living amidst Chinese people, talking to people daily, shopping, going to parks, traveling a bit, observing babysitters interact with my daughters, and visiting friends. Random observations usually made it into my field notes, though some things did not necessarily strike me as useful at the time yet remain in my memory (Simon Ottenberg calls these "headnotes," cited in Sanjek 1990:92–95). This aspect of fieldwork has to do with the unpredictable encounters in daily life; it is the hardest to elucidate in grant proposals or prospectuses or to explain to people outside the field. "Hanging out" when one has a set of questions loosely—or even precisely—formulated, with training in theory and a long history of reading other anthropologists' accounts of their field experiences and subsequent monographs or articles, is where the most important ideas come from, where mythical field "conversion experiences" stem from, and where one moves, allegedly, from an outsider's to an insider's understanding (see Bernard 1995:151–52, Wolcott 1995, Agar 1996). Indeed, I deliberately left certain areas open-ended, in case I was completely wrong about my understanding or off target with my assessment of the importance of certain issues. I wanted to let people tell me what mattered to them—even if sometimes this meant that out of hospitality they talked about what they thought mattered to me. This too reveals Kunmingers' understanding of the outside world.

CHAPTER TWO

DESIRE FOR DIFFERENCE: COGNITIVE PROTOTYPES OF ETHNIC IDENTITY

The seven portraits that constitute the core of this book present ethnic minority groups in southwest China as they are perceived by the Han majority. Each group is known for particular reasons, and it is my aim to explain their salience. I explain the salience of particular groups as stemming from four sources: (1) they provide a kind of maximal contrast with the Han (for example, the Wa), or (2) they reaffirm the qualities that the Han themselves are proud to have (for example, the Bai), or (3) they yield a kind of cognitive dissonance as principles heretofore taken for granted and confirmed by other groups are questioned (for example, the Zang and Hui), or (4) they represent a desire for a different kind of life, romantically portrayed (for example, the Dai). The portraits are prototypes, amalgamations of experience not replaceable by lists of features. They aim to convey something of the spirit of the groups represented, much as painted portraits of individuals seek to convey persons' enduring nature through a medium more insightful than mere photography. As such, each portrait may be considered a prototype of ethnic identity.

PROTOTYPES OF ETHNIC IDENTITY

Prototypes provide models by which Chinese in Kunming make sense of the tremendous human diversity all around them. In many ways this diversity is irrelevant to ordinary Han, who take their goals as standard and universal. Indeed, many urban Han have little personal experience with ethnic diversity, which operates at the geographic and psychological margins of Chinese society. Yet it is at least partially an ordered diversity, organized by notions of Han selfhood. Han selfhood is idealized and made into an implicit point of comparison. I find it helpful here to refer to George Lakoff's notion of "idealized cognitive models," presented in his work *Women, Fire, and Dangerous Things: What Categories Reveal about the Mind* (1987). Idealized cognitive models "structure . . . mental space[s]" (p. 68) and provide models of how we think the world works. People often unconsciously posit typical, prototypical, or central members of categories. In this case, the idealized cognitive models are of an "ethnic other" on the one hand and a "Han self" on the other. Actual cases differ from this central, idealized model of ethnic others to varying degrees. Pejorative views of ethnic others may exaggerate differences from the unmarked "Han self" in ways that appear prejudiced, disdainful.

I suggest that the prevalence of social stereotypes follows to some extent from general properties of cognition. Categories are held apart by means of extreme contrasts. "Barbarians" is a useful category for people who are interested in their own "civilization." As Saussure pointed out in his study of language as an exemplar of a semiotic system, "In language, there are only differences" (1983:118; translation modified). So if cultural and social categories, like all categories, require contrasts that are easy to process, these can be furnished by cataloguing categories at maximal distances from one another, by exaggerating differences.

All this is, arguably, true of human cognition in general. Hence the Chinese way of conceptualizing ethnicity, with its concomitant excesses and oddities, can be explained largely even before we consider the role played by political factors, without having to attribute conspiracies to groups in power. We generalize, conflate experiences that have commonalities, give them labels—name them—thus solving the problem of understanding with finite brains an infinitely complex world. This strategy is universal in its essentials, but societies differ in the degree to which they tolerate ambiguity and in the areas they tolerate as ambiguous. In China, identity is not an area that is accepted as ambiguous.

The concept of cognitive and linguistic prototypes as developed by Eleanor Rosch and elaborated on by George Lakoff and other cognitive anthropologists is useful for examining the types of social stereotypes encountered in Kunming.[1] Lakoff demonstrates that human cognition is efficiently organized around prototypes, and that these prototypes can frequently be discovered by looking at language use. His position is strongly opposed to a traditional "objectivist" or representational approach to cognition, where words are taken as labels for things in the world (see also Quine 1960, Lakoff and Johnson 1980, Quinn 1982, and Silverstein 1996 for a basic discussion of this ideology). Rather, he and Mark Johnson argue that it is our language and especially the structural metaphors (among other factors) that create the organization for our thoughts about complex matters. A consequence of this premise is that we can gain access to thinking processes by examining people's language use (see also Lucy 1985, 1992a, 1992b, 1996, Gumperz and Levinson 1996) without having to assume absolute consistency of use. In fact, often there are contradictions in both our language and our culture, though these do not usually cause trouble for users of them (see also Strauss and Quinn 1997).

Cognitive prototypes are the mental models we hold of phenomena of all varieties: pronouns, prepositions, colors, categories, social roles. When we encounter new phenomena, we compare them to our existing prototypes and assess their "fit." If they do not fall into the middle range of our category, we may still be able to process them cognitively, but it may take longer or we may be more reluctant to do so. The notion of prototypes was presented as a solution to many shortcomings in a feature analysis or componential analysis approach to cognition, in which researchers proposed that people break concepts down into specifiable features or components. Prototypes involve, rather, central typical members of categories with which new cases are compared. Category membership is then a matter of degree rather than absolute.[2]

Most research on prototypes in cognitive linguistics, cognitive psychology, and cognitive and psychological anthropology has centered around (1) color and other perceptual categories, (2) classification of physical objects, such as birds or pots, or (3) single terms like "anger," "commitment," and "lie." This work has been extremely careful and painstaking, usually using experimental psychological or discourse analytic methodology and demonstrating conclusions through statistical analysis of, for example, reaction time.

The conceptual model of prototypes has not, to my knowledge, been used to analyze identity and has definitively not been used to analyze identity in China. Most of the work has been carried out in the United States and has led to the description of conceptual metaphors or underlying assumptions expressible in single sentences. Recent work by Hirschfeld (1994, 1997) on categories of human kinds suggests that such categories are innate, easily learned because of specific "domains" of the mind dedicated to organizing such ideas. Without disputing this possibility, I argue that this has not yet been adequately demonstrated ethnographically (see Hacking 1997), especially since the category of "race" as indexed by something like "skin color" is far from a universal concern. Indeed, even a sociobiological explanation would not require it since humans likely evolved without such differences.

The notion of prototypes sometimes contrasts with that of "schemata" (plural of "schema"); a third approach, used by cognitive anthropologists, involves "scenarios." Fillmore (1975), Lakoff (1987), and, following him, Coleman and Kay (1981) discuss the notion of an "idealized cognitive model." While the refinement of terminology does indicate conflicting ideas about how the mind works, we should remember that these are all models, each with its own blindnesses and insights (the term is, of course, Paul de Man's [1971]), just as all translations include exuberances and deficiencies (Becker 1984, following Ortega y Gasset 1957). The model then becomes a kind of grid through which the observer may see. (Note all the visual imagery.) Clearly we all use models—implicit or explicit—in our processing of information. The molds through which we see—literally, figuratively—are mostly given by our cultural context. This is the question addressed in part in George Lakoff's work on metaphor (Lakoff and Johnson 1980) and in his later work on perception (Lakoff 1987), just as it is addressed by Stephen Pepper (1942), terming these "world hypotheses." The question of how our thought worlds are organized—possibly through language—is related to the so-called Sapir-Whorf hypothesis, for which see Sapir (1921), Whorf (1956), Friedrich (1986a), Hill and Mannheim (1992), Lucy (1985, 1992a, 1992b, 1996), and Gumperz and Levinson (1996). But here I would like to borrow elements of many of these theories to describe what informants do and to point out common regularities, without necessarily positing the details of the mental processes involved. Employing a variety of approaches to analyze an assortment of data may permit us to triangulate, to get a sense of the terrain by overcoming one method's limitations through another method that has different limitations and different illuminations. As Alessandro Duranti says so brilliantly in his book *Linguistic Anthropology,* "All theories are mortal" (1997:48)—or at least they should be!

While these ideas from psychological anthropology are extremely helpful, I do not constrain myself to operating within this field. Many aspects of the Chinese situation—the politically saturated public sphere, the long and complex history of ethnic interactions, tourism and other economic phenomena—require nonpsychological perspectives. Psychological and cognitive anthropologists, such as Strauss and Quinn and Bock, are quite justified in arguing that we must correct the exaggerated denial of psychology in traditional anthropological accounts that privilege publicly observable behavior. At the same time, an exclusive focus on psychological aspects of cultural meaning overlooks the importance of other factors. I attempt here to walk not a middle ground but both grounds, all possible grounds, in accounting for observations I made on the ground in China. If my account is messy rather than elegant, eclectic rather than loyal, difficult to assign to a subdisciplinary position, then my faithfulness to accounting for Chinese practices is borne out.

Let me summarize what I will draw on from this field: I assume that people have certain prototypical models of ethnic others in southwest China (modal ethnic others) that operate both in the realm of generalizing about minority nationalities as a group and about typical individuals of a given nationality. Some minority nationalities fit the prototypes better than others do and are consequently invoked more readily, just as some reds are better examples of "red" than others and would be selected more often to illustrate the quality of redness (see Berlin and Kay 1969). Beyond that, each minority nationality has a prototype as well, so that some individuals are more "typically Bai" or "typically Sani" than others.

Even encountering an atypical individual does not automatically lead to re-
vision of the prototype, or at least not immediately. An amusing instance of
this situation occurred when I was buying shoes at a Kunming department
store. The clerk wondered whether I was from Japan, Fujian province, or
Hong Kong, given my selection of a linguistic variety other than the local dialect, Kunminghua (I spoke in Putonghua, standard Mandarin) and noticing
my accent in speaking it. My appearance is not that of a Chinese or even an
Asian person. But Japan was apparently at the far limit of the range in which
actual speaking, intelligible persons exist; more remote foreign countries
could not possibly produce human beings with whom communication is
possible. Prototypical persons who speak are, according to her model, Chinese or East Asian.

Much of what is said about minority nationalities in Kunming might strike
a reader as exaggerated—both positively and negatively. It may be understood in part as a way to keep prototypes separate. The exaggerated prototypes are what are commonly referred to as (social) stereotypes. I argue as
well that thinking and talking about various sorts of "others" in China is
stereotypical as a result of (1) educational, propagandistic, and linguistic
background forces; (2) a tendency to dichotomize the world into full persons, such as the self, and shadowy others who are fundamentally different,
possessing many fewer distinctive traits than are attributed to one's own
group (see also Hsu 1971); and (3) a tendency of human thought in general
to think in terms of prototypes (Miller 1982, Lakoff 1987). Following
Lakoff, I believe that the stereotypical contents of statements about various
others may be regarded as inseparable from the stereotypical formulations of
such statements. Hence part 2 looks closely at verbatim statements or reports, based on the belief that summarizing is not sufficient in many cases.

The exaggeration may also be explained as based on the desire of Han to
discover extremes in the nature of the other, desires answered in the imagi-
native construction of the other's silent—because idealized—movements in
an alien, faraway world.[3] The minority nationalities exist at the borderlands,
removed in space both horizontally and vertically to harsh stretches of unknown territory. Foreigners too are viewed in terms of extremes, with the
United States seen as a land of divorce, guns, children alienated from their
parents, and drugs—all described in great detail in the Chinese media—
along with modernization and riches beyond one's imagination.

We will see some of the uses to which these categories are put and what
function they serve in China's contemporary endeavor to construct a "modern" national identity. This has much to do as well with inchoate notions of
Han selfhood.

"SELF" AND "OTHER" IN
INDIVIDUAL AND SOCIAL PSYCHOLOGY

The terms "self" and "other" have two different uses in scholarship on identity, meaning both (1) an individual person and particular individual persons, and (2) a group of individuals and groups differentiated from that group. The former tends to be the province of psychological anthropology and developmental psychology, while the latter falls under the rubric of "ethnicity."[4] Using social psychological terminology, much contemporary writing on identity mentions "the other" and "othering" without considering the intriguing move of attributing volition and intention to groups, usually dominant ones. Talk about the "self" and "other" of a society conflates discourses of individual psychological development with social processes. The relationship between individual and society—the heart of much anthropological work since its earliest formulations by Durkheim—needs to be spelled out rather than assumed (see Cohen 1994). Here an unconscious extension of the image of society as an organism, used by early anthropologists like Spencer and Tylor, is used by people who would critique its older incarnation.

According to developmental psychology, following insights of the social psychologist G. H. Mead, very young children develop a concept of self as they progressively differentiate themselves from the others around them. While psychoanalytically and for individual development this is undoubtedly true (Lacan 1977, Bruner 1990, Rothstein 1993), for the study of socially constructed "selves" and "others" such a model can be only metaphoric and inspirational. Societies develop in ways profoundly different from individuals. Individuals are born into already-existing societies, where at least many of their actions are shaped by cultural constraints. Even those choices over which they have control are largely shaped by the types of selves permissible within their society.

Given our very imperfect understanding of the relationship between the self and society in psychological development, to extrapolate from notions of identity to notions of self requires complex argument. This book focuses much more on notions of identity than on notions of self, but in the final chapters I speculate on such a relationship,[5] looking at Han Chinese notions of "self" as a form of contrast with people who are different from them.

HAN IDENTITY

China is often considered a quite homogeneous nation-state, with the Han majority constituting 92 percent of the population at the last census

(FBIS 1990). There has been a sudden increase in the proportion of those claiming minority status, from 6 percent to 8 percent in only ten years, indicating that even by official ethnic criteria, the Chinese nation-state may be less ethnically "pure" than had previously been believed. Add those desiring but not granted minority status, add those who choose to follow the ethnicity of their Han parent, and add the distinctions between vast regions of China, and it seems that critical reflection on the issue of China's homogeneity is warranted.[6] Western analysts such as Edward Friedman (1994) have begun to question the very possibility of China remaining unified in the face of much ethnic and regional diversity and identification. The way one regards the possibility of Chinese unity depends on one's model of a nation (see, for example, Duara 1995). It is evident that the idea of a timeless, homogeneous, well-bounded polity underlies some such conceptions, but that the only sorts of states that approximate such a model (such as Japan, but see Fowler 1993) do so only through sometimes violent suppression of memory and difference.

China is considered a new nation-state in the sense that, with the founding of the Republic of China in 1911 and that of the People's Republic of China in 1949, a new, nonimperial identity for China had to be forged. With the improvement of transportation and communication (*jiaotong,* a term covering both "transportation" and "communication") and the increased complexity of participation in the nation-state, people's identification with their fellow Chinese—even with those from other regions, ethnic groups, or classes—had to be encouraged. One powerful way in which this identification was fostered was by renaming some of the entities in the Chinese universe; one central focus was on linguistic varieties, as China established an official, standard language. What had been merely *guanhua* (administrative vernacular, hence "Mandarin") was renamed twice: post-1911 saw coining of the term *Guoyu* (National Language)—a term that persists in Taiwan and many overseas Chinese communities—and post-1949 saw yet another name, *Putonghua* (Common Language). Sometimes linguists talk about *Hanyu* (Han language) to emphasize the fact that there are other languages spoken as well in the new Chinese nation-state—in an attempt to bring ethnic groups into the "family" of Chinese citizens.[7]

Ethnic groups were renamed as well, pejorative terms were changed, and all groups were encouraged to assimilate to the new socialist ideal. Despite repeatedly changing goals and methods for achieving them, the problem of integration of ethnic minorities has been salient to China's leadership since 1949 and indeed is one that troubled even the Qing rulers before Republican and "New" China.[8]

Han identity is a topic hard to approach directly. It is not discussed often in ordinary conversation among Han, just as "whiteness" is not often discussed in Anglo communities in the United States. A new body of research on whiteness in the United States has been proliferating since the mid-1990s, following bell hooks's admonition that this category requires examination (see Dyer 1997, Hill 1997, Johnson 1999, Nakayama and Martin 1999). In ways that may be fruitful for understanding Han identity, these works tend to emphasize the changing definition of "whiteness" and of which groups are included at which times. For example, Jews, Irish, and Italians were considered to be members of a Jewish race, Irish race, and Italian race at the turn of the twentieth century, as Haney-López (1996), Brodkin (1998), and Jacobson (1998) have shown. Other authors emphasize the lack of markedness on whites while all other groups are marked. Still others emphasize the privileges that attend to whites. As Dru Gladney points out so aptly, "Majorities are made, not born" (1998c:1).

HOW IS HANNESS (NOT) THE SAME AS WHITENESS?

In some interesting ways, "whiteness" in the United States is similar to "Hanness" in China:

1. They are both the unmarked category. That is, people so classified will often be unaware of their own classification—at least consciously (see Frankenberg 1993, Berger 1999).
2. Whites and Hans tend to occupy positions of economic, political, and cultural dominance (Roediger 1999).
3. There are "affirmative action" programs in place in both countries that attempt to redress the balance of economic opportunity. These programs are often protested by those excluded from them—that is, the majority group—on the grounds that they are unfair. (See, for example, Kincheloe et al. 1998).

Yet whiteness is different from Hanness in several instructive ways. First, though all writers on whiteness are careful to contrast this category with one for "people of color," there is often an implicit black-white dichotomy. Certainly the focus on "color" points to the uniquely American preoccupation with skin color as a marker of identity, which emphasizes the putatively biological dimension of American identities. In China, by contrast, descent and "blood" are much less central (*pace* Dikötter 1992) in the construction of ethnic categories. As I show below, in some cases people in China mention physical features as indices of belonging to particular categories, but in most cases these categories are dependent on other, more visible, markers: clothing, language, hometown, and so forth.

Second, in the case of whites in the United States, as many have shown, a "single drop" of "black blood" is sufficient to move a person into the "black" category. In China, because there is no official category of "mixed" ethnicity, children in this situation are free (forced?) to choose the identity of either parent. The classification is thus somewhat voluntary and is not biological or categorical.

Third, though discussions of ethnicity in the United States may include a handful of choices—African American, Native American, Hispanic/Latino/-a/Chicano/-a, Asian American, Pacific Islander, White—the number is far less than in China. The existence of the fifty-six categories of ethnic groups—however constrained and artificial—still means that the discourse of ethnicity is less simple. At the same time, the percentage of people in the nonwhite category is quite large (approaching a majority) in the United States, while in China the percentage of people in the non-Han category is relatively small (8 percent).

Fourth, though classification in China has voluntary dimensions, once an individual has chosen to belong to a particular group, this choice becomes part of the individual's official biography and is recorded on official documents such as identification cards *(shenfenzheng)*. In the United States, there are cases of "passing" as a member of a group other than the group one's parents claimed. Usually this involves a person of color passing as white (but see McBride 1996).

Fifth, the histories of these nation-states and their relationships to ethnic and national groups are different. In the United States, it is easy to trace the roots of many minority groups, especially African Americans, to sources quite clearly distinct from those of the dominant, white group (England, Germany, France). In China, by contrast, there has been little immigration and much "ethnic" mixing from its earliest recorded history. The Shang and Zhou of the earliest attested periods differed from one another in many ways, including religion, art, and subsistence. Whether we would call these differences "ethnic" or not depends on the purpose of making such a determination. During the Zhou period, there were groups that were quite different from one another, yet they communicated and competed as virtual equals. The Qin conquest of China brought a new style of governance, but there is no mention of "blood." China was surrounded by groups of "barbarians" and "semi-barbarians" and, for half its history, the "barbarians" (usually pastoral nomads from the north) ruled China. As Chinese civilization spread southward, the people it encountered were often incorporated into China, bringing some of their own customs into the new hybrid culture.

The Han identity was never articulated as such until this century, when nationalist ideas propelled China's politicians and intellectuals to establish a "nation" (*minzu*, from Japanese *minzoku*) at the core of the new nation-state. "Han" was one term in circulation and had a long history, though it did not yet mean exactly what it came to mean later. Sun Yat-sen, one of the leaders of the Nationalist party, posited the Han as the center of the new nation-state, with the four "younger brother" nationalities at the peripheries: Tibetans, Mongols, Manchus, and Uighurs/Huis. The Kuomintang (KMT) party in power at the time envisioned assimilation of the younger brothers to the illustrious example of the elder brother.

Other ways of speaking of the dominant group included *Zhonghua Renmin* and *Zhongguoren*. Terminology has been a key battleground because of the implied inclusions and exclusions.

With the founding of the PRC in 1949, some continuities may be observed, especially a concern with how to include differences within an ideal unity. Positing ethnic minorities alongside a majority and giving everyone a *minzu* seemed to make this aspect of identity equally shared. Yet the importance of belonging to a *minzu* varies for the Han. In places like Beijing and Shanghai, where ethnic minorities are very rare, Han identity might scarcely ever come into prominence. In places like Kunming, it is evident only when certain issues are in the air. In places like Lijiang or Dali—autonomous areas in Yunnan with numerically dominant minority populations—the Han are aware of their Hanness much of the time. But Han identity is scarcely discussed. This does not mean there is no conception of Hanness, merely that a researcher has to use methods other than direct inquiry to elicit the notion.

Though asking directly and indirectly about ethnic minorities gave rich data, sporadically I tried another approach as well. I wondered how Han imagined ethnic minorities looking at Han (see table 2.1). Since this research was conducted among urban Han, I did not ask the reverse question of ethnic minorities ("What are Han like?"); surely colleagues focusing on various minorities are in a better position to pursue this line of inquiry.

HAN GUESSES OF MINORITY VIEWS OF HAN

Han students asked to write about how they imagined minorities would view Han made the following characterizations:

From my point of view, I think, compared with the Han nationality, the minorities are backward in the fields of economy, culture, and science, etc. The

Table 2.1: Han Attributes from the Point of View of Minorities, as Reported by Han

Good Points	Bad Points
intelligent, wise	cunning
thoughtful	cruel
happy	imperious
good culture	ruthless
kind	proud
friendly	not to be believed, cheat
advanced science and technology	tricky
hard-working	Han chauvinism (*da Hanzuzhuyi*)
fashionable clothing	
self-confident	
non-religious	
receive outside information, accept outside influence, change	
clever	
strong	
help minorities	
better at things than minorities	

main reason is that most of them live in far and remote mountain areas. They hardly exchange with the other nationalities because of backward communication and transportation. Certainly there are some reasons of history; I think this problem is very complicated. As far as I can see, I think the Han nationality, on the whole, gets on well with the other minorities. I'm a student from a coal mine; in our mine the leaders and workers come from different places and nations. But I have never seen and heard that they quarreled and fought because of national contradictions (i.e., conflicts). . . . How do the minorities think about the Han minority? Perhaps they think Han persons are very cunning and cruel, maybe some of them think they are kind and friendly. I think different persons' ideas are different, but I'm sure, at least most of them can't regard the Han nationality as their enemy.

In China, the Government advocates and carries out a policy of "Regional autonomy of minority nationalities" and "policy towards nationalities"; it makes allowances for minorities. It appears in different forms. I don't think it's fair. As I know, in Sichuan province, if a Yi minority's people or Zang [Tibetan] minority's people killed or injured a Han person, he might not be sentenced to death. But if a Han person killed or only injured a Yi or Zang person, the trouble is different. He has only one way, to be sentenced to death. From this, I

think in some cases, the Han people are like Indians or Negroes in the United
States of America, though the Han people are an advanced and civilized nation.

Describing Hanzu in the minorities' eyes, for me it is very difficult, because I'm
a Han person. In fact, I really don't know, the only thing I can do is imagine.
Before Liberation, most of the minorities were controlled by chiefs and the nationalist party [KMT]. They had no freedom and lived in hunger and cold. Because of cheating by their chiefs, many of them hate us Han people. In their
eyes, maybe we Han people are very proud and are not worth trusting so when
the first batch of technicians came to the minority districts, they thought Han
people must have invaded them and occupied their land. But with the time
going by, they were moved by Han people's profound sentiments of friendship.
Now we have become good friends.[9]

Such self-conscious descriptions supplement the attempt to understand
Han identity in general. These essays show some awareness that many minorities resented and resisted Han efforts to intervene in minority lives. The
dimension of advancement is pervasive.

Minorities and Han are seen to contrast in part along dimensions of simplicity and complexity, leading to differing degrees of honesty and craftiness
(wiliness). Minorities express concern, as do peasants coming to the city, about
their own naïveté and the likelihood that they will be deceived by city Han.
Zhao Ling, my Yi friend, lamented the difference between Kunming and her
hometown: in her hometown, everybody knew everybody, so it was not possible to commit crimes without everybody knowing about it. But Kunming was
so dangerous that she preferred not to go out in the evening even with friends
and did not even attend dances of people of her native group.

RELATIONS AMONG HAN AND MINORITIES

I also wondered about relations among Han and minorities. Ethnic conflict
is rarely mentioned in any sort of official setting, but it can be observed.
Some students mentioned it as well, giving rise to the sorts of observations—
often contradictory—listed in table 2.2. We have already encountered some
accounts that suggest such relations, but here they are enumerated clearly.

In general, students repeated the official position of equality, fraternity,
and harmony, though some gave voice to the remaining tension that is a sub-
text to the ideological position of harmoniousness.

A saying attributed to the Miao is this: *"Shi bu neng dang zhentou, Han-
ren bu neng zuo pengyou"* (A stone can't be a pillow, a Han can't be a friend)

Table 2.2: Relations between Han and Ethnic Minorities as Mentioned in Student Essays

Positive	unity
	equality
	mutual (economic) dependence
	"both the yellow race"
	happy family of nationalities
	peaceful coexistence
Negative	hatred
	pride
	some dissatisfaction
	maintain distance
	unbridgeable gap
Neutral (?)	past oppression, discrimination, and inequality
	enumeration of policies to improve relations or position of minorities
	assimilation (?)

(Dreyer 1976:108). Han hearing such an expression explain it as having arisen during periods of harsh policy and excessive *da Hanzu zhuyi* ([great] Han chauvinism). In general, all Han I spoke with, except a few who work exclusively with minorities, expressed incredulity at the ingratitude of minorities toward Han or certainty that the minorities admire the Han. Yet people were aware of "hatred" and the need to "maintain distance" between Han and other nationalities, even though they knew the official line about all fifty-six nationalities belonging to a happy family.

SELF AND IDENTITY IN CHINA

Not only is Hanness little discussed, a preoccupation with self-definition is similarly uncommon in China. There is little terminology used to discuss the abstract matter of "identity." As Perry Link points out with some frustration (1992:175), "identity" is a modern term, introduced under Western influence in the unsatisfying *rentong* (recognition of similarity), a term rarely heard, without resonance, and not even included in common dictionaries. *Shenfen* (status, capacity, identity) is an official term of identification and includes one's job, work unit, and the other information about a person that appears on identification cards. Still, the morpheme *fen* has the richly associative meaning of "lot, portion" (see also Munro 1985:265), which does get close to the Chinese notion of identity: it is one's allotment, one's place within a system.

English "identity" has an entirely different origin, from the Latin *idem* (OED 1971:1368) for "the same; is,"—implying self-sufficiency and consistency as hallmarks of personality.[10] In Chinese thought, self-containment has always had negative connotations, with traditional thought especially opposed to selfishness *(si)* (Munro 1985:268) and lack of group awareness—an opposition that is similarly found in the socialist rhetoric of the twentieth century. Words for "self" are given in the dictionary as *zi, ziji,* and *ziwo,* or as *benxing* and *benzhi* (both meaning "basic nature") and as *gerende zhengchang qingkuang* (an individual's normal situation), rapidly fading off into connotations of selfishness: *sixin, sili, zisi* (all meaning "selfish"). One of Mao's exhortations was to "Fight self (-ishness) and repudiate revisionism" *(Dou si, pi xiu.).* So the term "self" is almost entirely associated with the evil of selfishness and self-absorption.

The term "other" is usually translated as *taren* but can also be *lingwaide ren, bieren,* or *qitade ren.* "Otherness" is *lingyi(wu)* or *butong(wu).* All of the associations are of things aside, physically apart, outside. In Chinese, the term "difference" can be expressed as *butong* (literally "not the same"), implying the negation of identity, or *fenbie* (literally "to divide and differentiate"), implying discrimination. *Qubie* suggests putting things in their places.

If the Chinese notion of identity as a category is intrinsically bound up with a person's place within a system rather than with individual essence, it is particularly important to locate those other elements with which a system is formed and then to identify the contrasts that are involved. It is common to contrast an implicit judging "self" with selected "others": materialistic foreigners, backward minority nationalities, counterrevolutionaries, unfilial Westerners, immoral drug users (see also Thongchai 1994).[11] These "modal others" form ideal-type templates against which new experiences and information are assessed.[12] One way to get at the meanings of identity is to make explicit the cognitive prototypes people hold of ethnic identity, often through talk, even though such talk is rarely explicitly about this identity.

Unlike in the West, and especially in the United States, where people devoutly seek to "find themselves" or "be an individual" or engage in "self-actualization" or "find the real self" (cf. Bellah et al. 1985, Linde 1987, 1993)[13]—all hallmarks of recognized mental health—in China people are much more likely to define themselves relationally: daughter of XX; from XX village or work unit; parent of XX (Hsu 1967, Bond 1991:33–34). Terms for identity and difference, self and other, do not come as readily because discourse about the self does not have much currency in China. Identity is both relational and contrastive: one is from the XX department to a coworker at a work unit, from the XX work unit to a neighbor, from the XX neighborhood to a fellow resident of the city, from XX city to someone from another city, from XX province to someone from another province, a northerner to a southerner, a Han to a minority nationality, a Chinese to a foreigner. Berreman (1982) makes much the same point about India, where informants can identify strangers by their appearance or their specific remarks depending on the context.

The discourse of identity is fraught with moral evaluation in China and likely elsewhere, where difference is sometimes negative and sometimes positive but rarely neutral. Moral relativity is not a stance one finds readily in China. Description of the state of affairs is often seen as a point of departure for the evaluation that must precede action. Who is John Smith? He is a foreign businessman. So my relationship to him is ABC and this means our expectations are DEF, so what I should do and say is XYZ. If Chongchai is a Tibetan party member, a different set of entailments follows.

But such evaluations are rarely an individual matter in contemporary China. Without denying the possibility of an individual idiosyncratic viewpoint, it is necessary to acknowledge the various collective influences on an individual's moral formation. One such influence is of course political, in the guise of the nation-state. However, the state does not function as a sui generis entity but rather operates in a cultural milieu on which it also has some degree of influence.

POPULAR AND OFFICIAL, COEXISTING AND CONTRADICTING VIEWS

In exploring the cultural and psychological meanings of identity in China, including in my analysis political factors, I assume that individuals, like "states," can hold mutually contradictory views. One of my favorite exercises in teaching an introduction to anthropology is to inquire into students' views about causality. The first response is usually that everything has a proximate, material cause. This belief leads them to reject witchcraft as an explanation for disaster and suffering. At the same time, most express the belief that some things "just happen" (coincidence) or are "meant to be" (fate)—views in direct contradiction to their previously articulated views of causality as well as to each other. Similarly, the Chinese state can embrace and encourage ethnic diversity while believing it is bound to fade away, and individuals can believe that minorities are colorful and innocent while disliking the way they act in local shops.

While I am more interested in popular views held by individuals than I am in official views, there is some relationship between those two types. Experts may have one view of, say, the difference between trees and bushes, while regular people hold a related but different "folk" view. Experts can hold folk views too, when they are acting as "just folks"—astronomers may speak of sunset and sunrise, knowing full well that it is the revolution of the earth that is responsible for our relative motion. Yet ordinary educated Americans are also aware of this and might speak of it this way in some contexts—when helping their children with science homework, for instance. When a person admires the colors of the western sky while on vacation, the folk view will likely prevail (see the papers in Holland and Quinn 1987 and D'Andrade and Strauss 1992 for examples of cultural models).

Charlotte Linde terms these views "expert systems" and "explanatory systems" in her work on life stories (1987, 1993). She has extracted three different psychological explanatory systems used by middle-class white American informants in accounting for their life paths to that point: Freudian, behaviorist, and astrological. Though experts have elaborated on all of these systems, the explanatory devices used by informants telling their life stories may, according to Linde, reveal a system of beliefs "midway between common sense, the beliefs and relations among beliefs that any person in the culture may be assumed to know, if not to share, and expert systems, which are beliefs and relations among beliefs held, understood, and used by experts in a particular domain" (1987:343). These are similar to some of the judgments made in China by ordinary people about ethnic others, in which "expert judgments"—necessarily officially sanctioned—filter down in the form of generalizations and enter popular consciousness, especially among the educated nonspecialists. The popular explanatory systems involve simplification of the original expert models, "reducing both the number of themes and concepts [they use] and the complexity of the connections between them" (1987:356). There is mutual influence as well; the "expert systems" are made by people who share the common sense of their culture. From this perspective, all "science" is ethnoscience (see Haraway 1988, Lutz 1985), just as all anthropology is ethnoanthropology.

One aim of this book is to make explicit the explanatory systems regarding ethnicity. Many other works have specified the expert systems. The relationship between them can only be clarified after we know what they both are—assuming they can be separated.

One can see such mutual influence at play in the Chinese case in the popular recitation of categories, often appearing in the form of ill-remembered quotations from official discourse: "There is a very lively saying to describe our large national family, that is fifty-six nations are fifty-six flowers. It shows our country is a multinational country. For a long time, there have been all kinds of exchange among these nations and so all different nations are a united whole." This writer recalls the categorization, enumeration, and ideological goal without going into detail about ethnic relations and processes. Unable to speak from personal experience of the overall situation of China's minority populations, people often report things heard or read elsewhere (see Link 1992:9–11, 174–91). It is not that these views are inaccurate, merely that they reveal a lumping together that prejudges the nature of ethnicity in China.[14] A Han woman who talked to me of ethnic groups in her school said, presumably offering her own views (since her opinion is not officially sanctioned), that "Tibetans are very bad, a lot of trouble . . ." and then later gets involved in enumerating the nationalities and slipping more into received wisdom: "China has fifty-six nationalities, that's right. Like in Yunnan they are very numerous. . . . They, those, are similar to the Han, without much difference. Maybe now in general their productivity is increasing rapidly." Her sentences become longer, less wisps and hedges than complete sentences, using more abstract terms: *shengchanli* (productivity) as opposed to the very colloquial *mafan* (trouble, bother). When she slips into the official language of modernization, she need not pause to consider her next words, for many of the phrases are already constructed.[15] Such talk may be taken as evidence for a prototype held perhaps unconsciously.

What interests me is not the accuracy or inaccuracy of the models offered by social scientists and ordinary people but the models themselves and the ways they relate to similar models of other domains, seeking an "implicit theory of personality" (Jones 1982) by means of which Chinese in Kunming explain behavior of selves and others. According to social psychologists, we all construct theories about personality traits and about which traits are likely to co-occur; we assign individuals or groups to categories and exaggerate sameness or difference, depending on the circumstances and the perceived distance from self (see Jones 1982 for a review of this literature).

Using these concepts—prototypes, idealized cognized models, explanatory systems, folk theories—I turn to the substance of the analysis with a summarized overview of the portraits.

CHAPTER THREE

CHINA'S MINORITIES THROUGH HAN EYES: A PRELIMINARY SKETCH

HAN VIEWS OF ETHNIC OTHERS:
A KEY TROPE OF EXAGGERATION

A frank student wrote the following essay on the topic of the *shaoshuminzu* (minority nationalities).

> Minority nationalities always live in remote places and mountains. Many of them still keep an original (i.e., primitive) life style—self-sufficiency; their means of production are very far behind. Some of them do not even have enough food and clothes. The conditions are very bad, and they don't even have schools or entertainment. A few of the minority nationalities are still living in forests, depending on hunting and gathering. There is no competition; it is not like a big city, so they don't know how to work hard if they want to be winners. They only know how to depend on each other, help others, to prevent them from being hungry and cold. But, Han people live and work by their own efforts.
> Minority nationalities' character is straightforward and uninhibited. They think they are sons of mountains, sons of forest, sons of grassland. They don't care so much, just do anything they want. But you know, because of their limited conditions, they don't pay attention to hygiene. So, Han people always think they are so dirty. But, they treat others with earnestness. If you treat them true, they will get rid of their guard and help you unselfishly.

In many ways, this brief passage captures the overall feelings that Han harbor with regard to their minority nationality brethren:[1] a feeling of superiority combined with appreciation of the ethnic others' greater simplicity and ruggedness, along with some fastidious inclinations to maintain distance. After a very clumsy song-and-dance performance at an overpriced restaurant, my dear Yi friend whom I'll call Zhao Ling observed, "They like our clothes, music, and food, but they don't like us *(Yifu, yinyue, fuzhuang tamen xihuan, dan tamen bu xihuan ren)*."

In essays students wrote about minority nationalities (see chapter 1), they frequently mentioned categories that are very similar to those reported in all of the official discourse about ethnic others (see section 1 in table 3.1): customs and habits, clothing, festivals, and so on, mostly traits that can be observed objectively and externally, things that can be represented by photographs or other visual media. Mention of these attributes reveals familiarity with the common discourse concerned with ethnic minorities.

Table 3.1 lists all of the attributes students mentioned for minority nationalities, divided into general, positive, and negative categories, based on my understanding of the values placed on such attributes, which is derived in large part from extensive interviews about these matters.

Table 3.1: Minority Attributes Reported by Han

Attributes mentioned for minorities in general include

festivals
"customs"
clothing
singing and dancing
handicrafts
weddings, funerals, courting behavior
folk tales
their own characteristics/customs/language/clothing
self-determination, autonomous regions

Positive characteristics

Never said of Han/selves	Might be said of Han	Fetishized
straightforward	clever, intelligent	handmade, exquisite clothing and jewelry
simple	diligent	beautiful skirts
honest	self-confident	good at sports
natural, involved with nature and animals	kind	sturdily built
unconstrained	generous	long-lived
shy, modest	rugged	simple but nourishing food
direct	brave, bold	different building styles
hospitable	enthusiastic	interesting marriage customs
beautiful girls and women	industrious, active	tasty food
warmhearted	clean (primarily said of Dai)	magic
easy to get along with		mysterious
unconstrained		
learn from Han, e.g., Yuan and Qing dynasties		
now socialist ("leapt" into socialism)		

(continued)

Table 3.1: *Continued*

Negative characteristics

Nearly neutral

Material	Social and cultural	Grievances
nomadism	still in matriarchy	specially privileged (relief
relied on hunting	savage	from one-child policy,
bull/cow sacrifice	patriarchy	extra points on college
nonmonetary exchange, barter	believe in Islam, Buddhism, or Christianity	entrance examination,
pastoralism	free relations between the sexes	special schools)
eat with their hands	superstitious	don't abide by national laws
drink alcohol	religious	
eat strange things (corn, moss, ant eggs,		
sour meat, milk, raw meat, no pork, no wine)		

Pejorative

Level of development	Consequences of historical situation
backward	ignorant of outside world
wild	live in closed places, mountains
rude	no entertainment
(semi-) primitive	hard life (mountains, bad climate, no water)
uncivilized	poor
	ignorant
	no schools
	foolish
	no notion of competition
	uneducated, much illiteracy

Table 3.1: *Continued*

Dangerous characteristics	Distasteful characteristics
enforce cruel punishment	conservative
fearless in fighting (especially Hui)	conventional
united	stubborn
weapons (especially Hui)	dirty, unbathed (especially Zang)
separatist (especially Hui and Zang)	bad temper, nationalities' temper *(minzu piqi)*
hate Han (especially Hui and Zang)	rough
nongregarious	covetous
	lazy
	dark skin
	greed

I divided the positive attributes into three categories: (a) never said of Han/selves, (b) might be said of Han, and (c) fetishized. Attributes in the first category involve the simpler, more natural temperament of the minorities, very similar to ideas Europeans held of the innocent "noble savage," untainted by the corrupting influence of knowledge and worldliness. The connection of minority nationalities with nature and animals is a common theme, often appearing in visual representations of minority nationalities (see Schein 1997). This is strikingly like Christopher Columbus's first contact with the natives of the New World, where he collected specimens of interesting flora and fauna—and people (Todorov 1984:48; Greenblatt 1991:90, 154 n. 13). He moved from a position of total appreciation and enjoyment of the natives, finding them the best people in the world, to anger and disdain, finding them intolerably violent and duplicitous. Compare his views with the negative attributes mentioned in table 3.1 (negative characteristics: pejorative), especially dangerous and distasteful characteristics: conservative, bad tempered, lazy, dark skinned, stubborn.

There are many contradictory attributes: generous and covetous, industrious and lazy, clean and dirty, beautiful women and dark skin (considered ugly by most urban Chinese, especially because dark skin is said to characterize peasants). We can explain the apparent inconsistency of viewing ethnic minorities as both wonderful and terrible by recognizing these views as extremes united by the common trope of exaggeration. As Todorov describes Columbus' descriptions of the native peoples he encountered, their goodness and badness were both exaggerated because both derived from his preconceived understanding of these people as essentially different from himself. Todorov explains this apparent contradiction:

> How can Columbus be associated with these two apparently contradictory myths, one whereby the Other is a "noble savage" . . . and one whereby he is a "dirty dog," a potential slave? It is because both rest on a common basis, which is the failure to recognize the Indians, and the refusal to admit them as a subject having the same rights as oneself, but different. (1984:49)

Some positive traits that might be said of the Han are the ones that narcissistically confirm Han self-confidence, whereby the ethnic other acts as a mirror to reflect Han self-understanding, allowing the Han, as Greenblatt (1991:95) puts it, "to imagine [them] as virtual doubles." Such traits include industriousness and intelligence. These are the characteristics that are often used to socialize children (*yao nuli* [be industrious]) or to describe the Chinese nation (*Hanzu shi yige qinlao, ai laodong, congming de minzu.* [The Han nationality is an assiduous, hard-working, intelligent nationality.]). Kindred minority nationalities such as the Bai are seen as possessing those traits as well, a fact that goes a long way in explaining the Han comfort and enthusiasm with regard to their Bai brethren. Others, such as the Dai and Yi, may have certain of these traits, such as generosity, yet others, such as Zang and Hui, are not mentioned as having any of these traits other than bravery—and that trait is implicitly linked to their purported eagerness for violence.

Some of the more interesting traits are those "never said of Han." These show a desire for a different kind of life from the one lived most commonly by Han.

The traits I've assigned to the category "fetishized" have much to do with frequently repeated characteristics that appear in the official media. Most of them are understood at a superficial level ("good at sports," "different building styles"), and no attempt is made to connect these apparently arbitrary facts to any more systematic notion of culture. In many ways the attributions of "mystery" and "magic" have everything to do with justifying the lack of comprehension and connection. Exoticization keeps the ethnic others at a distance, obviating any need to draw nearer.

The "negative" characteristics involve either "nearly neutral" or truly "pejorative" traits. The former are very much social-scientific descriptive terms ("barter," "still in matriarchy"), but in a teleological system with a clear-cut hierarchy of values, anything differing from the pinnacle must be regarded as inferior. Indeed, as I argue later in this chapter, the metaphor of modernization pervades the discourse about ethnic others, as it does much discourse in general in the contemporary PRC. The leap from the description of (weird) social practices to the conclusion that the group in question is "backward," "primitive," and so forth is small and is taken as purely factual.[2] "Nomadism," for instance, is placed within the "bad characteristics" category but under the "nearly neutral" subcategory, because in general Han find pastoral nomadism—like shifting agriculture or boat dwelling—to be a strange and not entirely legitimate form of subsistence (see Lattimore 1951, Barfield 1989, Williams 1996). During the Great Leap Forward, nomads were required to settle down and participate in Han-style agriculture; this policy was later repudiated, and currently official talk about nomadism attempts to be value-neutral about it, even going so far as to criticize earlier "ultra-left" policies (see, for example, Ma Yin 1989:14–15, 31–38).[3]

The official discourse of ethnic otherness posits several not always consistent characteristics of minorities:

- They are less advanced.
- They are "simple" and grateful for guidance from the Han "brothers."

- They are in the process of "modernizing," which is inevitable and desirable.

The image of unilinear evolution applies here, though such an account runs into difficulty with regard to some of the less tractable nationalities (Hui, Zang). Positive attributions that imply unilinear evolution include the following: straightforwardness, simplicity, honesty, naturalness, ruggedness, handmade clothing and jewelry, simple but nourishing food, magic, and mysteriousness. The corresponding negative associations with such evolution include the following: nomadism, hunting, pastoralism, sacrifice, nonmonetary exchange, matriarchy, savagery, free sexual relations, superstition, backwardness, rudeness, lack of civilization, primitiveness, ignorance, dirt, and dark skin.

This characterization may be seen as contrary magic or taxonomic alchemy: all of these characteristics ward off doubt and ambiguity with a familiar magic. What is inherently unstable is lent an air of stability, much as socialist enumeration and jargon in general have fixed experience—at least in succeeding paradigms—so that exceptions appear impossible.

PORTRAYALS OF MINORITIES IN NEWSPAPERS AND OTHER MEDIA

Newspapers are filled with photographs of (male) Han cadres demonstrating new scientific agricultural methods to grateful minority peasants or to impressed minority mothers wearing traditional clothing. Minority "primitiveness" contrasts with the ideal "scientific, modern" Han self.

This type of image is repeated in photos of male urban Han cadres assisting female minority peasants—the "us" going down benevolently to the "them." In 112 issues of newspapers, mostly concentrated during six weeks or so, I found thirty-eight photographs of minorities or minority artifacts, of which seventeen (44.7 percent) included minority females. Only five (13.2 percent) represented minority men. Gender, politics, and ethnicity combine here, fetishizing the exoticism of the backward, female "others."

The breakdown of images in the thirty-eight representations of minorities or minority artifacts is detailed in table 3.2. The vast majority of photographs of ethnic minorities are either of beautiful young women in native dress or of middle-aged women in native dress being aided by middle-aged male Han cadres in Zhongshan clothing ("Mao jackets"). A casual reader—most read-

Table 3.2: Images of Minorities in the Popular Press

Image	Number of occurrences	Percentage of sample
Women	17	44.7%
Houses/buildings	7	18.4
Men	5	13.2
Scenery	4	10.5
Festivals/dances/songs	3	7.9
Elderly	3	7.9
Work activities	2	5.3
Markets	2	5.3
Children	1	2.6
TOTAL 44		115.8*

Note: Six photographs were assigned to two categories, as they contained more than one image. Hence the total exceeds 100 percent.

ers—would conclude from these representations that ethnic others are almost always female, while selves are always male; there are no female Han pictured with ethnic minorities.

The superficiality of these images and the fact that photographs appear without accompanying articles or with suggestive captions that read only "Yunnan's colorful minorities" are ingredients in the soup of ethnic issues in China. For all of the resources devoted to promoting a view of China as concerned with its minorities, most Han interest in minorities is superficial and limited. The minority nationalities serve merely as colorful embellishments to otherwise dull news.

Articles about minority nationalities cover various aspects of their lives, especially those most salient in the popular imagination, from economic development to festivals to songs to houses. The only critical remarks I found showed that, owing to great population increases, minority nationality illiteracy and poverty had increased (a promotion for population planning, from which minorities are in part exempt).

From my sample I concluded that interest in minority nationalities, as conveyed by the press, lies in the domains of festivals, the need for improvement in their material lives, unusual physical artifacts and practices, and improvements in higher education and political life. At least in the popular press, one finds little mention of dire poverty, illiteracy, religion, morality, struggle between ethnic groups, marriage and family structure, or indigenous art forms. A nonexpert general reader would perhaps be expected to absorb the lessons here about the features of ethnic identity having to do with colorful clothing, songs and dances, gratitude for Han benevolence, and so on.

A sample list of article titles follows (the abbreviations are explained in the bibliography):

1. "15,000 nationality cadres in county seats" (YNRB 6/2/91)
2. "Glorious 40th anniversary of the Central Nationalities Institute" (QNB 6/12/91)
3. "Take care of nationalities' trade, encourage nationalities' economic development" (RMRB 6/12/91)
4. "Shanghai workers donate Yongjiu bicycles to their Tibetan compatriots" (RMRB 6/12/91)
5. "Our province will send superb books on nationalities to Hong Kong exhibition" (YNRB 2/12/91)
6. "Spring sayings at Spring Festival" (about each group's New Year customs) (YNRB 2/12/91)
7. "The richest person in Yijia Mountain Village" (YNRB 2/12/91)
8. "Wooden drums and Wa traditional culture" (YNRB 6/14/91)
9. "Nationalities' and folk prescriptions cure myopia" (CCWB 2/22/91)
10. "The profound thought in nationalities literature" (YNRB 4/30/91)
11. "100 youth from all nationalities in our province go to Shenzhen for employment" (GMRB 6/10/91)
12. "Bai hero: A brigade leader who dared to die" (YNRB 5/24/91)
13. "Houses among Dali's Bai people" (WZZK 5/24/91)
14. "Good reception for the Tibetan Arts Troupe" (RMRB 7/24/91)
15. "Tibetan compatriots in Beijing celebrate the year of the golden sheep (yak?)" (RMRB 2/12/91)

SPECIFIC CHARACTERISTICS OF MINORITIES

In compiling a prototype of ethnic others, I found that people's comments fell into several common categories. These categories are explained below, following which I develop a single model. The portraits each focus on one or more of these characteristics.

Cleanliness and "Dirt"

One characteristic attributed to virtually all minority nationalities, and especially to the Zang, is that they are "dirty" (*zang;* first tone). (Exceptions are the Dai and the compulsive Hui.) Could it be that the near homophony of *Zangzu* (fourth tone; "Zang nationality") and *zang* (first tone; "dirty") unconsciously echoes and reminds speakers of this equivalence? An alternative explanation comes when one looks at the other groups that are also considered dirty.[4] Dirtiness is said to characterize the Miao and the Wa as well and is in some ways regarded as typical of the "primitive" nationalities. While there may be some truth to this description, it is used as more than a factual remark; it is also a standard dismissal of any ethnic group and indeed of Han from different regions. Ida Pruitt's account of the life of an illiterate woman, Ning Lao Taitai, in the early twentieth century reports her saying that southerners have a less fastidious sense of hygiene than northerners like herself (1945:113); northerners use latrines, but southerners use "night pails," which need emptying. Nym Wales repeats the stereotypes she heard in Yan'an in the 1930s of Mongols bathing only twice during a lifetime (1939:85). While there may be a substantive basis to beliefs about the "two or three baths in a lifetime" of Mongols and Tibetans, the exact repetition leads one to suspect the formulation. Why three (or two) baths? Why are these particular "others" so dirty?[5]

Hui consider Han to be unclean, but it is difficult to sort out whether this is because of physical dirt or of pollution since the Han fail to perform the symbolic purifications of the Hui. The Dai are "clean," bathing frequently— sometimes as much as twice a day, compared to the typical urban Han who bathes once a week—but this does not lead the Han to regard themselves as dirty. Most groups regard themselves as the standard and, depending on their relations with other groups, will consider the others either similar to themselves (only to a greater degree) or overly fastidious. Hui cleanliness rituals appear to be regarded with a degree of incredulity, while the more generally liked Dai are seen as delightfully sensual and hygienic.

Groups like the Yi, who sleep on the ground rather than on *kangs* (platform beds), have fire pits rather than stoves, and eat with their hands rather than with chopsticks, are considered unclean. A lack of latrines— used by the Han to collect human wastes for fertilizer—is considered dirty to the Han, while many minorities, such as the Hua Miao, consider Han practice disgusting (Norma Diamond, personal communication). Peasants are regarded as dirty by urban Han, but the minorities are seen as dirtiest of all. As the protagonist, Liang Rui, in Bai Hua's novel about the Mosuo, *The Remote Country of Women*, loses his passion for his Mosuo wife, Sunamei, he suddenly notices how dirty everything is around him in her village:

> During the day, I could see more clearly that every Mosuo courtyard was too dirty for me to set foot in. Everywhere there was manure, and the worn-out clothing of the children and the elderly seemed to have never been washed.

Although beautiful girls wore beautiful clothes, their necks were dirty. Sup-
posing I had met Sunamei here but not in town: could I have brought myself
to kiss her? (1994:350)

Bai Hua demonstrates awareness of the common Han perception that
Mosuo are dirty. It is instructive to recall here the exhortations seen all over
Chinese cities not to spit on the streets, not to urinate or defecate in improper places, and so forth. If even urban Chinese are not in fact as clean as
they like to believe, at least they are clean in contrast to others they know to
be both dirtier and more backward than themselves.

Rural-Urban Schisms

While professional identity seems to be critical for self-definitions and presentations among middle-class Americans (see, for example, Linde 1993), for most
Chinese the paramount identifications fall along urban-rural lines. When I asked
people in interviews about their ability to speak the languages associated with
the minority nationality to which they belonged, they laughed nervously and
immediately reminded me that they were urban (often from the *xiancheng*,
"county seat") and thus more sinicized *(Hanhua)*, suggesting the profundity of
this point. (An equivalent response might occur in the United States if someone mistook a person's gender.) Such a distinction is critical and foundational;
errors are virtually impossible. Those who are urban see themselves as more advanced, more modern, and as having more "culture" *(wenming)*. This, along
with other important schisms, can be seen as we examine closely what people
say when they talk about themselves and others.

During a discussion with a group of students about educational levels, I
once asked what the most common level of education was for various sorts
of people. There was some agreement; a typical person from the countryside
is believed to have three or five years of education, while a typical city person is seen as having eight or ten years.

The prototypes of each minority group thus include an assumption about
whether they are typically rural or urban and about their likely level of education. Of the minority groups sketched below (the six mentioned in the linguistic identification and evaluation task), the Hui are believed to be most
urban and the Yi the most rural, beliefs accompanied by corresponding views
of their degrees of modernization.

The Metaphor of Modernization

Modernization has been promulgated in China as a paramount goal since
Zhou Enlai announced it in 1975 and especially since Deng Xiaoping reap-

propriated it as his own policy in 1978. "The Four Modernizations" (*sige xiandaihua,* or *sihua*) is a shorthand phrase that pointed to the goal of catching up with the West by the year 2000 in the areas of industry, agriculture, defense, and science and technology. During the 1980s, the Four Modernizations figured prominently in slogans in many incongruous contexts: one studied in order to realize the Four Modernizations; one made oneself attractive for the Four Modernizations. While this campaign has largely faded away, the language of modernization is pervasive and virtually unchallenged. Arguments revolve only around what form of modernization is best and how much "Westernization" to include.

Constant exposure to evaluation of every society, every ethnic group, every city and region in China in terms of how *xiandaihua* (modernized) or *fada* (advanced) they are would shape the way citizens themselves think about the same things, just as in the United States we talk about "growth" and "competition" and "the business cycle" and "recession" as if these were actual, uncontested things in the world rather than hypotheses and metaphors used for conceptualizing events, around many of which revolve heated theoretical debate.[6]

The language of modernization freezes talk about ethnic groups along a reified continuum. I had intriguing talks with people in trying to discuss the United States. *Meiguo fada* (America is developed), I was told over and over again. Knowing as I do how these models are organized, I nonetheless tried to engage people in talk about preconceptions. I mentioned American inequalities, the growing feeling among many people of economic insecurity, Americans' exaggerated sense of "needs." Yes, yes, that was all true. But in the terms of the description, America was still *fada:* almost everybody has cars, microwaves, and college educations (never mind illiteracy and high school dropouts). The only possible way to categorize America was as "advanced." And similarly, the only possible way to categorize the Wa or the Yi was as "not advanced, backward," and as "primitive."

Food

E. N. Anderson suggests in *The Food of China* (1988) that food can serve as a marker of identity. The most well-known generalizations with regard to food are that northerners eat noodles and other wheat foods while southerners eat rice, or that Chinese eat rice and Westerners eat bread (or meat), or that Chinese eat cooked food and Japanese eat raw food. The idea of *zhushi* (staple) assumes that a single grain food is the basis for each society's foodways. Ohnuki-Tierney (1993) has shown that the Japanese regard themselves as rice eaters despite a relative decrease in rice consumption (and increase of protein foods since the end of World War II) and despite the rarity with which commoners were able to eat rice in the past. Nonetheless, they see rice as central to their diet for many symbolic reasons.

Han Chinese also tend to regard rice eating and rice cultivation as the principal markers of civilization. Indeed, minorities can be divided into rice-eating and non-rice-eating groups: Dai and Bai eat rice; Miao, Yi, Zang, and Wa, for example, do not usually eat it. (Some Yi are noted to be "rice-field Yi.") Hui seem to eat more bread than the Han, and many bakeries in Kunming are run by Hui. Many people commented to me about the horrifying foods eaten by minorities: yak-butter tea (Tibetans), "birdseed" (*xiaomi*— actually millet, though someone once described it to me as similar to bird-seed, which it is in appearance—eaten by Miao), fatty pork (Naxi), strong and abundant liquor (Wa), potatoes and corn (Yi).[7] Though the Han diet is quite hospitable to outside innovation, these foods occupy emblematic positions in which their meaning is "inferiority."

Writing

Groups that have a *wenzi* (writing system) fall into a different category from those that lack one. *Wenzi* resonates with *wenhua* (culture) and *wenming* (civilization, enlightenment), and possession of one implies the other. The government has made providing romanization for each group a priority, but those that originally have their own system are popularly regarded with more favor (see also Bradley 1987, Ramsey 1987, Harrell 1993).

Naxi, Yi, Dai, Mongol, Manchu, Tibetan, and Miao (among others of the groups in Yunnan) have their own writing systems. Some (such as Tibetan) are based on Sanskrit, some (such as Uighur) use Arabic, and some have completely innovative systems, such as the Yi scripts and the Pollard script, invented for the Miao by the British missionary Samuel Pollard. Even if the government has replaced an original script with a new, romanized one, the fact that one existed remains salient.

Chinese writing occupies a remarkable place in Chinese self-conception. As scholar Yang Jingchu wrote in an article titled "How the Han Became the World's Greatest (Most Numerous) Nationality," the longevity and prevalence of Chinese writing is one of the Han's greatest accomplishments.

> China has one of the richest and most developed languages in the world, with a history of several thousand years. In China, in addition to the Han, several minority nationalities also use Chinese characters. There are more than one billion people altogether who use Chinese characters—one of the most widely used writing systems in the world. It is also one of the five written languages of the United Nations. (1989:155)

Writing is the basis of China's most admired art form, calligraphy. It is believed that people's moral character can be revealed through their handwriting. Yearly, people put fresh couplets on their doorways, whether or not they can read or write. Writing is the way spirits communicate through their mediums to send messages to those seeking relief from some affliction. A word, a *zi*, is synonymous with "character" or "ideograph," no matter what linguistic analysis would like us to distinguish.[8] The primacy of writing is evident in linguistic studies, in studies of dialects, in what counts as "history." What has not been written is "folklore" *(fengsu, minjian chuanshuo)*. The more it is like Chinese writing, the more admired is the writing of other societies.[9] *Pinyin*, the alphabet in common use in the PRC and abroad, is seen as a tool for certain limited purposes, but it has no place in people's hearts. Children learn pinyin before they have adequately mastered characters, it is used for alphabetizing in dictionaries, and it is used for teaching foreigners. But once people learn characters, they would never prefer pinyin to using characters. Native speakers of Chinese who teach Chinese to foreigners often believe that they are teaching the real word only when they include the character. It takes years of training for them to dissociate the sound from the character enough to represent it phonetically (just as English speakers persist in using spelling rather than phonetic representation when studying introductory linguistics).

Minority groups that have no lovely, tradition-filled writing system of their own are given a workaday set of symbols that can represent the phonological system of whatever dialect comes to have dominant status. To outsiders, this writing resembles all other romanization schemes, has no possible beauty, and so is not a *wenzi*, a writing system. This provided system is necessary for introducing students to their own language, but in most cases there is little literature and no science written in minority languages (see Harrell 1993).

Sexuality and Marriage: Family Morality as Key Symbol

In Sherry Ortner's classic formulation (1973), a "key symbol" can be identified because (1) "the natives [*sic*] tell us [it] is culturally important," (2) "the natives seem positively or negatively aroused about [it], rather than indifferent," (3) it comes up in many different contexts," (4) "there is great . . . cultural elaboration surrounding it," and (5) "there are great . . . cultural restrictions surrounding it" (1973:1339). Based on these criteria, the family is a key symbol in China. Emperors were to be like a father and mother to the people. Family relations were to set the tone for a peaceable kingdom. Though Mao Zedong was a chairman and a helmsman, the party is to be loved like a family member. The strength of feeling for family is evoked on television, in poetry, in film. Symbolically, the family—with its central unit of a couple married as virgins through their parents' efforts, along with their ancestors and offspring, coexisting harmoniously and working side by side, each person with her or his duties—sets the tone for a well-ordered universe.

The family—courting, marriage, residence, inheritance, and sexuality—is one way that writers claim the Han to be superior to minorities (and the Chinese superior to Westerners). There is frequent invocation of minority practices, such as premarital sexual relations, easy divorce initiated as often by wives as by husbands, marriages initiated by young adults fancying each other at festivals, and (a most peculiar institution) Tibetan polyandry.

Scholars often describe ethnic minorities as having "colorful" marriage customs (for example, Gao 1990, Yang and Gong 1990:90–94, Mei et al. 1993:100–102). This version emphasizes the festive, positive aspects, such as the Dai exchange of *xiangbao*, fragrant embroidered bags tossed by unmarried young people of the opposite sex at the Water Splashing Festival. In other contexts, the focus is on the negative, such as the way wives are taken by their husbands: stolen, eloped, struggled with, or wept over (Yang and Gong 1990:90).

Many writers focus on the order of childbearing, cohabitation, and marriage. The idealized Han marriage begins with engagement, then marriage, followed by cohabitation, and finally childbearing. Some shock is expressed that this order is sometimes violated. The well-known anthropologist Lin Yaohua, writing of the Yi of Liangshan in Sichuan, states that up to five years might elapse between marriage and cohabitation, with the bride moving in with her husband only when she becomes pregnant—whether it is his child or not (1961). At the extreme, weddings occur after children are born: "Who could believe that some weddings take place after a child is born?" *(Shei ye xiangbudao, youde hunli shi shengle haizi hou juxingde?)* (Yang and Gong 1990:90).

Other aspects of minority kinship practices are also criticized, including "bride purchase" and the levirate (the practice of a widow being married by one of her husband's relatives—a brother, father, or cousin). This idea of culturally encouraged widow remarriage violates strongly held Han ideals of women's chastity, whatever the actual frequency of widow remarriage among the Han.[10] Some texts mention the minority lack of a sexual division of labor or a failure to differentiate properly women's roles from those of men. The Wa, one of the most "primitive" ethnic groups, are noted for the lack of separate gender roles in the production process (Wazu Jianshi Editorial Group 1986:40–41).

Harrell (1995a) explains the frequent mention of sexuality and marriage in discussion of minorities by the existence of a metaphoric comparison of minorities with women. Norma Diamond (1988) discusses Han fears of Miao sexuality and their manifestation in frightening stories told about a powerful invisible poison, *gu*, that Miao women administer to keep Han men returning to them. Schein (1997, 2000) writes about Han fascination with minority women and their equivalence to nature. Gladney (1991) writes about insults to Hui through a book that made sexual innuendoes about Hui towers (as phalli) and so forth.

All this can only be understood within a general perspective on popular Chinese notions of sexuality. In contemporary China, sexuality is not discussed openly. Anthropological treatments of sexuality are still quite rudimentary; one noteworthy beginning was Jankowiak's work on sexuality (1993, chs. 7–9; see also van Gulick 1974, Feng 1994, Brownell 1995, Liu et al. 1997). What is relevant here is the way focus on sexuality presupposes an overarching system of morality to which all groups must aspire. But people demonstrate fascination toward alternative systems, suggesting that patrilineal monogamy is cognitively not the only possible system. Han imagination can include alternative forms of living, even to the most basic matters of morality and family structure—although in the end it dismisses those forms.

Clothing

Clothing is the paramount emblem of ethnic difference in China. Though I was told on occasion that ethnic identification can be made on the basis of facial features, this was not usually offered until after many other features had been mentioned. Clothing—especially women's clothing—seemed the most obvious marker of difference (see also Leach 1954, Moerman 1965, Friedlander 1975, Nash 1989, Lutz and Collins 1993). Clothing is also interesting because it can be donned and shed, leaving no trace. Focus on clothing suggests a certain degree of voluntary identification with minority status; those who wish to "pass" can master new ways of walking, talking, and dressing and are not forbidden from doing so (cf. Berreman 1982). Han can dress up as any minority they choose, favorites being Sani and Dai. They can "try on" this alien identity but return from it (see figure 3.1).

Festivals and Religion

Festivals are the single most mentioned aspect of minority life. When I spoke to a group of junior-high-school students and invited them to ask me about

Figure 3.1   A Shanghai Han going ethnic at a Guizhou ethnic theme park (Photo by Tim Oakes)

the United States, their first question was about festivals and holidays. Conversations with Han invariably mentioned the Water Splashing Festival of the Dai or (a far second) the Third-Month Fair of the Yi or Bai. Spontaneous singing and dancing, in contrast to official Han organized parades, appear liberating. These minority festivals are basically perceived as remnants of earlier, more licentious celebrations and are explained through a kernel of folklore that contains an origin story.

Festivals of the Hui and Zang, however, who are both quite religious and have many religious celebrations, are not mentioned. Their festivals do not necessarily include singing and dancing, nor donning of colorful costumes, but are incorporated into the round of religious worship that occupies a very central part of both societies. This less-colorful aspect of religion is a source of discomfort for Han—likely a result of over fifty years of official atheism and anti-superstition campaigns. Despite the restoration of some mosques and temples in recent years, there are clear limits to religious practice; in the summer of 1994, a crackdown on Muslim practice was announced in northwest China. In fact only a handful of the religious buildings originally in use have been restored, though these have been very noticeable. But many more have been transformed into factories or schools or have been abandoned.

Architecture

Classification of groups seems to depend in part on whether their houses are permanent or temporary. Permanent architecture in stone attracts praise. Bai houses are regarded very favorably. Attention to architecture seems to be directed at houses rather than at more communal edifices such as religious buildings. Tibetan buildings may indeed be "permanent," but they bring with them the reminder that they were built at great cost, with families "forced" to contribute a large portion of their livelihood to the temples, and that they were built for "superstitious" purposes. The Potala palace in Lhasa is mentioned, but no one ever pointed out Hui mosques to me as demonstrative of the sophistication of Hui building techniques.

Honesty and Simplicity

In *The Remote Country of Women,* Sunamei's relatives lament her having been out in the "outside world, a Han place full of dishonesty and turmoil" (Bai 1994:347). Indeed, this marker of ethnic difference was mentioned to me by both Han and minorities. Han are crafty, cunning, smart, and cheating. Minorities are simple, honest, gullible, and ignorant. The emblem of difference between ethnic minorities and the Han is actually a boundary that applies as well to the differences between urban and rural Han, or urban Han and peasants: the tendency for the Han/urban dwellers to be what is often called *congming* (clever) and the minority nationalities/peasants to be *laoshi* (ingenuous) or *sha* (dumb). This is a euphemistic way of saying that the Han are in many cases duplicitous and that the minorities are easily duped (Blum n.d.[a]).

A student with one Han and one Hui parent—I'll call her Ma Qing—told me of a source of unhappiness when we talked frankly and privately about ethnicity, family, identity, and many other topics. "My parents taught me to lie," she said, "because they wanted to protect me. I learned not to tell anybody the truth, especially Han. Out in society, in the world, we had to know how to keep the truth from other people."

She spoke rapidly, and earnestly, as if unburdening herself to a safe listener, a foreign anthropologist, someone outside the system that oppressed her. A line was drawn: life in society versus life in the family. Yet this line was not clear enough, and the fact that exigencies of dissembling were taught by her own mother and father, that the stain of society's demands spilled over into the pure life of home, was still painful for this young woman in her early twenties.

This contrast between honesty within her family and dishonesty in the larger Han world was connected, too, for her and for many others in China to the question of her ethnic identity. Her father is Han, her mother Hui. She chose, at eighteen, to be Hui like her mother, and her younger sister chose to be Han—to balance things out, she said. She told me of her grandmother's sister's trip to Mecca, of the separate bathing facilities for Hui at her parents' factory and work unit where they all lived, of marriage customs and food taboos. But as the child of a "mixed marriage," and an intellectual, she herself did not believe in Islam necessarily. Still, she was known as Hui.

For all the epithets directed by Han at Hui, I rarely ever heard anyone accuse the Hui of being duplicitous. Hui were called violent (see, for example, Lipman 1990), unreasonable, separatist, and superstitious, but where ethnic stereotypes were concerned, only the Han were considered anything but honest.

Simplicity and honesty—being *laoshi*—is a hallmark of most ethnic minorities, according to Han, just as it is of peasants. This trait is admired, at least officially. In the 1960s, when urban youth were supposed to be educated by peasants rather than by books and teachers, one of the qualities most often mentioned was that peasants were *laoshi, pusu*—ingenuous, unassuming, natural—and that others should emulate them.

A recent book concerned with morality among China's southwest minorities (Gao 1990) claims that one of the moral qualities that characterizes most ethnic minorities is their *chunpuxing* (honesty, simplicity, lack of sophistication). This quality used to characterize all people in primitive societies, the author claims, and is often overlooked but should be valued: "They treat others sincerely, honestly and reliably, giving people a sense of security. They do things extremely clearly; one is one, two is two, come and go straight, their moral sentiments are directly expressed externally" (Gao 1990:229). Words used to describe them are *chengken* (sincere) and *dushi* (honest and sincere, solid).

The implied contrast is clear: peasants and minority nationalities are simple and honest. Urban dwellers and Han are complex, not gullible, not naive. "Clever" *(congming)* was the term often used, usually mistranslated as "intelligent." Intelligence is often understood in China as the ability to use words properly and cleverly for pragmatic ends. In China, talking is not principally conceived of as a vehicle for revealing one's inner truth, except on those rare occasions when one finds a *zhiyin*, a hearer of one's music. (This is an allusion to the well-known story of Yu Boya and his friend Zhong Ziqi, who understood perfectly Yu's *qin* [Chinese lute] playing.) Language is used for many other purposes. It soothes children; it chants the name of the Amidha Buddha and brings paradise closer; it recites statistics that increase enthusiasm for hard work (Banister 1987); it deprecates one's own accomplishments to avoid the envy of others, including god's; it gives answers to questions that preserve face all around; it is a weapon that can destroy one's enemies.

Language is regarded with great nuance in China. If one is asked a question, one must answer. Truth, all other things being equal, is better than falsity, but the other things are never equal. If one tells "the truth"—yes, I was the one who picked your apples—what will the consequences be? For me? For my parents/spouse/siblings/children? For the others involved? If one tells "a lie," will one be discovered? By whom? When? Does the discoverer have enough influence to matter? All things considered, which way will produce the most desirable results? (See Blum n.d.[a] for more on deception and truth.)

Lies are related to deception in Chinese; *sahuang* (spreading untruths) is a form of gossip; *pian* (to cheat or deceive) is used when people harbor ill intentions. At its best, a clever use of language can save a life. This adage is learned not so much through explicit instruction as through stories, schemata. One such schema is learned in the delightful classic Tang story "Sung Ting-po [Song Dingbo] Catches a Ghost" (Institute of Literature 1979:17–18), in which Sung fooled a ghost into revealing ghosts' secrets by claiming to be a new ghost and therefore heavy when they took turns carrying each other.

At worst, people can be cheated, robbed, or led into great misfortune. Pu Songling's story "Fraud (No. 3)" (1989) tells of a man who cheated through a most clever and patient combination of verbal lying and misleading actions. A Taoist named Cheng bought a post in a certain district in order to forge an apparent friendship with a man named Li who possessed an ancient and magical lute. For at least a year, Cheng never mentioned the lute; then he left one lying around, causing Li to admit that he too was a connoisseur of the lute. After more time passed, they played for each other. One day, Cheng lamented that he did not have a better lute to play with. Li finally took out his magical lute. Cheng said his wife could play even more skillfully than he could so he passed the lute behind a screen for her to play. Li, who had been drinking much wine, was urged to return the following day to retrieve his lute and to hear Cheng's wife play masterfully. When Li returned, the entire compound was deserted and his lute gone with Cheng and his wife. Pu Songling concludes with the moral that "there are many angles from which to practice deception in this world. In the Taoist's case, there was a certain refinement in his trickery" (Pu 1989:291).

In cases of trickery when people are harmed, it is lamented, and yet—and here we detect something important—in other cases there is a certain admiration for cleverness, patience, perseverance, refinement. To set up a person over a period of several years for a robbery demonstrates much cleverness. In such an enterprise, language is a tool like others. There is desire for honesty and simplicity, as my Hui friend described it, when situated in the Han world. Her longing is not unique.

Yet the longing for honesty and simplicity coexists with recognition that it may be impossible. When asked playfully what "paradise" might be like, one young woman answered, "In my heart, I only wish the world had less hatred, more fraternal love and kindness, less craftiness and more sincerity, fewer tears, more happiness. I also wish that people who live in the same area would treat each other sincerely instead of each trying to cheat or outwit the other and life would become easier." But this woman, like Ma Qing, knows that such simplicity is impossible for them; the returned urban youth made quite clear that they could not function like Chinese peasants. Still, the longing can be directed outside the boundaries of one's own group toward those others who embody so many desires. As the authors of our essays make so clear, without ever having had much contact with ethnic minorities they are able to recite many of their attributes.

IDEALIZED COGNITIVE MODEL OF MINORITIES

Thus the "idealized cognitive model" (Lakoff 1987:68–117) of minority nationalities is that they

1. wear different clothing
2. speak different languages
3. believe in religion
4. eat different foods
5. have no state-level political organization, but retain "primitive" types of social organization
6. have festivals
7. have music, dance, costumes, and ornaments
8. may not have an indigenous writing system
9. occupy particular territories
10. have different marriage patterns and kinship systems
11. have different ("primitive") material culture
12. are ingenuous.

Not all aspects of this model apply to every ethnic group, but groups with the most of these attributes tend to be the most salient.

SALIENCE

The seven minority nationalities examined here are among the most salient for Chinese[11] in Kunming. This can be explained by these groups being prototypical or by their fulfilling stereotypical notions of ethnic others. These groups are brought to mind most often and most quickly, leading to repeated use of the same examples and even of the exact phrases. We can compare the frequency with which they are mentioned by different people in different fora and can draw some conclusions about which groups might be considered significant in the cognitive universe of Kunming residents.

In the linguistic identification and evaluation task, listeners guessed about the ethnic identity of speakers they heard on a tape. Many groups were mentioned who were not actually speaking, a fact that I take to indicate their salience in the minds of the respondents. Table 3.3 lists groups mentioned and their frequency. As is readily apparent, the Yi and Bai far exceed the other nationalities in terms of salience, both guessed fifty-five times. There was one actual Yi speaker, in guises ten (speaking Yi) and sixteen (speaking Putonghua), but the attribution of "Yi" was made for speaker ten only six times, and for speaker sixteen only eight times, with the greatest number (fifteen) guessing "Yi" for a person speaking Naxi and the next greatest (nine) guessing "Yi" for a person of the Kucong (unrecognized) minority speaking a local, accented variety of Yunnanhua. (Quotation marks indicate ethnicities attributed to speakers by respondents.) There was no Bai speaker.

Table 3.3: Frequency of Minority Attribution in the Linguistic Identification and Evaluation Task

Group guessed	Times (no.)	Group guessed	Times (no.)
Yi (one actual speaker)	**55**	Lahu	3
Bai	**55**	Kucong (one actual speaker)	2
Naxi (one actual speaker)	**22**	Nu	2
Zang (Tibetan)	**21**	**Wa**	1
Miao	15	Yao	1
Dai	**11**	Aini (Hani)	1
Hui	**9**	Mongolian	1
Zhuang	8	Uighur	1
Lisu	6	Tujia	1
Hani	6	Jingpo	1
Sani (Yi)	4	Dong	1
		SUBTOTAL	227
	"minority" or "non-Han" (unspecified)		99
		TOTAL	326

Note: Groups treated in the following chapters appear in boldface type.

The three next most frequent attributions were of "Naxi" (twenty-two), "Zang" (twenty-one), and "Miao" (fifteen). As was the case with the Yi, there was a speaker of Naxi ethnicity, though there were none of Zang or Miao identity. Following these were fairly equal numbers of attributions of "Dai" (eleven), "Hui" (nine), and "Zhuang" (eight), followed by diminishing numbers of other minorities. "Wa" was guessed only once, a fact that may be explained by the extreme unlikelihood of Wa being found speaking to a foreigner in Kunming. Using this instrument, most salient were Yi, Bai, Naxi, Zang, Miao, Hui, Dai, and Zhuang.

Slightly different groups seem salient in student essays (see table 3.4). The essays were divided into a batch that required students to describe a personal experience with minority nationalities and a batch that merely asked about minority nationalities. In the latter case, I counted only those mentions that were "substantive," in which people wrote at least a descriptive sentence about the minorities, not merely in which they listed their names. The descriptions could be based on either personal direct experience or hearsay to varying degrees.[12]

Table 3.4: Frequency of Mention of Minority Nationalities in Student Essays

YD essays (personal experience)		YZM essays (substantive: hearsay or personal experience)	
Dai	6	Dai	13
Yi	6	Yi	12
Bai	3	Hui	8
Hui	2	Tibetans	7
Lisu	2	Miao	4
Jingpo	1	Bai	3
Miao	1	Mongol	3
Hani	1	Naxi	2
Naxi	1	Lahu	2
Lahu	1	Lisu	2
Mongol	1	Kucong	2
		Hani	1
		Manchu	1
		Jinuo	1
		Mosuo (= Naxi)	1
		Hezhen	1
		Korean	1
		Achang	1

YD = Yunnan University
YZM = Yunnan Metallurgical Institute

Groups most often mentioned in essays involving personal experiences were the Dai (six) and Yi (six), usually in descriptions of the Water Splashing and Torch festivals. These were followed by the Bai (three), Hui (two), and Lisu (two). There was no essay that includes personal experience with the Zang.

In essays that could incorporate either personal experience or secondhand information, in contrast, Dai (thirteen) and Yi (twelve) were still most frequently mentioned, followed by Hui (eight), Zang (seven), Miao (four), Bai (three), and Mongols (three). Tibetans (Zang) are quite salient in people's minds despite their lack of contact with them.

A third source of evidence of salience is a glossy book with colored photographs of China's ethnic minorities, *Highlights of Minority Nationalities in Yunnan* (n.d.) (hereafter *Highlights*). *Highlights*, written in both English and Chinese, includes "all the 24 minorities of Yunnan," but a cursory analysis of the representation of various groups reveals much about the importance placed on each. The photographs serve to illustrate the "colorful diversity" of China's ethnic minorities. While we cannot be certain of the manner in which such a book was compiled—was it according to a fixed ideological/propaganda formula or was it the intuition of the editors?—it seems, with a few exceptions, to be fairly representative of popular portrayals of Yunnan's minorities, especially with regard to the Hui (who are very prevalent, as we shall see, in people's consciousness but scarcely even appear in *Highlights*) (see table 3.5).

Clearly, the groups are unevenly portrayed, with more emphasis placed on some than on others. Population alone is insufficient to account for a given group's degree of salience (see table 3.6).

Another explanation for the salience of each group is that each typifies a certain type of minority. Yet another is that those that are more salient for some reason—yet to be explained—capture the imagination or are considered picturesque and photogenic. While the Water Splashing Festival of the Dai is clearly popular and receives much attention, we must seek a cultural explanation for that very popularity.

The groups that require particular explanation with regard to their degree of salience include the Dai, Yi, Bai, Zang, Wa, Naxi, Hui, Zhuang, Hani, and Miao. Some are overrepresented and others underrepresented in terms of population. Why are the Dai, with a population of only 836,000 in Yunnan (840,000 in China) given so very many pages (thirty-three pages)? They are not the most numerous, but are they somehow the most important? Why are the very numerous Hani (1.1 million in Yunnan; none in the rest of China) given such short shrift (eight pages)? Are they too insignificant? Chapters 4 to 7 treat the six most salient groups (Dai, Yi, Bai, Tibetan, Wa, and Naxi) as well as one strikingly overlooked group (the Hui). The Hui are depicted

Table 3.5: Ethnic Groups in Official Publications

No. of pages		Order of appearance	
Dai	33	1	Yi
Yi	22	2	Bai
Bai	16	3	Naxi
Tibetans	13	4	Lahu
Wa	10	5	Lisu
Naxi	10	6	Hani
Hani	8	7	Pumi
Miao	7	8	Nu
Yao	6	9	Dulong
Zhuang	5	10	Jingpo
Mongol	5	11	Jinuo
Jingpo	5	12	Achang
Lahu	4	13	Tibetans
Achang	4	14	De'ang
Lisu	4	15	Bulang
Dulong	4	16	Mongolian
De'ang	4	17	Hui
Hui	3	18	Yao
Bulang	3	19	Buyi
Nu	3	20	Shui
Pumi	2	21	Miao
Buyi	2	22	Zhuang
Shui	2	23	Wa
Jinuo	2	24	Dai

Source: Highlights of Minority Nationalities in Yunnan

Note: Groups treated in the following chapters appear in boldface type.

in three pages like the Nu are, even though they have nearly twenty times the population in Yunnan alone (438,000) compared to the 23,000 Nu in Yunnan. There are approximately 7.2 million Hui in China as a whole; there are no Nu in the rest of China. I will explain what makes certain groups prevalent in the popular imagination and what makes others virtually absent.

Assuming that groups are placed to maximize contrast—usually between "advanced" and "backward" groups—the ordering of the appearance can be understood. Assuming also that for some reason these groups were selected to represent typical minority qualities, photogenic and appealing, one can account for the greater number of pages devoted to the Yi, Wa, and so on, and for the fewer pages devoted to the Hui.

Table 3.6: Minority Population

Ethnic Group	Population in Yunnan (1982)	Population in China (1990)
Yi	3,352,000	6,572,173
Bai	1,120,000	1,594,827
Hani	1,060,000	1,253,952
Zhuang	894,000	15,489,630
Dai	836,000	1,025,128
Miao	752,000	7,398,035
Lisu	467,000	574,856
Hui	438,000	8,602,978
Lahu	300,000	411,476
Wa	298,000	351,974
Naxi	236,000	278,009
Yao	147,000	2,134,013
Zang	96,000	4,593,330
Jingpo	93,000	119,209

Sources: 1982 census; 1990 census: Zhongguo Renkou Tongji Nianjian 1990 (Kexue jishu wenxian chubanshe, Beijing, 1991, pp. 56–57, 12–15.)

Beginning with the ubiquitous and varied Yi (featured first, with twenty-two pages), one has an impression of tremendous diversity and color. The Yi costumes photographed are far from daily attire, but they are recognizable as belonging to the Yi. (My friend Zhao Ling looked at the book and said, incredulously, "That looks a little like our Yi traditional clothing!" The experience of seeing people similar to those she might know photographed in such an important book was a new one for her.)

The Hui have few recognizable, colorful traits and have very few (three) pages devoted to them, despite their great salience for ordinary people and despite their great numbers in the population. The Wa have much to do in their role as quintessential negative other, for they must represent the formerly unreachable minority now brought within the brotherhood of unified nationalities; ten pages are devoted to them.

Tibetans are featured quite prominently, with thirteen pages, despite their small numbers in Yunnan. Given the intended audience of this sort of publication, however, we can understand this coverage as a demonstration of the great respect with which the Tibetans and their culture (including religion) are treated.

The Dai and Bai are prominent as well because of their ability to represent the best of minorities, both those needing assistance from the Han (the Dai, with thirty-three pages) and those who scarcely need much (the Bai, with sixteen pages). Both groups are "colorful," with well-known and quite presentable costumes, are famed for their beautiful women, and are without any of the troubling violent or separatist tendencies of such groups as the Zang and the Hui.

PROJECTING DIFFERENCE

The linguistic identification and evaluation task, essentially a projective test in which groups and their characteristics were projected onto unknown stimuli, reveals important differences among the groups invoked (see tables 3.7a and 3.7b). Six of the seven groups for which I have sketched portraits appear frequently in this test. (The Wa alone do not.) Comparing attributes imputed for the six groups, we can see important differences. In some cases the number of responses was quite low. There may be no statistical significance to these figures. Still, to the extent that they correspond to the other accounts of these issues, they add up to a meaningful impression of the groups.

Pleasing Language

Haoting is ambiguous between "pleasing" and "comprehensible." The question of whether the language is *haoting* must be understood as vacillating between these two meanings. Responses are quite fascinating. Naxi are most *haoting* (27.3 percent), Hui least (10 percent). Since the Hui are known to be speaking Chinese dialects identical to Han around them, the interpretation can only be that they are unpleasing.

Decent

The question *Zheige ren bucuo ma?* (Is this person quite all right?) attempts to investigate overall attitudes toward the speakers. Dai were most *bucuo* (54.5 percent), followed (surprisingly) by Hui (50 percent); Yi were lowest (20 percent), at less than half the figure for Dai and Hui.

"Friends"

The question of *Zheigeren huibuhui zuo nide pengyou?* (Would this person be likely to be your friend?) attempted to get at some kind of perceived nearness. Most likely were Dai (54.5 percent); least likely were Zang (Tibetans) (23.8 percent).

Table 3.7a: Comparison of Attributed Identities in the Linguistic Identification and Evaluation Task

Rank	Language pleasing		Decent		Potential friend		Wealthy		Education (years)	
1	Naxi	27.3%	Dai	54.5%	Dai	54.5%	Dai	45.4%	Bai	6.75
2	Dai	18.2	Hui	50.0	Yi	38.2	Zang	33.3	Dai	6.33
3	Yi	16.4	Bai	30.9	Bai	34.5	Hui	33.3	Zang	6.20
4	Zang	14.3	Naxi	27.3	Hui	33.3	Naxi	27.3	Naxi	6.00
5	Bai	9.1	Zang	23.8	Naxi	27.3	Bai	18.2	Hui	6.00
6	Hui	0	Yi	20.0	Zang	23.8	Yi	10.9	Yi	5.47

Table 3.7b: Comparison of Attributed Identities in the Linguistic Identification and Evaluation Task: Profession

Rank	Teacher		Cadre		Worker		Peasant		Getihu		Teacher+Cadre	
1	Dai	14.3%	Dai	21.4%	Hui	37.5%	Hui	50.0%	Naxi	15.9%	Dai	35.7%
2	Hui	12.5	Bai	18.3	Yi	26.7	Yi	48.0	Bai	14.6	Bai	26.5
3	Naxi	9.0	Naxi	15.9	Zang	24.2	Naxi	40.9	Zang	12.1	Naxi	24.9
4	Bai	8.5	Zang	12.1	Dai	21.4	Bai	37.8	Yi	9.3	Zang	18.2
5	Zang	6.1	Yi	10.7	Bai	18.3	Zang	36.4	Dai	7.1	Yi	13.4
6	Yi	2.7	Hui	0	Naxi	15.9	Dai	28.6	Hui	0	Hui	12.5

Wealth

The question of the wealth of the speaker gauged perceived economic standing. Most likely to be wealthy were Dai (45.4 percent), Zang (33.3 percent), and Hui (33.3 percent); least likely were Naxi (27.3 percent), Bai (18.2 percent), and Yi (10.9 percent).

Education

At first the educational figures guessed for those speakers believed to be minorities seemed low and the result of snobbishness to me, but looking further into it, they are actually fairly high—in some cases impossibly high—for many of the categories. If the minority nationalities are predominantly peasant (see below), then the educational levels guessed were unrealistically high.

Mean educational levels guessed range from a high of 6.75 years for the Bai to a low of 5.47 years for the Yi. These guesses reflect, to some extent, impressions people have about degree of "advancement" as well as urbanness, with the Hui most urban and the Yi most rural.

Occupation

As table 3.7 shows, nearly all of the attributed ethnic minorities were guessed to be peasants and of five likely types of employment: cadre, worker, peasant, teacher, or *getihu* (independent entrepreneur, often on a very small scale). The relative proportion of different professions is, however, not identical among the six groups. The most prestigious job could clearly be deemed that of "teacher." The Dai were guessed to be potential teachers in 14.3 percent of the cases, while only 2.7 percent of the Yi were so judged. The least prestigious occupation is that of "peasant," guessed to be that of the Hui in 50 percent of the cases, in contrast to only 28.6 percent of the Dai. The most urban occupations are those of "worker" and *"getihu,"* with rather different figures for various groups: 37.5 percent Hui worker compared with 15.9 percent Naxi worker, and 0 percent Hui *getihu* versus 15.9 percent Naxi *getihu*.

Getihu include some of the independent people who are often newly arrived from the countryside into the city, who are without the regular employment of workers but who construct their own employment, often through very small enterprises. Sometimes they become very successful businesspeople. Hui are thus seen as more established, with jobs in the state sector; Naxi are seen as much more likely to have to create their own livelihood like others who arrive from the country.

	Negative		Positive
Less "advanced"	Wa	Yi	Naxi
More "advanced"	Zang		Dai
	Hui		Bai

Figure 3.2   Conceptual schema of various nationalities

ETHNOGEOGRAPHY:
THE WORLD ACCORDING TO KUNMINGERS

The overall impression one has from these sources suggests that some groups are especially salient. I have constructed two different kinds of diagrams that attempt to capture the overall importance of each ethnic category (see figures 3.2, 3.3, 3.4). Such exercises could be repeated in various domains. Figure 3.2 shows the relative positions of the seven ethnic groups that are covered in the following chapters on two scales: positive-negative and advanced-backward. This relies on all the information presented so far as well as the information that will be presented in the following chapters.

Figures 3.3 and 3.4 attempt to depict the relative importance of the places and groups represented, in large part based on how frequently they arose in conversations. Because of the need to assess first how wide the mental geography was of my informants, I asked people in interviews about places they had visited, places they had heard about, and places they would visit if they could go anywhere they wanted.

If I were to represent the salient elements of the world according to a Han resident of Kunming, based on interviews and other interactions, I would put (following Hsu 1971) family at the center with decreasing importance indicated by increasing distance from the center. Some geographic locations would be included, while others might hover at the margins (see figure 3.3). Most respondents mentioned Beijing and Guangdong, a few mentioned Hainan (which had just separated as a province separate from Guangdong), and occasionally someone would mention the United States. But for most of them, the knowable universe ended with the borders of China, and few included areas of predominantly minority population. Minorities are intriguing embellishments on an otherwise uniform human world, but they are not seen as intersecting much with the world of the Han.

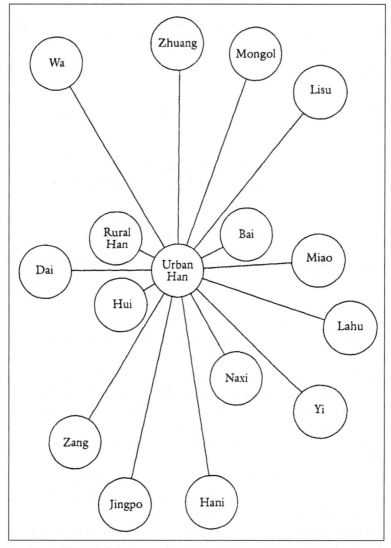

Figure 3.3   Ethnogeography: Ethnicity According to Kunmingers

CONCLUSION

This chapter has discussed the notion of cognitive prototypes and the value these have for making sense of identities attributed to minority groups in China. Though ethnicity is not an especially important aspect of identity for members of the majority group, the so-called Han, the state has promoted

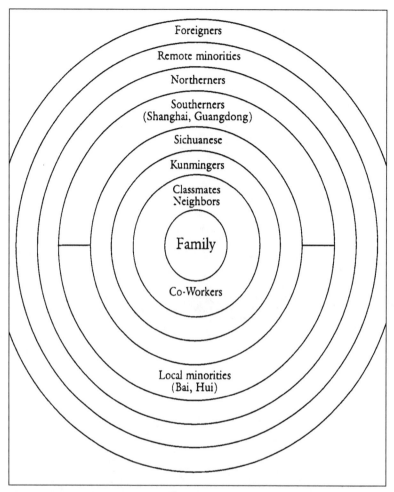

Figure 3.4   Ethnogeography: The world according to Kunmingers (after Hsu 1971) (created by Hal Aqua, Aqua Design)

certain views of minorities; the official views, in turn shaped by the pervasive models of desirable and undesirable traits, influence popular views. Popular views of ethnicity focus on certain traits believed to be possessed by minority groups: primitiveness, dirtiness, backwardness, honesty, colorful clothing, exotic food, festivals, and so forth. Those groups that are particularly good fits with these cognitive models are the groups that are salient—that is, mentioned frequently in a wide variety of contexts.

PROTOTYPES
OF OTHERNESS

PART II

THE FETISHIZED
ETHNIC OTHER: THE DAI

Dai Nationality

The Dai, related to the Thai of Thailand,[1] are in many ways the prototypical, best-case model of ethnic otherness. Nearly all of the general attributes for minorities are applicable to the Dai example: they have famous festivals (Water Splashing Festival), distinctive customs (hospitality) and clothing (narrow skirts), singing and dancing, handicrafts, rituals, foods (eating moss and sour meat), and their own autonomous areas (Xishuangbanna and De-hong prefectures; see map 4.1). Such prototypical criteria are included nearly every time the Dai are mentioned, with Poshuijie, the Water Splashing Festival, receiving the most coverage. The Dai are mentioned in Kunming almost every time minorities are invoked.

I call the Dai "fetishized" because in many presentations they are abstracted from their actual social life and detached from their individual characteristics, reduced to picturesque and simplified versions of their full human character. According to Michael Taussig, "Fetishism denotes the attribution of life, autonomy, power, and even dominance to otherwise inanimate objects and presupposes the draining of these qualities from the human actors who bestow the attribution" (1980:31). One of the major aspects of the "cross-cultural spaces" filled by the term "fetish," according to William Pietz (1985, 1987, 1988), is that "African fetish worship (and hence African society) was . . . revealed to be based on the principles of chance encounter and *the arbitrary fancy of emotion conjoined with desire*" (Pietz 1987:43; emphasis mine). In this sense the Dai are the ideal, modal ethnic other, made into a fetish of colorful otherness and desire. Though the Dai are clearly animate, images of them are often employed to adorn objects, whether key chains, murals, or figurines, divorced from any living meaning. Our task in this chapter is to explain some of the arbitrary conjoining of emotion and desire.

The following two student essays give some flavor of the reports made about "personal experiences among minority nationalities"—in this case, the Dai. The first is essentially a matter-of-fact description of the events, while the second includes more enthusiastic and even gushing praise.

"Celebrating the Water Splashing Festival"
I come from Xishuangbanna, so I have had a chance to celebrate the Water Splashing Festival with the Dai Minority people.

The Water Splashing Festival is held during three days. Before the Festival boys and girls of the Dai Minority go to the mountain together to pick flowers, making houses of flowers. Preparations for all kinds of activities in the Festival are going on in the streets in Jinghong (the capital of Xishuangbanna).

On the first day of the Festival, the main activity is the Dragon Boat Race. Thousands of people including foreign visitors from different countries, Dai

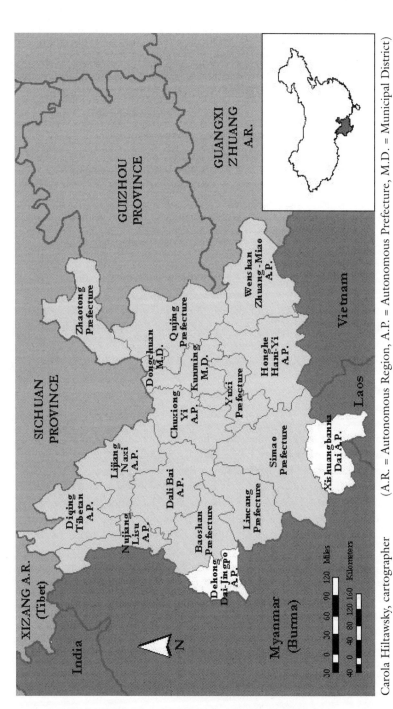

Carola Hiltawsky, cartographer   (A.R. = Autonomous Region, A.P. = Autonomous Prefecture, M.D. = Municipal District)

Yunnan Province Prefectures

Map 4.1   Dehong and Xishuangbanna Dai Autonomous Prefectures in Yunnan

Minority, Han Minority and other minorities go to the Lancang River to watch the race. The race begins at 10:00 A.M. and finishes at 4:00 P.M. People stand around on both sides of the river. I can see there are about seven wooden boats on the river. The boats are decorated with many beautiful dragon pictures. There are ten young strong men of the Dai minority in each boat. The seven boats start rowing together to see which boat goes fastest. The winners of the boat will be given a reward by the government. Near the bank, some people beat drums and gongs. Some actors and actresses who wear Dai Minority clothing perform excellent programmes. Some people are selling ice-cream and some other sorts of things. This is a really happy scene!

On the second day of the Festival, all of the people gather at Mang-Ting Park. They want to see an entertainment called "throw bags." But the bags are different from ordinary bags. The bags are five square *cun* [inches]. They are made of cloth. These bags are full of cotton seeds. There is a cloth ribbon, about three or four *chi* [feet] long, which hangs on the bag. Boys stand on one side of the square, girls stand on the other side of the square. They "throw bags" to each other. If one fails to hold the bag, he or she will be punished. If the boy fails to hold the bag, he has to give the girl his money. If the girl fails to hold the bag, she has to give the boy her ornaments. But the hosts and guests "throw bags," too. The guests are of course the foreign visitors, and the hosts are usually the girls of the Dai Minority from nearby villages. The foreign visitors can scarcely stand still when the girls throw more than fifty bags to them. Of course, most of the bags fall to the ground. So the girls run to the losers to get their prizes. If the girls fail to hold the bags, they give several wisps of flowers to the guests. This is a very wonderful game. So I tried to throw bags with the boys or the foreigners.

The last day of the Festival, of course, is splashing water on people. On this day, men and women, young and old splash water on each other. The Dai Minority believe that it is auspicious if one is splashed with water on this day. So many people go to the streets for a special purpose—to get splashed. The high point of the Water Splashing is at 12:00 o'clock, because the sun is very hot at this time. When I went to the street, I met many men carrying basins of cool water who were chasing me. When they caught up with me, they splashed water on me. This was an exciting moment to me. The Water Splashing finishes at 4:00 P.M. If you go to the street after the Water Splashing has finished, you will find the streets all covered with water.

The Water Splashing Festival is held in the Dai Minority area. This is the new year of the Dai Minority. Dai Minority splash water on each other in order to be lucky, and with best wishes for the new year!

This account introduces most of the basic themes commonly associated with the Dai—themes of performance, public courtship, and rational explanations for apparently irrational behavior (the water throwing culminates at noon because of the heat). The following account is a bit less generic in feeling:

"An Unforgettable Journey: A Personal Experience in Water Splashing Festival"

As is known to all, China is a great country with vast territory, large population and diversified national minorities. There are 56 minorities in China which constitute 6% of China's total population and there are altogether 25 minorities in Yunnan province. Minority people have peculiar characteristics in appearance, dress, food, customs and languages.

In the early spring last year, I happened to have a wonderful chance to go to Xishuangbanna for the famous Water Splashing Festival. All the way, I listened attentively and patiently [to] the legend of the Water Splashing Festival told in minute detail by my older sister. It is said that once upon a time there was a vicious demon who seized seven beautiful sisters to be his wives. The youngest of them all was very clever and took a hair of the demon to strangle and kill him when he was sleeping. His head fell to the ground and it rolled with unceasing flames. It was only when the girl held it up that the fire went out. So the girls held up the evil head in turn to prevent it from burning. From then on, the Dai people splashed cool water on the girl who was off duty to relieve her of her fatigue. Hence, the Dai people splash water on each other to celebrate the victory and the coming of a new year. The Water Splashing Festival is celebrated on new year's day in the Dai calendar, and the exact date changes slightly each year.

As soon as our bus arrived in Jinghong, capital of Xishuangbanna, we were surrounded by splashing water from all sides and shouts of joy. The first person to get off the bus was welcomed by a mugful of water which made him wet through the vital organs of the body. We were carried away by a sudden impulse in an undulating sea mixed with the sound of splashing water and cheers of great joy. We joined a grand and rejoicing group without knowing the passing time.

In the next day, we went out to wander in the street. There were green palms on both sides of the street. A couple of girls were walking elegantly in front of us. They wore long skirts with beautiful peacock designs and short shirts that matched fittingly. One after another Dai girls passed me in a flash with colorful umbrellas, and I was at a loss to tell whether they were dainty goddesses or proud peacocks. What a gentle and graceful carriage!

In the last few days, we visited the local Dai people. We were fascinated by the architectural style of their bamboo houses. They are dainty works of art built completely with bamboo to prevent extreme hot weather there. There are two stories and people live on the second floor. One must take off shoes before he or she enters into the house. The hostess is always friendly and hospitable to offer you raw and cold foods which are their favorites, and delicious tropical fruits such as pineapple and mango. What is more, they entertain guests with fragrant rice wine and the guests must accept and drink it at once without exception to appreciate the kindness.

On our way back, we indulged in a dream filled with the fragrance of the wine and the sweetness of the round moon.

In these essays one can find fascination with graceful women, hospitality, and exuberant festivals, with minorities' unusual foods and clothing. If the Dai represent the quintessence of ethnic otherness and as such are the prototype, the "modal ethnic other" against which all the minorities are compared, we might ask why. What benefit is derived from the emphases placed on festivals, autonomy, and the other features that make ethnic others intriguing? Why, for instance, is the Water Splashing Festival famous?

Xishuangbanna, one of the two Dai autonomous prefectures in Yunnan (the other is Dehong), is a showcase of exoticism, nature, and prosperity for foreign visitors, with great infusions of supplies and funding from outside. Though it was closed to foreigners until the mid-1980s, without a single hotel deemed appropriate to house non-Chinese, there is now a hotel as well as a guest house. Planes fly directly from Kunming, and foreigners are greatly encouraged to visit. In 1991, foreign teachers were granted a week's vacation if they were interested in spending 800 *yuan* (in foreign currency, of course) for first-class accommodations and a special tour created just for invited "foreign guests" to the limited-attendance Water Splashing Festival. "The Dai Lunar New Year, commonly called the Water Splashing Festival, is marked each April by three days of unbridled celebration, drunkenness and hilarity. It is a wonderful time to be in Xishuangbanna, but because of transportation and lodging constraints only about 300 foreigners, many of them students studying in China, are able to attend" (Booz 1987:168).

In the first essay quoted above, notice the clarity with which the author identifies the guests with "foreign visitors." Many Chinese, even those who live in Xishuangbanna, are unable to attend the Water Splashing Festival; it is considered a privilege that requires a certain stature.

The Water Splashing Festival is an especially well-hyped event, dehistoricized and spoken of as if it were timeless. Photographs of Zhou Enlai wearing a Dai head covering during his 1961 visit to the Water Splashing Festival are prominent everywhere, even in textbooks of Chinese for foreigners (see figure 4.1). (Zhou also visited Dehong Dai Autonomous Prefecture to meet the premier of Burma, U Nu.) The Dai section of the first-floor exhibit of all of Yunnan's minority nationalities at the Yunnan Provincial Museum features this photograph. When I went to dinner at the home of a woman who was a retired member of the performance troop of the People's Liberation Army (PLA), sure enough she displayed a photograph of the turbaned Zhou in her home, but this variant included my host's visage as well since she had been on that trip.

Figure 4.1 Zhou Enlai visits
the Dai during the Water
Splashing Festival in 1961

In addition to demonstrating the support—however token—for minority religion, Zhou's presence is a kind of harbinger of the tourism that has recently been so encouraged. (A cynic might ask if it were the case that no noteworthy official has visited the area since Zhou's visit three decades ago. But another question is what was made of his visit during the intervening years.) In any case, although the Water Splashing Festival is reported to be celebrated as well by other nationalities who live near the Dai, it is most completely associated with the Dai. An answer to the question of why, of all "festivals," this one has received so much official attention may be found in Mikhail Bakhtin's notion of "the carnivalesque" (1984).

In his study of Rabelais, in part as analogue to the straitening of culture taking place in the Soviet Union, Bakhtin describes the demise of "the carnivalesque," a concept partially but fortuitously applicable to the analysis of China's appropriation of minority festivals. Bakhtin means by "carnival" something ribald, unconstrained, earthy, where status differences are suspended and laughter prevails. The laughter of carnival is social and universal yet ambivalent because it mocks while it also affirms (Bakhtin 1984:10–12). Many elements of this carnival have been removed from the festival, as a result of the official embrace and then sanitizing of minority ritual, which sounds oddly like the Stalinesque "soviet realism" (or socialist realism) for which the Middle Ages Church stood as metaphor in Bakhtin's work. "Sanitizing" has occurred for all of the officially sanctioned minority festivals in China, with changes ranging from dates to costumes to length of time, making them more rational, predictable, convenient, and harmonious with Han morality. (What is preserved is a shadowy suggestion of greater liberty. But this presupposes a "pure" and "authentic" past version.) In the current version, one finds contradictions, in this case both the eroticization of the ethnic female other and the sanitization of that eroticism.

One could also read the Han longing for carnival as a sign of the degree to which the straitjacket-official socialist Han culture is unconvincing to those subject to it, even though the suggestion of a more exuberant life has been planted and embraced by the state itself. A safety valve that always threatens to burst, festivals are viewed as the quintessence of exotic otherness and are carefully co-opted by the state.

Han festivals, in contrast, tend to be somber, marked by ancestral remembrances, reiteration of hierarchy and the social order, and often gender separation. Bakhtin describes "the official feast" of the Middle Ages, and by inference those of the Stalinist Soviet Union, as asserting, "all that was stable, unchanging, perennial: the existing hierarchy, the existing religious, political, and moral values, norms, and prohibitions . . . [of which] the tone . . . was monolithically serious and . . . the element of laughter . . . alien to it" (1984:9). Dai festivals are no longer quite as unconstrained as they were in the past, and now, in addition to the participation of guests and hosts, there is a clearly staged, costumed element of performance about them.[2]

Similar transformations have occurred in the realization of other official festivals, such as the Dragon Boat Festival and "Teachers' Day" in Taiwan. The former is ostensibly a tribute to the loyal minister of the ancient southern state of Chu, Qu Yuan, who chose exile rather than speak the false words his master wished to hear (see Schneider 1980). It is an occasion for political speeches (ironically consisting mostly of the "false words" in current favor [see Link 1992:3–11, 79–89]) and staged performances, as well as officially sponsored boat races that "the masses" can observe. The latter, Teachers' Day, is a day chosen by the Manchu Qianlong emperor (reigned 1736–1796) to commemorate Confucius's birthday. Confucius has become the "patron saint" (if we may appropriate terminology from an entirely alien tradition) of teachers, and thus his birthday has become linked to the newly constructed "Teachers' Day," now construed as "timeless." Interestingly, foreigners are often taken at dawn to watch the ostensibly ancient rites of this solemn "festival" as well.

These official Han festivals are often said to be pale remnants of what was once an extremely vibrant tradition, at least in ancient times. Marcel Granet (1926), Wolfram Eberhard (1968), and Chow Tse-tsung (1978) find convincing the evidence of a time when sexual relations were consummated at festivals, of which the purpose was precisely this pairing off. (Are they guilty as well of exaggerating the exotic?) Many Han believe that contemporary Han festivals are in some way rational, but that in the past they were more exuberant.

Sexual relations provide an undercurrent in the interest Han feel toward the Dai. One aspect of the Water Splashing Festival frequently mentioned is the tossing of bags between unmarried women and men as a signal of interest in courtship. This frank expression of interest would be improper for Han[3] and is often used to signify a (mythic) time in the past when actual pairing off for sexual relations was the outcome of such games. Though most minorities had clear standards for courtships and proposals, they are commonly believed to have had no standards and to have "mated" easily and casually— almost like animals. The line between propriety and licence provides part of the titillation implicit in the embrace of this alien, myth-driven (but now fiercely areligious) holiday.

The Water Splashing Festival, as interpreted in its official manner with a regular but controlled date of occurrence, flouts the conventions of contemporary Han festivals while hearkening back to a time when the conventions were different. Dai gender and sexual relations are two aspects of Dai culture that have captured the imagination of Han everywhere. The "exotic Dai woman" is a sort of icon of ethnicity—and unobjectionable ethnicity at that (Charles McKhann, personal communication). In the local press, the frequent images of benevolent Han cadres, always male, are accompanied by the grateful rural Dai women (or other minority women) whom the Han are assisting (see figure 4.2). The Dai are seen as gentle and, like the Hui, quite concerned with cleanliness. But their softness mitigates any strangeness the Han might feel in contrast, for instance, to Hui fierceness (as will be evident in the following chapter).

Highlights of Minority Nationalities in Yunnan, the glossy book on Yunnan's minorities, culminates in thirty-three pages about the Dai, giving them the preeminent final position—the last pages of the entire book. In Chinese writing, films, and other sorts of representation, the final sentence is frequently reserved for the moral message implicit in the preceding work. (Narrative analysts call this the "evaluation," the explicit mention of the point of a narrative.) In this case, the Dai occupation of the final position suggests some sort of pinnacle, some achievement of ultimate ethnic otherness that must be understood.

Figure 4.2   Enthusiastic assistance (Source: YNRB 91.7.9,
p. 1) Photo by Zhu Yuhu.

The Dai have a "high level of civilization" yet do not surpass the Han.[4] Interestingly, as George Moseley points out, "Alone among the peoples with whom the early Chinese had contact, the T'ai [Tai; the Thai in Thailand] were not regarded as barbarians *(man)"* (1973:17). They are gentle and amenable to guidance from the Han. They are religious, being adherents of Theravada Buddhism, a world religion with ties to southeast Asia. Their clothing is seen as modest and graceful. (Compare the Wa, said to be devoted to clothing that is very inconvenient, while nothing comparable is said of the Dai wearing long skirts while working in rice paddies.) Women hold recognizable places within the family and society, unlike, for example, the Wa, who are said even to not have a clear division of labor along gender lines. They eat rice and grow it in paddies. They have writing, but it is not as esoteric as the Naxi *dongbawen* (see chapter 6). Their language belongs to a well-attested language family (the Zhuang-Dong family, Zhuang-Dai branch [Ramsey 1987:232–34, 243–44]), and thus they can be categorized without difficulty. Their festivals, especially the Water Splashing Festival, may be appreciated by outsiders without much effort, at least at a superficial level. The festival's religious aspect may be summed up in a simple phrase and treated as a harmless, quaint folk remnant, much as the Han Dragon Boat Festival is said simply to have originated in the suicide of the loyal and honest minister Qu Yuan—though such historical reflections are inessential to universal enjoyment of the festival. The Dai look different enough to appear quintessentially "other," but many of their values can be assimilated to those of the Han. (They bathe frequently—more frequently than the Han—but unlike with the Hui, there is no barrier to Dai/Han commensality [eating together].)

Two other English-language books published in China focusing on Yunnan's minorities also pay special attention to the Dai: *Travels through Xishuangbanna: China's Subtropical Home of Many Nationalities* (Zheng 1981) and *Yunnan Travelogue: 100 Days in Southwest China* (Zhong 1983). They have photographs of lovely Dai girls (see figures 4.3, 4.4, and 4.5), typifying the best of ethnic otherness. The books describe the cruel pre-Liberation slave system (more technically, feudal serfdom) of the Dai and their "leap into socialism" (bypassing the stage of capitalism believed necessary before accomplishing socialism), something possible because of their "advanced" level. Indeed, the terms *xianjin* and *fada*, both meaning "advanced," are frequently associated with the Dai, at least in terms relative to the other minority nationalities. The scale of advancement peaks with the Han, so the Dai can be only relatively advanced. Their level of education is difficult to establish in fact. Heberer (1989:48–49) gives attendance for elementary school for the Dai in general as 244,554 out of 723,118. This is not to say that all of them graduated or were

Figure 4.3   Young Dai lasses (Source: Zheng 1981:12)

Figure 4.4   "Sugarcane (rear) grows high in Xishuangbanna" (Source: Zheng 1981: between 20 and 21)

Figure 4.5   A Dai mother with her child (Source: Zhong 1983: between 30 and 31)

even able to do so, since many villages have schools with only grades one to three after which the only available school is a boarding school. An article on elementary school graduation rates for Xishuangbanna gives an estimate of 2 to 12 percent. Temple schools are presumably excluded from these figures. Still, according to Liu Yan (1988:28), only 1 of 346 Dai in Xishuangbanna enters middle school compared with 1 of 41 Han.

Although most student essays about the Dai depict the beauty of Xishuangbanna and the hospitable Dai people, much like the stories in the travelogues (Zheng 1981, Zhong 1983), one essay stands out in contradistinction. Here is evidence of instability of interpretations, not entirely consistent with the official views of the Dai. This essay is full of rich implications about attitudes toward modernization, gender, ethnicity, and the sociology of fear. We learn how a young adult conquered his childhood prejudice and expectations.

"The Old Window"

When I was a boy, I lived in a remote town in the southern part of this province, inhabited by many Dai People and Jingpo People. It has spanned a long history, suffered from calamities and plunder by bandits. There are many irregular stairs down the slope of the hill.

That year I went to school. Every day, I had to pass through a frightening road to go to school. The walls of the building were so high, covered with thick moss and dried grass, among which you could find small dirty windows, like dark holes, high in the walls.

One day, from one of these windows, I caught sight of the wrinkled face of an old woman, still in the shadows; beneath the tough-skinned palm lay a sleeping cat, whose fur was good-looking.

She casually looked onto the street, like a mummy; only from the slowly moving eyes could you make sure that she was living. I trembled and ran away quickly. Since then, whenever I passed by the window, I looked up at the window, though I dreaded to do that. It was always the same face. Once, I felt I was caught by her sight.

One day, my mother and I passed the dreadful area. I asked mother who the old woman was. Mother said, "She is a Pipagui (Sinister Woman)."

"What is a Pipagui?"

"A Pipagui is not liked by others," Mother simply answered. According to the outdated customs of the Dai people, if a woman is pointed out as a Pipagui, she would be killed or expelled. It was said she left her village as a Pipagui, when she was young, and she lived in a kinsman's house. Then they left. The woman was lonely.

Then, my fear changed to curiosity. Every time I met her, I smiled at her. She returned my smile. Later, we usually said hello to each other silently.

One day in the dusk, when I passed the window, I heard the old woman calling me to visit her house.

I agreed. Entering into the pitch-dark corridor, I felt greatly scared. I opened the door and peered in. I will never forget the way she was outlined by golden twilight. She was sitting at the window, smiling benevolently at me.

"Come up, son" she said. "I'll give you something to keep." She gave me a lovely pet—a lovely baby cat. We chattered.

After this, I often visited her and she gave me sweets.

Before long, my family moved to Kunming, where I continued to study in primary school, then middle school. The small cat had been given to others before we moved to Kunming, but the old window still always came into my mind.

Eventually, I got a chance to go back to my hometown. The Town was a brand new one then. The minorities still wore the traditional costumes, but the colors and the patterns were brighter. I walked down the familiar stone way to find the window among the new buildings and shops.

That house was not torn down yet, but a giant billboard covered the window. The window had disappeared any way, as well as the old "Pipagui" and the cat. In the ad picture, a pretty woman was saying "Yongfang make-up series of high quality keeps you young forever . . ."

As the remote rural areas develop, Dai people don't believe in the superstitious concept of "Pipagui" any more. They are fond of studying science and constructing their towns. But behind the bright appearance of the new town, there are many, many old stories.

We do not learn about the writer's ethnic group but can assume it to be Han from the way in which the mother feared the "witch" (much of the underlying feeling about minority nationalities is fear, but it is covered up by laughter and disdain). This is similar to Shen Congwen's short stories "Fenghuang" and "Qiaoxiu and Dongsheng," which describe "jinxes" and the connection between adultery, sexual repression, and accusations of witchcraft (1982a, 1982b). This story is also reminiscent of Norma Diamond's analysis of Han views of Miao women as able to employ *gu* poison, forcing men to return without themselves being at risk (1988). In anthropological literature, there is no shortage of cases in which "others"—especially women—are accused of dangerous, mysterious powers, in which the majority group is at risk and must establish some defense. Such judgments excuse all extraordinary measures taken against that group as necessitated for the greater good, the safety of the majority. In some settings, it is individuals who are ostracized because of their personal characteristics on the charge of witchcraft (see, for example, Bowen 1954). This accusation is also available in China to direct against those seen as especially threatening to the accuser's sense of rationality and morality.

Of course the majority of the Dai are seen as too simple to have such magical powers. In fact (according to popular account), they had nothing at Liberation, and the majority of the population was enslaved (Zheng 1981:7–12, Daizu Jianshi Editorial Board 1985:63–70; but see Hsieh 1995 for a radically different account of Dai history). Now they are fairly prosperous. The old practice of ostracizing women as *pipagui* has ostensibly been eradicated (Zheng 1981:15–16, 27, 30), though it is still known and associated with the Dai.

The other autonomous prefecture in Yunnan with a majority of Dai, Dehong prefecture, contrasts sharply with the backward simplicity of pre-Liberation times and with Xishuangbanna until very recently. Dehong is well known for being well-off. A visitor to its capital, Mangshi, finds well-stocked stores, a plethora of goods not found in Kunming, and a vibrant nighttime market with goods from Burma and Thailand. As early as 1991, there were refrigerators in every restaurant—very different even from Kunming. Simplicity along with prosperity makes possible the construction of the Dai as a prosperous, nonthreatening, and exoticized other.

A new association has been forged, however, between the Dai and drugs. Dehong prefecture borders Burma; passage is virtually unrestricted, especially in the town of Ruili. When I visited Ruili in 1991, the Han I met mentioned the recent increase in both drug use and the drug trade. By 1994, the connection was even more salient. Photos of drug sellers condemned to die showed "ethnic" clothing on some—long skirts on men and women. By 1996, a reporter for the *Philadelphia Inquirer* did an entire week-long report on drugs and Ruili, complete with executions, addiction, law-breaking, and AIDS (Tofani 1996). The Communist Party permits the Dai to cultivate opium, though with certain limitations. In this context, we find increasing mention of Shan tribes in Burma, of Lue people in Laos—both different "branches" of people considered Tai. The transnational connections of the Dai are seen as threats to the health—both moral and physical—of China (see Davis 1999). The more crafty and degenerate Dehong Dai are thus contrasted to the charming and simple Banna Dai, who appear not to be mentioned as much for their cross-border drug trade nor for AIDS. Popular images of ethnic groups are not static; half a decade of a "social problem" associated with a group—in this case, the drug traffic of mainland Southeast Asia, moving from Burma through Ruili in Yunnan, to Kunming, and out through Hong Kong, with its concomitant corruption, prostitution, and AIDS—can drastically alter its prototypical representation.[5] By the late 1990s, Banna Dai were also connected in the popular media with AIDS (Hyde 1998, 1999).

Table 4.1: Dai Statistical Portrait (Attributions of Persons Guessed "Dai" in the Linguistic Identification and Evaluation Task)

N = 1

	Language pleasing?/ Easy to understand?		Person decent?		Potential friend?		Wealthy?	
Yes	2	18.2%	6	54.5%	6	54.5%	5	45.4%
Avg.	2	18.2	2	18.2	0	0	1	9.1
No	7	63.6	1	9.1	3	27.3	4	36.4
Blank/ Don't know	0	0	0	0	2	18.2	1	9.1

Profession (N = 14)			Mean educational level
	(number)	(%)	
Teacher	2	14.3	
Cadre	3	21.4	
Worker	3	21.4	6.33 years
Peasant	4	28.6	
Getihu	1	7.1	
Blank/Don't know	1	7.1	

Note: Total of number of guesses for professions usually exceeds the total number of guesses for that ethnic identity because some respondents checked *every* profession they thought likely, while others checked only the most likely one.

When people in Kunming think quickly and automatically of the Dai, they are likely to picture the more celebrated Banna Dai. The evaluations evoked of "the Dai" are likely to be favorable.

As shown in table 4.1, in a statistical portrait of people guessed to be "Dai" in the linguistic identification and evaluation task (though there were no Dai speakers, in fact), the overarching impression is one of a group fairly likely to be regarded favorably in several areas.

In many categories, the Dai are the absolutely most preferred. They were rated the most decent (54.5 percent, compared to the runner-up, the Hui, at 50 percent); most likely to be the listener's friend (54.5 percent, compared to the next-most-likely, the Yi, at 38.2 percent); and most wealthy (45.4 percent, compared to the next-wealthiest, the Zang, at 33.3 percent). The Dai were only guessed to be speaking eleven times—though there were no Dai speakers—which suggests that listeners regarded it as possible though unlikely for Dai to be speaking in Kunming.

CHAPTER FIVE

RESISTANT, DISLIKED ETHNIC OTHERS: WA, ZANG, AND HUI

Wa Nationality

Tibetan (Zang) Nationality

Hui Nationality

121

If the Dai are the most advanced and the most appealing other, the Wa epitomize backwardness, the primitive, the other who must be changed. Their position just preceding the Dai in the final section of the book *Highlights of Minority Nationalities in Yunnan* appears far from accidental, maximizing the contrast between these two groups that represent prototypical extremes among Yunnan's minority nationalities. The Wa in many ways represent the quintessential negative ethnic other: backward, dirty, ignorant, without a single feature of civilization. The Zang (Tibetans) and Hui (Chinese-speaking Muslims) are also regarded with extreme distaste, though not for being primitive. They are numerous and have ties to world religions, but they are seen as having "separatist" tendencies, not fitting in with China's modernization and rationalization plans. This chapter presents portraits of these three groups, showing the importance of subsistence, marriage practices, religion, hygiene, and foodways in classifying and evaluating ethnic minorities. All of these groups are also resistant to Han assimilation and resisted the Chinese Communist Party (CCP) takeover during the early years of the PRC—another trait seen as evidence for their backwardness.

THE "SIMPLE" ETHNIC OTHER: THE WA

"The Wa" (also romanized as *Va*) is an umbrella term referring to some groups known more commonly in pre-1949 times as the "Kawa" (with the "Ka" representing a glottal stop). With conationals on both sides of the Burmese border, the language of the Wa is classified as belonging to the Wa-De branch of Mon-Khmer. They were the last group "pacified"—that is, brought into the state system of the PRC—in southwest China. Chinese texts treat them as patriotic and anti-imperialist; George Moseley, in contrast to the mainland texts, mentions their enduring anti-CCP activities (1973:35). A British scholar, G. E. Harvey, calls them "indescribably filthy and often stark naked, . . . nevertheless stronger and harder-working than the surrounding races, the Burmese and Siamese" (Harvey 1957:126).

Few people other than the People's Liberation Army (PLA) dared approach the Wa, because of their notoriety for headhunting.[1] Before their recent transformations under Han stewardship, they employed slash-and-burn agriculture, used no fertilizer (at least none recognized as such by the Han, who consider only human and animal wastes—not ashes from burning fields—to be appropriate fertilizers), and what little rice they grew was dry-field rice. They had nuclear families, and Han observers noted that the Wa had little division of labor at all, even along gender lines. This allows them to be treated as the "primitive" *(yuanshi)* ethnic other par excellence—a category taken as both scientific and descriptive.

The Wa were mentioned twice in student essays and guessed once in the matched-guise test; they are imagined neither as speaking nor as sharing interactive space with Han. Yet the Wa are spoken of frequently in conversation, precisely as the most extreme example of primitiveness. Headhunting is the most common association with the Wa, just as it was among the Ilongot in the Philippines (Rosaldo 1980:ix–x), though the Wa have not found a sympathetic ethnographer seeking "the native's point of view" as the Ilongot found in Rosaldo.[2] These remote practices, relayed as tidbits of information that most people could not possibly know firsthand, are recounted in similar fashion in many contexts, often in identical phrasing, much as beginning anthropology students mention that "the Eskimos have thirty-two [or sixteen, or however many] terms for snow."[3] Without any means of examining the truth or falsity of such claims, people remote from areas where they might encounter the Wa merely take such "facts" as evidence for the great gulf separating such prototypically primitive people from the obviously more advanced Han. Han superiority is thus confirmed through recitation of paradigmatic case material.

In two books devoted to the Wa—*Wazu Jianshi* (A brief history of the Wa) (Wazu Jianshi Editorial Group 1986), and *Wazu* (The Wa) (Tian and Luo 1985)—many topics are repeated nearly verbatim, suggesting that the same sources and the same organizing principles were used in writing both texts. Further, we may surmise that very few scholars have had personal experience, or have conducted fieldwork, among the Wa, resulting in the necessity of relying on the accounts of those few pioneer researchers.[4] The authors' reliance on one another or on a third source is evident. The first two sentences are, respectively:

> *Wazude hunyin shi yifuyiqizhi, dan ye you gebie duoqizhe. Zhe gebie duoqizhe, bing bu goucheng duoqizhi de hunyin xingtai, ershi yifuyiqizhi paisheng de huo biran dailai de xianxiang.* (Wazu Jianshi Editorial Group 1986:97)
> [Wa marriage is monogamous, but there are also occasional cases of polygamous unions. This does not constitute a polygamous marriage system, but is a phenomenon that arises perhaps necessarily with monogamy.]
>
> *Wazude hunyin shi yifuyiqizhi, ye cunzai shaoshu duoqi de xianxiang, zhe shi nanquantongzhi de yi zhong biaoxian.* (Tian and Luo 1985:63)
> [Wa marriage is monogamous, and there also exist a minority of cases of polygamous unions; this is a manifestation of patriarchy.]

These references to their kinship system affirm that the Wa belong to the proper evolutionary category ("primitive"), so that they may be understood properly. Monogamy and patriarchy imply that the Wa are not so far back in primordial times that inclusion within the Chinese fraternity is impossible, but the Han are clearly the leaders in the move forward.

The Wa are rarely extolled for their beauty or even their strength but simply for being *"teshu"* (unusual). Their clothes may be homemade, but—in contrast to Dai or Bai clothing—nobody is rushing to buy Wa clothing. Wa backwardness is further supported by the fact that they are barefoot, with skirts and trousers that are, for the most part, short. In fact they are ridiculed for their aesthetic judgment: "This kind of clothing and ornamentation [silver earrings and bracelets, and bamboo knee bracelets] is actually too great a burden, and is very inconvenient, but the Wa find it beautiful" (Wazu Jianshi Editorial Group 1986:104). This is the last sentence of a scholarly book describing Wa culture, leading us to conclude that it gives us the message implicit above: standards of beauty vary and may even overcome rational considerations. A further possibility is that, as the Wa become more sensible under the guidance of the Han, they will discard these cumbersome ornaments and opt for efficiency.

Once I was waiting in a small restaurant for the summer rains to stop. Two ragged and dusty women in dark, distinctive clothing came by to beg. The proprietor sent them off rudely and without hesitation. When I asked what group they were in, she appeared not to have given it much thought (and was perhaps a little surprised at my being interested enough to ask). "I don't know. Minorities. Maybe Wa," she answered.

Descriptions of the Wa include mention not only that their clothing is mostly homemade, but also that they are "hospitable" and serve wine to their guests. The book-length treatments of the Wa mention that much of their grain is employed in the production of an alcoholic drink, that virtually every Wa can make his or her own *shuijiu* (water-alcohol), and that alcohol is necessary for all occasions—festivals, hospitality for guests, ceremonies, and sacrifices to the spirits (Wazu Jianshi Editorial Group 1986:43).[5] (Again the British observer Harvey is less guarded: "The amount of beer and opium they consume would kill any other race" [1957:126].) From this, the more "advanced" Chinese would draw the following conclusion: starving yet wasting grain on the immoral and irrational production of alcohol, the Wa clearly need help in transforming their food production along more rational lines. In figure 5.1, notice the conflation of "intoxication," dance, and young women. In a book such as this, aimed at demonstrating the richness of Yunnan's ethnic resources, it would be inappropriate to point out negative aspects of any nationality, yet the words chosen here reveal the common, even unconscious, association between the Wa and drunkenness. The Han are implicitly compared for their possession of much better techniques and more reliable methods of producing desired grains, including irrigation, the use of night soil, and terracing. Deviations from this standard method are taken as evidence of backwardness.

Further proof of apt classification of the Wa as "primitive" comes from a detailed description of their stage of development in terms of the classic Marxian (from Marx, Engels, and Morgan) categories of economy and political structure. In this view, Wa society is said to be in the process of developing into a class society from primitive society, with different Wa localities having features of either primitive communal society (areas centered around Ximeng) or feudal society (other areas). Its religion is primitive nature worship, its technology extremely rudimentary. Any tools other than those of bamboo or basketry (including plows, iron woks, and knives) are explained as having been bought ("bartered," with an implicit evolutionary scheme of economic development) from other ethnic groups. Even the structure of their houses is said to be learned from the Dai.

In addition to consumption of alcohol, short skirts, and stage of development, headhunting is definitive evidence of the primitive state of the Wa. Though they resisted CCP efforts in the early years of the PRC, their relations with other groups appear now to be peaceful, and successful guidance by the Han appears welcome—and available for public relations promotion.

Yet despite a kind of implicit deprecation (or because of it?), and because they exemplify the extreme position, the Wa are awarded ten pages and placed in the penultimate position in the book *Highlights*—just before the concluding section on the Dai. The ten pages devoted to the Wa contrast with, for example, the Miao, who have only five pages yet have three times the population of the Wa.

In terms of exemplars, the Dai and the Wa fit the bill. The Wa occupy the opposite corner from the Dai in a conceptual square-shaped schema (refer back to figure 3.3), though both epitomize the types of groups that must be led into modernity by the advanced Han. The Naxi are generally favorably regarded, with some aspects of "civilization" such as writing but with other aspects of "primitiveness" such as matriarchy. Occupying a third corner are the Zang and the Hui, who are often mentioned together. Among other shared qualities, both are regarded as fierce.

THE FIERCE AND SEPARATIST
ETHNIC OTHERS: ZANG AND HUI

By "fierce" *(lihai, baozao)*, the Han mean something like recalcitrant, stubborn, and uninterested in assimilation, as well as prone to fighting. These reputed traits of the Zang (Tibetans) and Hui are puzzling to Han; these two

Figure 5.1   Wa girls "intoxicated with dance" (Source: *Highlights*, p. 144)

groups appear to reject the otherwise evident Han cultural superiority, a superiority rejected by groups with no interest in being guided by their "elder Han brothers" to a more "modern" life. The Han bewilderment—and ultimate anger—at such effrontery and delusion is reminiscent of eighteenth-century Chinese responses to the British monarch George III, who did not demonstrate the proper understanding of China's position at the center of the universe to which all other nations paid tribute (Fairbank 1968; Spence 1990:122–123; but see Hevia 1995 for a different understanding). The Chinese expectation that all within their known universe will respect Chinese superiority is bolstered by relations with most other ethnic groups. Those groups like the Tibetans and Hui who reject such notions are regarded with distaste and a good bit of fear, as may be seen in the following excerpt from a student essay:

> In my opinion, most minority nationalities are kind and satisfied with national policies of all kinds; they try their best to build up a happy family of nationalities and make our own country stronger together with the Han people. But a few of them, I don't know why, are against the Communist Party and its policies. They vainly attempt to get away from the Central Government through outside power. For several times in the Tibet Autonomous Region, the Tibetans have rebelled against the Party.

In another case, I was wondering why some minority nationalities are always so rude and so savage such as Huizu and Zangzu (Tibetans). They used to fight fights for some infinitely small problems. In Wenshan, Yunnan, it is true that Huizu often rise up and conflict with local police and Han people. It's very unfortunate that Han people always fail in accidents involved in national problems in China. I am afraid of Huizu and Zangzu in my life.

The conflation of the Hui and Zang is not coincidental but is based on views of both groups as separatist, violent, and to some degree incomprehensible. The backwardness and primitiveness of most of the minority nationalities (in terms of technology) can be explained by appeal to history and are invoked in the rather more comfortable discussions of such groups as the Dai and Wa. The Hui, however, are primarily an urban nationality, with the same level of technology as the surrounding Han, and Tibet has long had an "advanced" and to varying degrees independent civilization, even if it remained at the level of a "feudal" society until its "peaceful liberation" in 1951 (Avedon 1984, Grunfeld 1987, Goldstein 1989). Yet the writer of the above essay calls them "rude" and "savage"—quite indicative of the attitudes held toward the Zang.

In conversations and essays many people mentioned that the Zang were dirty, taking the proverbial three baths during their lives (at birth, marriage, and death). I also heard that they were *"yeman"* (wild barbarians) from many Han, including a peasant woman, this description sufficing for her as justification for dismissal. One young student expressed interest in visiting Tibet because the religious atmosphere there is thick *(zongjiao qifen hen nong)*. Polyandry was known to a slight extent. Many people commented on the low standard of living and the generous help offered by the Han, sometimes adding a comment indicating astonishment at the ingratitude of the Zang who inexplicably want the Han to leave. Even a well-educated Taiwanese woman living in the United States stated definitively that Tibet has always been part of China, and that attempts to suggest otherwise are ridiculous.[6]

The majority of the Zang (nearly four million) live in the Tibet Autonomous Region and neighboring provinces (Sichuan and Qinghai), but Yunnan's Zang population is 95,915 (1982 census; Yang Yucai 1989:27). Responses on the part of Yunnan natives to queries about the Zang are shaped by the twin factors of the situation within Yunnan and the national perception of Tibet. As the latter is of grave interest in China, it is likely quite effective in shaping people's attitudes.

In China as a whole, a great effort is placed on presenting Zang willing participation in the life of the nation. During the fortieth anniversary of the "peaceful liberation of Tibet" during summer 1991, stories appeared almost every day in the newspapers and programs aired on television demonstrating the backwardness of pre-Liberation Tibet and the gratitude with which the Tibetans welcomed the materially advanced civilization of the Han. Westerners who know the history of Chinese-Tibetan relations may find this "spin" horrifying, lamenting the continued unwelcome Chinese presence in Tibet. In justification for their intervention, Chinese invariably mention the pre-1949 poverty and "slavery" suffered by the majority of Tibetans.[7]

Tibet is loudly included in all treatments of China's ethnic others, lest there be any tendency to consider it a different nationality with its own country. Interestingly, despite the great number of articles about Tibet (45 in 112 issues of the newspapers I studied), there are very few photographs of Tibetans—especially in the Chinese-language press, in contrast to the English-language press directed at foreigners. In the Chinese press, I came across two photographs of Tibetan women—one singing in a performance, one being treated by a Han doctor—and one of the Potala Palace. There were three photos of Tibetans in the much smaller English-language *China Daily*: one of a Tibetan clinic, one of students, and one of herdsmen's children being given gifts by soldiers. Is Tibet too dangerous to photograph? Is it too dangerous for representation of those particular others? Is it simply unappealing, so that where ethnic otherness is to be depicted, the more appealing groups such as Dai are used instead?[8]

This lack of photographic representation in the Chinese press may be viewed as being guided by an attempt to withhold information about the actual situation in Tibet. Or it may be that everybody knows that the general populace is not truly interested in Tibet. However, in the case of representation of picturesque features, the Tibetans might even be considered overrepresented. In *Highlights,* the Zang are allotted thirteen pages, nearly double the number given, for example, the Miao, even though the Miao population is greater both within Yunnan and in China as a whole.[9] The Miao population numbers 752,226 in Yunnan (more than eight times that of the Zang in the province) and 7,398,035 in China (almost double that of the Zang) but is given just seven pages in *Highlights.*[10]

The spectacular scenery included in the photographs of northwestern Yunnan, especially mountainous Diqing County, cannot fully explain the heightened treatment of Zang, nor can the impressive full dress in "native costumes." (It is obvious that certain of the photographs are staged, particularly where masses of colorfully dressed people in orderly lines form the central focus while those at the margins of the photos are dressed in less vibrant colors [see figure 5.2].) But the overrepresentation of the Zang is mostly to be explained by their salience, if not their prototypical nature as a minority nationality.

Figure 5.2   Traditional dance (Source: *Highlights*, p. 100)

The English-language treatment of the Zang is much more extensive than the Chinese treatment, though there is no shortage of that either—especially in the official Party newspaper, *Renmin Ribao (People's Daily)*. But in the *China Daily,* the English-language official newspaper, articles about Tibet appear with astonishing frequency. They unfailingly portray the great respect had by the Chinese for Tibetan tradition, even religious tradition, as well as the material advantages bestowed on the Zang by the constant modernizing effort of the Chinese: new airports, new weather stations, new roads, new schools, and so on. Each of these contributions may also be read, cynically, as an attempt to foist Han culture and, literally, Han people on the otherwise remote Tibetans.[11] Roads are not welcome when they bring conquerors with ever greater speed and efficiency. John Avedon (1984:42, 316–17) and June Dreyer (1976:132–35) mention the building of roads into Tibet, both suggesting motives that are not entirely noble. It is true that with improved transportation goods can be moved more easily—but such movement can go in both directions: taking rice in to support Han technicians and taking out minerals and other resources so sorely needed by industrializing China, in addition to taking in necessary and desired supplies for the Tibetans, along with Han personnel.

Two facts must be explained: (1) Tibet is seen as a threat to China, and (2) Tibetan culture is seen as distasteful. I do not believe that simple

political explanations can adequately account for the ardor of these sentiments. It is necessary to consider at least the unity of the Tibetans and their
ardent desire for independence, a desire that has only increased with forty
years of occupation and one that is defended with force if necessary (though
even more of the force comes from the Chinese). World opinion is partially,
idly, against China, though not thoroughly for Tibet; no country recognizes
Tibet as a sovereign state. The Dalai Lama did not visit the White House
until 1991, for instance.

China acts as if it has a great myth to perpetuate. It limits contacts between
foreigners and Tibetans, even beyond the natural limits imposed by geography and language: independent travelers are periodically forbidden to ven-
ture into Tibet, though permission has occasionally been granted. Organized
tours into Tibet, in contrast to independent travel, are enormously expensive
and hence are a wonderful source of coveted hard currency. Such tours also
permit the Chinese state to exert strict control over what tourists see in
Tibet. Tourism is clearly a way to improve foreign relations—if the tourists
are shown the positive aspects of China.

Since few Chinese will ever have a chance to go to Tibet, their knowledge
of it, as of many places, comes entirely from what they absorb from official
sources. (I was surprised to see a poster at Yunnan University in the spring
of 1991 advertising a summer program in Tibet for students.) Official
sources are working hard to insist on a single interpretation: the grateful but
still backward Tibetans were rescued from their ignorance by the advanced
and rational Chinese. Repetition ensures that people will absorb the proper
message, and distance ensures that they will rarely see Tibet personally.

Polyandry is mentioned as a trait that places Tibetan society at a more
backward stage of development, along with the slave society (feudal serfdom) that existed to some degree before Tibet's "liberation." Tibet's religious life is usually described in Chinese sources as wasteful, with nobles and
monasteries said to have owned 30 percent of the land in Tibet before Liberation (Ma Yin 1989:205)—a figure comparable to those for the situation
in China proper before land reform. According to Chinese religious policy,
freedom of belief is permitted, and freedom of practice is tolerated as long as
it does not *pohuai shengchanli* (destroy productivity). The interpretation of
how much freedom is permitted has varied widely, from the grossly restric-
tive and humiliating cultural revolution to the more tolerant atmosphere of
the 1980s and 1990s, in which restoration of a handful of temples and
monasteries has been undertaken by the state and through local initiatives.[12]
As with the Hui, the amount of funding for restoration of religious buildings
has been broadly advertised, with variable increases in tolerance for religious

activity. In Kunming, official notices and even bronze plaques announced the amount of money spent by the state to restore several big mosques, but people told me that during that same period arrests of Hui increased.

Religion is regarded with great ambivalence in contemporary China. Officially it is tolerated. Popularly, especially among younger people who were raised to "believe in atheism," it is perplexing and even to be suspected. The common understanding that Tibetans, like the Hui, are almost uniformly devoted to their religion combined with their "unity" and violence gives rise to views quite unlike those of most other ethnic groups. The two excerpts from essays below illustrate many of the features of Han views of Tibetans:

> In our country, the most remote and backward area perhaps is The Tibet Autonomous Region. There live the Tibetan people. How can they live there? How do they live? Do they live better or worse? Many Han people couldn't understand why they could live there. The Qinghai-Xizang Plateau is the highest place in our country, even in Asia. There corn can hardly be planted. [This is the easiest crop to grow, at least in Yunnan. If even corn won't grow, it must be infertile indeed.] Zang people's life depends on herding sheep and cattle also. They believe in their own religion. There is a very famous palace [the Potala] in the place. Zang people's living standard is very low. Every year our government will give them more help in food and money. Many Han people think that they are very dirty and lazy. It is said that a Zang person just takes baths three times in his whole life. How dirty it is! They look stronger than Han people for they drink milk often.

> Han people think the minority are another kind of people in China: some habits, customs, life-style of minorities are so strange and fresh for Han people. In Yunnan, every year, about the 4th month, at a festival which is called "Pouring Water Festival," all the people are together with a bowl of water in their hand, put olive leaves into the water and use it to spray at people. Those actions express a kind of blessing and wishes, these are a symbol of happiness, so, we Han people very much appreciate it. When this festival is coming, some Han people go there to share the happiness of that holiday. But in XiZang [Tibet], the ZangZu [Tibetans] only have three baths in their whole life, one is when they are born, one is when they get married, and another time is when they die. For us, we can't bear the dirty and foul smell, but they just take it as a habit; if you make them have a bath, maybe they will be angry. So, although the government said, we are the great family of nationalities, we should have national unity. Yes, it is necessary, we should do it, but I think, we can't understand each other completely, we unite together, but have a distance.

Remoteness, low standard of living, Han assistance, nomadism, poor hygiene—all are recited as a matter of course. The first writer is a bit surprised that despite these flawed conditions, the Zang look stronger than the Han. (She attributes it to their drinking milk, which most Han find nauseating—though milk drinking is increasing, especially along the eastern coasts.) The second writer contrasts the easily appreciated Dai Water Splashing Festival with the repugnance of Tibetans' lack of bathing, arguing against an easy unification of all nationalities despite the state policy with regard to the great fraternity of nationalities in China. But she distances herself from the stereotype slightly by saying, "Han people think . . ."

Tibetans are seen, then, as backward but in the process of being modernized, though unwillingly. They are known to retain some cultural traits that most Han cannot fathom—bathing seldom, spending time and money on religious activities, eating much meat and dairy products rather than grain and vegetables (which, in any case, do not grow easily at Tibet's elevation). Their desire for sovereignty is an anomaly in the cognitive model of prototypical ethnic minorities, who are expected to be small enclaves of difference within a sea of powerful Han identity. Their resistance to Han efforts to modernize them makes them quite unsuitable to serve as examples of docility. While the centrality of modernization is supported by evidence from most other ethnic groups, it is greatly challenged by the Zang.

Statistically, the linguistic evaluation and identification test yielded some comparable contours, though with some surprising details (see table 5.1).

"Zang" were guessed as speaking twenty-one times (though there were no Zang speakers). They were regarded as least likely to be the listeners' "friends"—only 23.8 percent thought this likely, compared, for instance, to 54.5 percent of the "Dai." "The Zang" were seen as third most educated of our group of six reference categories with a mean guess of 6.2 years, following "Bai" (6.75) and just below "Dai" (6.33).

"Zang" and "Hui" cluster together in many ways: both are considered fairly successful and to have wealth, education, and status, but they are adherents of religion and have fairly insurmountable barriers with the Han.

RELIGION, FOOD, AND ALIENATION: THE HUI

For a very different set of reasons, the Hui—Chinese-speaking Muslims—violate Han notions of ethnicity, mostly because they are not backward, even if they are poor in many cases. The primary difference from the Han seems to be that the Hui are religious, with a few puzzling cultural differences thrown in for good measure. Some Chinese scholars argue that they are only

Table 5.1: Tibetan (Zang) Statistical Portrait (Attributions of Persons Guessed "Zang" in the Linguistic Identification and Evaluation Task)

N = 21

	Language pleasing?/ Easy to understand?		Person decent?		Potential friend?		Wealthy?	
Yes	3	14.3%	5	23.8%	5	23.8%	7	33.3%
Avg.	1	4.8	5	23.8	1	4.8	2	9.5
No	15	71.4	6	28.6	12	57.1	10	47.6
Blank/ Don't know	2	9.5	4	19.0	3	14.3	2	9.5

Profession (N = 33)			Mean educational level
	(number)	(%)	
Teacher	2	6.1	
Cadre	4	12.1	
Worker	8	24.2	6.2 years
Peasant	12	36.4	
Getihu	4	12.1	
Blank/Don't know	3	9.1	

a religious, not an ethnic, minority and wonder whether Chinese Christians and Jews should also be given minority status.[13]

The most automatic negative judgments I encountered in Kunming concerned the Hui, the nationality with which most Han have the greatest likelihood of personal contact, given the Hui presence throughout China. The belief that the Hui are "united" and "unafraid to die" and have volatile tempers makes them greatly feared by the majority of the Han, even if this fear is expressed with a certain degree of admiration.[14] My Han friend whom I'll call Lin Weiguo, a thirty-five-year-old college lecturer with a master's degree and some time spent abroad, offered the observation that the Hui were the only people in China in the 1990s who dared confront the Communist Party and the Army, since they had weapons and were both fearless and united. There are reputedly entire towns, including Pingyuanjie in the Wenshan Zhuang-Miao Autonomous Prefecture, far from Kunming in southeast Yunnan, where no non-Hui willingly goes—even the Army—because of recent incidents in which there were provocations and quite violent fights with outsiders.

While it is quite difficult to find officially-sponsored accounts of Han-Hui conflict, as opposed to accounts of the dissipation of such conflict (see chapter 3), many individuals brought it up. In student essays about minorities, the Hui were mentioned nineteen times. Almost all such accounts included talk about violence and sometimes about Hui (imagined) attitudes toward Han.

The following story from a student essay describes one such incident that the author himself witnessed and ultimately (as a Hui) deplored:

"Racial Pride"
My hometown is located southeast of Kunming, the capital of Yunnan Province. It is a large town of some five hundred houses among which the Hui minority, one of the 56 minority nationalities in China, believing in Islam, makes up 80 percent of the total population, and Han nationality, the majority believing in Buddhism, 20 percent. Since time immemorial, two different cultures and religions have co-existed in the town. There have never been any racial conflicts between them. My home is but four hundred metres or so away from the district where Han people live. In my boyhood, I often swam in a river near the town with many Han boys in split pants [standard clothing for young children] and received my primary education in the same school. Hui people have been much esteemed by Han people for their civilities and modesty, and Han people have also been respected by Muslims for their hard working. People with two different customs have lived in harmony for generations as though there were no cultural gaps between them.

But something happened four months ago that shocked me and made me worry . . . that Muslims in the town may fall into discredit.

One afternoon in the last winter vacation, my elder brother, a lorry driver, would drive to another town, which is some fifty kilometres away from my home town, to transport cement back. Before setting off, he asked me if I would go with him. To while away the boring day time, I eagerly said yes to him. It was a sunny warm day. We both were in merry moods on the way.

After going forth about twenty kilometres, we were blocked by two trucks and a crowd of people. "There must be a road accident," said my brother with assurance. Getting off the lorry, I elbowed into the crowd. Six lads were yelling with uproar at a man of some forty years old. "Pay reparations! Make a kowtow to us!" shouted the lads. "So . . . sor . . . sorry. I . . . I . . ." the man tried to defend himself. One lad abruptly hit him on the nose with his fist. With his nose bleeding, the man fell to the ground.

The crowd was silent. Another lad slapped the man on the face. "Pay reparations!" The man had no choice but to take out 500 Yuan (Renminbi [about five to ten months' salary]) with a trembling bloody hand and hand them to the lad. The fellow waved the bank notes and warned the man: "Get away! If there is a next time, we'll . . . !" The man nodded: "Yes, yes." Struggling up, he ambled toward his truck. The six young fellows burst into laughter and walked toward their shabby truck. I recognized the fellows, who are Muslims, Hui people, inhabiting my home town. I got a little puzzled about what they really did. A woman in the scene told me the truth. The six young men drove their shabby truck to the town where we headed to also. Half way there, when the lorry the man drove met theirs, they intentionally drove toward the lorry and broke their headlights by hitting it. Then they stopped and pulled the man out of the driver's cab, when I and my brother witnessed the scene that followed. The woman said that these fellows had done something like that before. By means of their old truck, they often blackmailed those who were Han people and not the inhabitants of the home town, and particularly those who were from other provinces; the man who was entrapped just now was from Guizhou Province [the next province to the east]. (They actually had a sense of fellow feeling?!) Many local Muslims were indeed proud of what the blackmailers had done, because they supposed that what the fellows did could make a show of strength to prevent them from being bullied and humiliated by Han people! What a thought of racial pride!

I said nothing. As a Muslim of the town, I feel too ashamed to mention it. It is true that one nation who wants to survive in the law of the jungle must resort to force, but that is not the only means, especially in the modern civilized world in which the essential means to survive is to develop national culture, science and technology. Furthermore, what the six lads did is illegal and immoral. As a nationality believing in Islam, their deeds have terribly infringed their sacred religious doctrine "the Koran." I would say nothing more but mourn for their so-called racial pride, and I hope they themselves would mourn over what they had done.

This story, from the point of view of an aghast Hui, an able storyteller even in a foreign language, has the feel of a "typical" account that might be given of the Hui. Many such stories are whispered among Han, though official accounts are nowhere to be found. Although this writer himself witnessed this event, many of the stories told about Hui violence are reminiscent of the sorts of urban legends or contemporary folklore collected by Brunvand (1984). Such implicit notions of the Hui tendency toward violence are supported by accounts of earlier Hui uprisings (*qiyi*, lit. "righteous uprisings"), demonstrating in the official organs Hui patriotism and righteous indignation against the indignities of imperialism and oppression (see, for example, Yang Zhaojun 1989, Jing 1986).

Another aspect of Hui behavior that is puzzling to Han and mentioned often is the Hui reluctance about and prohibition against eating pork. This has caused conflict with non-Muslims for a long time; in the Yuan dynasty, for a time Ghenghis Khan forbade Muslims from slaughtering animals according to Islamic laws, forcing them to violate their tenets (Rossabi 1981:261). Assimilated Hui, such as one Communist Party member I knew who was also an intellectual (I'll call him Liu Zhu), boasted of their willingness to eat pork just like everybody else and their courage in casting off the superstitions and *fengsu xiguan* (customs and habits)[15] of their ancestors (see also Gladney 1991:26). They said of themselves that they were not *zhenzhengde Huizu* (real Hui), since the quintessential criterion for Hui identity, even more than belief or religious practice, is enforcement of the pork proscription.

Han explanations for the Hui pork proscription are generally mythological: one version claims that the Hui believe pigs are their ancestors and out of respect refuse to eat pork. Another reports a story about Hui seeking refuge from Han attack in a pigsty, after which they showed respect for the pigs' kindness by refraining from eating their meat. Pigs are regarded in China in much the same way as in the West, as dirty, ugly animals (Thompson 1988:100), even though they are useful and desired for the nutritional or economic benefit that may be gained from raising them. So the purported Hui belief that pigs are their ancestors strikes Han as ludicrous, proof of a primitive mentality that is irrational and to a large degree disgusting.

Also, it is important to remember that pork plays a central role in Chinese views about food. It is synonymous with "meat" (unmarked *rou* "meat" means "pork" unless qualified: *jirou* means "chicken [meat]" and *niurou* means "cow meat," that is, "beef") and must be exchanged on many ceremonial occasions, such as weddings and funerals. It is said to stand for flesh and the matriline, in contrast to rice, which stands for bone and the patriline (Ahern 1974, Martin 1988, Thompson 1988).

Commensality (eating together) in China is the single most important act of social cohesion. Banqueting is one form, in which people forge obligations of reciprocity with one another and indeed force others to acknowledge relationships (Yang 1994). Most significant, of course, is the eating together that occurs in the family. K. C. Chang argued in his introduction to *Food in Chinese Culture* (1977) that the Chinese are more preoccupied with food than most people are. Indeed, it appears that food is a point of intersection among many aspects of Chinese culture, including family nurturance, physical well-being, medical treatment, a sense of harmonizing of diverse elements, aesthetics, time (food punctuates the day), relations with ancestors and descendants, and the well-run state.

Given the centrality of food in social life, the barriers to eating together imposed by Hui pork proscriptions force the conclusion that they must be excluded from many social and political interactions. Those with ambitions must renounce tradition and enter the food-sharing world of the majority group.[16]

Most Hui I met in Kunming were urban intellectuals and claimed to be quite assimilated. Yet Kunming also has a quite active and devout Hui community, with five active mosques and many *qingzhen* restaurants (following Hui dietary practices of cleanliness and propriety), whose proprietors are necessarily rigorous in their attention to matters of ritual cleanliness.

At a mosque, I met an unusual Hui, a young woman I'll call Ma Pingyi. She was a doctor and hence quite educated, but she admitted quickly that she was very much a Hui and *really* believed *(hen xin)*. Later she took me to see several festivals and to meet her family.

She spoke frankly, within the safety of a deserted mosque, of the scorn with which she—like all Hui—was treated as a child. Though she and the other Hui children were much smarter, in some cases, than the children of Han cadres, the latter got a better school and more teachers. The teachers of the Hui often scolded the children, beat them, and humiliated them. This treatment is not surprising, since she would have been in school in the 1960s, at the height of cultural revolution antireligious zeal.

Entering a mosque, I was invariably asked if I was Hui. Occasionally someone asked if I was a Muslim (Musilin), but usually the question was phrased in terms of being Hui *(Ni shi Huizu ma?)*. Though "Hui" has been interpreted to mean "Muslim Chinese," it clearly means "Muslim" in general for many who are self-designated Hui (see also Gladney 1991:18–21 and 1998a for the meaning and origin of the term "Hui"). The ethnic or racial-historical component that it holds for outsiders is not necessarily present for insiders, though there is also a sense of racial homogeneity among Hui. "I look like a typical Hui," several different people told me on different occasions, showing that for some Hui there is a phenotypical component to their notion of ethnicity.

Kunming Hui—at least those who are unassimilated—are for the most part a self-conscious community. There are streets that everyone knows as Hui streets. Directed to one of these, I chanced to visit it on a day when there was a great deal of hubbub: everybody was being relocated so that the street could be widened. Later when I asked the reason for this turmoil, I was told that the residents had petitioned the government to be allowed to remain so that they could be near their neighborhood mosque, or had at least requested permission to return after the construction was completed. The feeling was that this request would be disregarded and the neighborhood scattered. Many residents were delighted to live in newer buildings, safer and less rickety, with indoor plumbing; I heard no suspicion of less than noble intentions on the part of the city planners. Indeed, "modernization" has been so embraced by all residents of the PRC that even those clearly affected adversely by it cannot question its reputed benefits.

In addition to pork avoidance and violence, the Hui are renowned for being especially "clean." When I asked what this meant, one Han friend, Hong Weiping, explained that in the market, for instance, people would always prefer to buy food prepared by Hui, knowing that they used superior ingredients and cleaned them more thoroughly than did the Han. Despite that fact, she demonstrated no particular admiration for them. It was the only positive thing I ever heard said of the Hui, and there was a certain degree of amazement associated with it, as if they were hyperfastidious to a ridiculous extent. (A colleague of mine observed a nose-picking Hui on a long bus ride and concluded that certain hygienic practices of the Hui are similar to those of the Han.)

Hui also say that they are cleaner than Han. Hui have certain required ritual ablutions, and there is much more discussion of cleaning than I ever heard among Han. Utensils used in a Hui community ritual dinner were carefully cleaned by the women involved in preparation and were kept in cloth-covered basins until it was time to eat. They may even have used soap to wash the dishes—something unlikely to occur in Kunming in most group settings in 1991 (though increasing in the later 1990s).

At their simplest, ideas held of the Hui include only (1) descent from Hui parents, and (2) abstention from pork, with perhaps (3) some vague notions of greater cleanliness than the general Chinese population, and (4) a belief in the intrinsically violent nature of the Hui. An "expert" on the Hui might know of more technical, historical, or cultural features of Hui life: a Central

Asian origin, belief in Islam, practice of Islamic prayer five times a day, the fasting of Ramadan, and endogamy, in addition to the four aspects mentioned above. But for the general, especially the Han, population in Kunming, the cognitive model of the Hui is that they are a population very much similar to the Han with the exception of the factors mentioned above.[17]

Indeed, informants who are not particularly aware of the Hui mentioned just those aspects, emphasizing the idea that they are violent and unified. While the Hui themselves might say that they are courageous and unafraid to die for something in which they believe, the Han fear that fearless anger will be directed at them, and they convert the trait of courageousness into a source of dread rather than pride.

Hui levels of education seem to be similar to those of the Han. Some Hui and Han said that Hui were better educated than the Han, but others said the reverse. In any case, many people acknowledged that Hui can rise only to a certain level, especially in the government: How could they take part in the necessary banqueting ritual, if they did not eat the most important food? Besides, at the highest levels of government, patronage is vastly more important than any other criteria of selection, and naturally Hui would not be patronized by non-Hui.

Interestingly, though everybody I questioned agreed that Hui speak exactly as do the Han with the exception of a few special lexical items, in the matched-guise test people guessed that they were listening to Hui nine times. Three of these times, respondents said "Han or Hui," showing awareness of the difficulty of differentiating these two groups. It is unclear what they thought they heard in the tape that caused them to identify the speakers as Hui.

The Hui are always considered to be speakers of the Han language around them and in fact are conversant with such linguistic varieties. Some Hui, especially in the northwest, also command a large non-Chinese, Arabic-based vocabulary that is critical for communication within Hui communities (Gladney 1991: appendix B, 393–421). Given norms of interaction and politeness in China, however, this vocabulary would not be used with outsiders, so the outsiders would conclude on the basis of their own experience that the Hui are Chinese speakers. They *are* Chinese speakers but not only Chinese speakers.

Unlike the prototypical minority nationalities characterized by such traits as distinctive clothing and handicrafts, the Hui are seldom described or depicted for their physical nature. Occasionally an attempt is made to discover peculiarly Hui clothing, but generally they are simply disregarded as less than prototypical examples of ethnic others.[18] When I asked about minority nationalities in general, those that best fit the complete description for ethnic

otherness are the ones that were mentioned first, frequently, and easily. The
harder cases around the edges were mentioned much less.

Though Hui are mentioned often in conversation (and student essays),
they are treated very cursorily in the promotions of tourism and ethnicity.
Lacking picturesque qualities (other than old, bearded men reading from the
Quran), having no intriguing sexual tension, and without the ties to naturalness and the primitive that other groups have, the Hui are passed over as
representative of colorful ethnicity. And almost alone of all ethnic groups in
China, the Hui most typically represented in images are male. The most
common image is of a white-bearded old man praying with a thin book, his
head covered in a blue or white cap (see figure 5.3).

Hui emphasize female modesty, with greater gender separation than Han
and very clear proscriptions against adult opposite-sex contact. Hui women
act in many ways in a fashion that would be appropriate for Han women—
and even more so—but no one ever mentioned this to me. One might expect admiration for Hui women's shyness, but the focus was always on differences, especially characteristics viewed as negative.

Figure 5.3   An old Hui man (Source: *Highlights*, p. 117)

Table 5.2: Hui Statistical Portrait (Attributions of Persons Guessed "Hui" in the Linguistic Identification and Evaluation Task)

N = 6 (3 people who guessed "Hui" also mentioned "Hui or Han")

	Language pleasing?/ Easy to understand?		Person decent?		Potential friend?		Wealthy?	
Yes	0	0%	3	50.0%	2	33.3%	2	33.3%
Avg.	1	16.7	1	16.7	0	0	1	16.7
No	5	83.3	2	33.3	4	66.6	2	33.3
Blank/ Don't know	0	0	0	0	0	0	1	16.7

Profession (N = 33)	(number)	(%)	Mean educational level
Teacher	1	12.1	
Cadre	0	0	
Worker	3	37.5	6.0 years
Peasant	4	50.0	
Getihu	0	0	
Blank/Don't know	0	0	

A statistical portrait (see table 5.2) derived from the linguistic identification test shows that Hui were guessed to be speaking six, and possibly nine,
times, even though there were no Hui speakers. The educational level attributed to them is among the lowest of all the groups I discuss in this book
(a mean guess of six years), and they are viewed as a largely average, urban
cohort. Uncertainty about them is nonexistent (except for the question of
wealth) in the sense that few answers were blank or "don't know." Wealth
has become a valued attribute (Jankowiak 1993:77–81), but informants were
unsure about the position of the Hui: they didn't like them much, but was
this because the Hui were poor and unsophisticated or because they were
wealthy and cheaters? But people were more certain that the Hui were unlikely to be their friends: only two of six people (33.3 percent) thought the
Hui could possibly be their friends, compared to, for example, the 54.5 percent who felt the Dai likely to be their friends.

CONCLUSION

It might be logically possible to deny that the Hui are a legitimate minority
and to say that they are really Han with a different religion, but people are
generally convinced that the Hui are a significantly different ethnic group.
The Hui, like the Tibetans, are salient because they are a source of uncertainty
and discomfort, but they are scarcely typical. Attributes commonly mentioned
are strength, separateness, religion, cleanliness, and food proscription. None
of these are the most central features of ethnic groups, with the exception of
religion (but Islam is quite differently conceived in China from the variant of
Buddhism, for instance, practiced by the Dai). The Wa are prototypical of the
undesirable primitives, remote but lingering at the edges of possible contact.
For accessible and positively-valued typicality, one must look to the more
"docile" nationalities, such as the homegrown Naxi, Yi, or Bai.

CHAPTER SIX

COLORFUL, HARMLESS ETHNIC OTHERS: NAXI AND YI

Naxi Nationality

Yi Nationality

Two groups frequently invoked in Kunming are the Naxi and the Yi. Both are considered "primitive," though for different reasons, and both are considered fairly harmless (or at least powerless), though the Yi are sometimes thought to be strong, independent people.

THE PRIMITIVE BUT GLORIOUS NAXI

The Naxi are not widely known in China as a whole, but they are among the most salient groups in Yunnan. Yunnan touts them in its promotions of cultural diversity, and many people spontaneously mentioned them to me. A subject of anthropological investigation by Chinese and Western scholars alike, the Naxi are known primarily for some fascinating cultural traits.

The Naxi live largely in the Lijiang Autonomous Prefecture, renowned for its breathtaking mountainous scenery, and increasingly popular as a tourist attraction, beyond just the backpacking "adventurer" cohort that "discovered" it a decade ago. It is attracting missionaries as well; a new train line from Kunming is being completed, which will offer an eight-hour alternative to the current eighteen-hour bus ride. A new airport is functioning as well, connecting Lijiang to Dali and Kunming.

The Naxi have been described in Western scholarship for at least sixty years and were made famous (as the Na-khi) by the botanist Joseph Rock (Rock 1947, 1963) and by Peter Goullart (1955). But they are also on the anthropological map because they are one of the few groups who "still practice matriarchy." Though Western anthropologists such as Stevan Harrell view the matrilineal Mosuo as distinct from Naxi, in Chinese classification the Mosuo are a branch of the Naxi. The constant reference to Mosuo traits in discussions about Naxi make them appear indistinguishable. Hunting the truth, Western and Chinese ethnographers have headed off to Lijiang to investigate the facts (Shih 1985, 1993, McKhann 1995).[1]

But practicing matriarchy is not the only claim to fame held by the Naxi. As I describe below, they also have a script known as the *dongba* script, which works something like hieroglyphics. *Dongba* script has its own research institute (the Dongba Institute); Emily Chao, Sydney White, Charles McKhann, and Helen Rees (among others) have all done research through this institute.

The third aspect of the Naxi that is of interest and concern is the high rate of suicide, which is believed to stem from the changing courtship patterns imposed by the Naxi incorporation into the modern social system of the PRC. Naxi courtship patterns—as idealized by Han—are captured in their full romantic glory in a novel by Bai Hua, *The Remote Country of Women* (1994).

The Naxi speak a language classified by Chinese linguists as belonging to the Yi branch of Tibeto-Burman, because its phonological system is almost identical to that of Yi and other Loloish languages (Ramsey 1987:265), but this similarity could also be the result of long-term influence from surrounding languages, in a phenomenon known as "contact convergence" (see, for example, Dwyer 1993).

The Naxi ruled the Nanzhao kingdom in the seventh through twelfth centuries, with ancestors of what are now Bai, Yi, and Dai people (see Backus 1981), and relations among these groups are often quite close, even now. Charles McKhann is investigating this region as a "culture area" that includes interactions among several different ethnic groups (McKhann, personal communication).

This chapter discusses three features that explain why the Naxi are especially prevalent in the popular imagination in Yunnan:

1. *Dongba* "hieroglyphic" script;
2. *Azhu* "free" marriage, contrasted with a reluctant switch to monogamy and Han-style arranged marriages, which led to a high suicide rate; and
3. The Mosuo, a "branch" of the Naxi, who are matrilineal/"matriarchal."

The combination of these characteristics accounts for Naxi being considered "living fossils" *(huoshi)* and proof of cultural evolution. Their existence thus confirms the theoretical platform on which all social science research is conducted in China.

I take these traits in turn.

Dongba Script

The so-called *dongba* script *(dongbawen,* or *dtomba, tomba)* is a system of pictographs that are used in prompt-books for religious rituals conducted by practitioners known in Chinese as *dongba* (see figure 6.1). The remaining *dongba*—all old, all trained prior to 1949—no longer practice as ritual specialists and are employed principally as research assistants. *Dongba*-led ritual is said to be related to Bon, the pre-Buddhist religious system of Tibet. The script has attracted a great deal of scholarly and art-historical attention, and collections of texts may be found in libraries and museums throughout the world (Bockman 1989, Jackson 1989). Joseph Rock, though known more as a botanist, was largely responsible for placing thousands of *dongba* texts in the hands of non-Chinese collectors.

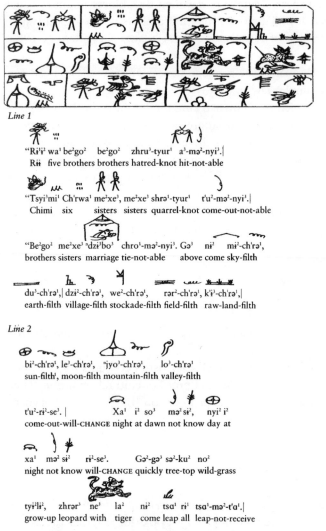

Line 1

"Ri¹i¹ wa¹ be²go²   be²go²   zhru¹-tyur¹   a³-mə²-nyi³.|
Rïï five brothers brothers hatred-knot hit-not-able

"Tsyi³mi¹ Ch'rwa¹ me²xe³, me²xe³ shrə¹-tyur¹   t'u²-mə²-nyi³.|
Chimi   six   sisters   sisters quarrel-knot come-out-not-able

"Be²go² me²xe³ ⁿdzï³bo³   chro¹-mə²-nyi³. Gə³   nï²   mï²-ch'rə¹,
brothers sisters marriage tie-not-able   above come sky-filth

du³-ch'rə¹,| dzï²-ch'rə¹, we²-ch'rə¹,   rər²-ch'rə¹, k'ï³-ch'rə¹,|
earth-filth   village-filth stockade-filth field-filth raw-land-filth

Line 2

bi²-ch'rə¹, le³-ch'rə¹,   ⁿjyo³-ch'rə¹,   lo³-ch'rə¹
sun-filth¹, moon-filth mountain-filth valley-filth

t'u²-rï²-se³. | Xa¹ ï² so³   mə²sï²,   nyi² ï²
come-out-will-CHANGE night at dawn not know day at

xa¹   mə² sï²   rï²-se³.   Gə²-gə³ sə²-ku² no²
night not know will-CHANGE quickly tree-top wild-grass

tyï²lï²,   zhrər³ ne³   la²   nï² tsɑ¹ rï¹ tsɑ¹-mə²-t'ɑ¹.|
grow-up leopard with tiger come leap all leap-not-receive

Figure 6.1   *Dongba* script (Source: Ramsey 1987:269)

Scholars from around the world come to the Dongba Institute in Lijiang (called Dayanzhen in Lijiang's Yunnanhua [White 1993:7]), principal city of the Lijiang Naxi Autonomous Prefecture, to study and translate. The texts have been viewed as curiosities, as historic evidence for the evolution of writing systems, as mystical keys to a foreign culture. When I accompanied a group of students studying *daoyou*, "tour-guide-ology," in Kunming to the museum attached to the Yunnan Minorities Institute, they all paused for a long time at the Naxi *dongbawen* display. They were intrigued by the writing, finding it to operate on principles rather different from those of Chinese and English. Symbols indicate moments in the chants and stories; I suggest that they are used similarly to prompt-books: much that is uttered is omitted from the written text.

Naxi social organization places the Naxi in the "primitive" category, but possession of a written script mitigates that primitiveness. A technical look at this script shows it to have very limited use and to be of very narrow currency. (A helpful explanation may be found in Ramsey 1987:266–270.) Yet its very existence places the primitive Naxi in a list of script owners that even the more "advanced" Bai can't enter.

Nonacademic non-Naxi, however, view the texts as mystical and perhaps intriguing, much the way American students in, say, Ithaca regard the *Yi Jing* (*I Ching;* usually referred to in China as the *Zhou Yi*). An "esoteric" script—known only to initiates—fits well with the notion that Lijiang is a remote, snowy, mountainous, cold place. Until recently it has scarcely been accessible to outsiders, though it now has a functioning airport and is slated to be developed as a Special Economic Zone. Missionaries are following this opportunity and setting up shop to convert the Naxi to Christianity—illegally and covertly, of course.

State control over religion has meant that the *dongba* texts are primarily of historical and theoretical interest. The state controls researchers' access to the texts and to their interpreters, all while offering the idea of these texts as evidence of Naxi tradition—very much the way the state promotes interest in (abstract) Tibet while denying access to it physically.

A similar, amateur, common sense interest has accompanied a second facet of Naxi culture, while the state and scholars have other interests in it as well: so-called "*azhu* marriage."

Azhu Marriage

Since the founding of the PRC, the Chinese have actively regulated marriage practices. Han marriage was declared "feudal" and "patriarchal" (*fengjian* and *fuquanzhi*). Stories of women's oppression were elicited, and the old system of virtual sale into slavery was declared impermissible. The Marriage Law of 1950 gave men and women equal roles; it eliminated child marriage, polygamy, and a host of other sources of misery. It also gave women as well as men the right to initiate a divorce, precipitating a rash of divorces in the early 1950s. A new marriage law was written in 1980, largely to emphasize family planning.

While this regulation may be easy for Americans to embrace, the corresponding actions that the state implemented among non-Han may be more troublesome. With a model of monogamy and patriliny (a system in which the family line is followed through males) as the highest form of marriage, other forms had to be "encouraged" to "progress" in a unilinear fashion as fast as possible.

Some strange and tragic consequences followed:

Minorities that had "free choice" in marriage (the Chinese term for "free choice" is literally "free love," *ziyou ai*) had to go through a stage of parent-arranged marriages, even while the Han were leaving this stage behind. "Freedom" for sexual liaisons had been practiced in the Communist enclave at Yan'an before the 1949 Communist victory, and sexual morality as applied to the masses was never quite what the leadership followed (cf. Li Zhisui 1994, Dai Qing in Gordon and Hinton 1995).

For the Naxi, this system proved to be a source of tremendous conflict with the state, and it is also a source of the popular notion of Naxi sexual activity as extremely free. Cadres entered Naxi society, collected reports about Naxi marriage and sexuality, and ordered its transformation (Chao and White 1990, Bai 1994). While "traditional" times saw nothing but "love matches," the arranged marriages imposed by the Han led to a rash of suicides that became institutionalized as the ultimate form of romantic love.[2]

In 1997, a scholarly expert on minorities told me that most Naxi now follow Han marriage practices because otherwise they can't get permission to have children. He also mentioned that he has had access to some remote groups because one of his students was Naxi from outside Lijiang city. Because he has this connection, people tell him the truth. This offhand statement suggests that it is difficult for Han from Kunming to learn what the actual situation is among rural Naxi; policies encourage duplicity in reporting.

A student at the prestigious Yunnan University wrote the following story about his personal experience with some Naxi. He must have been about ten years old at the time.

In the fall of 1981, I went to Xiaguan, a city which is 13 kilometers south from Dali, to visit my relative[s], the Hongs. They are Naxi people. There are five members in their family, the parents, two sons, and one daughter.

Miss Hong was a beautiful lady, twenty years old then. She often took me to the cinema to see films and to small restaurants to enjoy the flavorful local cooking. She was very kind-hearted and she really treated me well.

One day, a thing happened that impressed me deeply and surprised me a lot. It was a Sunday morning. I heard Mr. Hong quarreling with his daughter when I was watching TV. Their voices were muffled in the other room. I seemed to hear them disputing about Miss Hong's marriage. It seemed that Mr. Hong didn't agree to his daughter's hope to marry a certain young man. I heard Miss

Hong crying and her mother persuaded her daughter to obey her father. After a while, Miss Hong said that she would jump out of the window to commit suicide if her father insisted on his idea and his control of her. Mr. Hong became angry and shouted loudly to his daughter. Then I was watching TV and it sounded as if Miss Hong did what she said she would do. I rushed to the window, seeing Miss Hong lying on the ground. After a while, Mr. and Mrs. Hong ran out of the building. It was clear from their countenances that they were very worried and repentent. They carried Miss Hong on a cart and sent her to the hospital. Since I was then very young, I was scared by what I heard and saw. I just stayed at home that morning, waiting to see what the result would be. She was badly hurt. A few days later I went to the hospital. I saw her head was bandaged and she lay in bed. Not until half a month later did she come back home. She was never as beautiful as before. I helped take care of her till I had to be back in Kunming for the next school year.

From then, I began to realize that the Naxi people are not only kind, but also bold to do what they have said, though their deeds sometimes make burdens for themselves. I also find their patriarchal control is more firm than ours.

Whether himself Naxi or not—at least he has cousins who are—this story confirms the general public notion of the Naxi as romantic and passionate. What is intriguing as well, however, is his final comment about the Naxis' strong patriarchal control. This contradicts the technical classification of the Mosuo as Naxi (see below), with the Mosuo being clearly matriarchal. People told me over and over, instantly, far surpassing any other fact, that the Naxi are significant because they are still "matriarchal."

"Matriarchy"

The Chinese terms differentiate between *muquanzhi* (a system of "mother-right," that is, matriarchy) and *muxishizuzhi* (a system of family line coming from the mother, that is, matriliny). The former is a statement of relative power, while the latter refers to the more descriptive tracing of identity through the maternal line.

The Mosuo (pronounced "maw-saw") live in Yongning county, around Lugu Lake. A strenuous scholarly debate centers around the official Chinese claim that the Mosuo are a branch of the Naxi (Shih 1985, 1993, McKhann 1995).[3] The Mosuo seem to have a diverse set of marriage and residence practices, some of which are very similar to those of their neighbors, the Tibetans; these practices include the residency of men to a great extent in monasteries prior to Liberation and inheritance passing variably through either parent's line. Given the Chinese faith in unilinear evolution,[4] a decision must be made as to whether the Naxi or Mosuo system was primary. Some scholars suggest that historical pressures—forced sinicization—led to a concomitant shift to patriliny. Others suggest that the introduction of Tibetan Buddhism and the departure of many men into monasteries led to the development of matriliny.

Whatever the "facts" or scholarly squabbles, the classic folk model of Mosuo family life depicts children living with their mothers, their mothers' lovers (perhaps the children's fathers) living in men's houses, and these lovers visiting the women at the women's pleasure. Ill-fated policies in the 1950s, depicted with devastating humor in Bai Hua's wonderful allegory of freedom and control, *The Remote Country of Women* (1994), tried to force women to register "marriages" and to sleep only with the man who was registered as their husband. The ultimate threat to traditional Chinese ideals of male control over women, Mosuo society appeared to turn the world upside down—like Bakhtin's notion of the carnivalesque (Bakhtin 1984)—and to do so without apology. So Han control over marriage seemed necessary as a way of controlling the Mosuo politically.

In *The Remote Country of Women,* a sour Han cadre in charge of eradicating what two members of the Gang of Four had called "this most primitive, most backward, and most barbarous lifestyle"—that is, matriarchy and "free love"—talks to a Mosuo party member.

Bima, a twenty-year-old female party member, said in a thin voice, "During the year of the Great Leap Forward . . . they said the same thing. But later–"

"What happened later?"

"The women and men who married ended up separating and returning to their mothers."

"I can assure you that this year is not the same as '58. If that year saw a storm, this time there will be a hurricane! We will not give up until we have carried the revolution through to the end!"

"I can take the lead in all things except–" Bima stammered, "except in this kind of thing. I . . . I . . . I can't take the lead."

"Then you'll be expelled from the party!"

"So be it."

"So be what? You will still have to get your marriage certificate, even after you lose your party membership."

"I . . . I . . ." Raising her head, Bima suddenly found courage. "I don't see why the members of the central committee should give a damn about what's inside a man's pants or under a woman's skirt! We have been leading a decent, peaceful life, not a speck of chaos in it. No Mosuo has ever committed a crime, and none of us ever goes to court or picks a fight with her neighbor. Why are you forcing us to accept marriage? Why are you trying to separate us from our own kin and break up our matrilineal families? We are not accustomed to living in a family of strangers, separated from our own mothers and maternal uncles."

"Your head is on backward! Only monogamy fits current moral standards—can't you get that through your head?" (8–9)

In this allegory about freedom, in which Han culture is to Mosuo culture as totalitarian repression is to freedom and naturalness, the Han state's control over nature is clearly mocked. Written at the height of the *xungen* (searching for roots) movement in the mid- and late-1980s, the novel seeks an alternative to the present system by looking to the past. In this case, the past is believed visible in the Mosuo present. The author, Bai Hua, idealizes Mosuo freedom while nonetheless retaining the explanatory system of unilinear evolution: "Even today . . . the Mosuo people still maintain a prehistoric family structure and marital form. They regard the female as the root and trunk and the male as the branches and leaves" (373). His depiction of Mosuo paradise is irresistible, focused mostly on lovely women:

> The six-month storm finally passed [that is, the Han cadres left]. Lake Xienami, like a smooth mirror, calmly reflected the sky once again.
>
> The Mosuo were a simple people. They soon consigned the second political encroachment of the civilized world to oblivion, as if they were forgetting two invasions by mammoths or hordes of elephants. They healed instantly. No sooner had the engines of the departing work team started snorting than the *axiao* embraced each other. Apparently they had forgotten the taboos of heaven. Intoxicated, they embraced in broad daylight, during working hours in the fields. They believed that their ancestors and the goddess would forgive them because they had been forced to be apart from each other for so long.
>
> Those who had been forced into marriage also started to walk out of their muddy huts, carrying their bedrolls to their own *yishe*. (29)

In a description of a female puberty ceremony, one can see similar romanticizing of the beauty, independence, and "naturalness" of young Mosuo women:

> Five girls from the community were going to remove their linen gowns. On New Year's Eve they gathered under a row of pine trees along the lake in a place appointed for the annual meeting for thirteen-year-old girls. Every year there were up to a dozen thirteen-year-olds. In the previous years, Sunamei had been allowed only to stand watching at a distance. The bonfire on the grassy land and its reflection on the lake were like two large blooming flowers. Young maidens were dancing beneath the pines in a circle like a group of fairies. They opened their throats, singing unabashedly to the sky, as if they were already grown

Figure 6.2   Naxi women in "sun and moon" jackets (Source: Postcard series of Yunnan's ethnic minorities)

women. Their swaying arms and leaping legs churned the blazing fire into a dazzling sight. Then the girls sat and boiled tea by the fire in earthen kettles no bigger than their fists. Like the sixty-year-old *dabu*, they narrowed their smiling eyes and sipped hot tea with inexpressible satisfaction. They were drinking wine, too. Their cheeks, burned by flames and wine, were red as azaleas. (49)

Views of the Mosuo/Naxi are thus intertwined with Han notions of the primitive and of sexual morality. Naxi women are believed to flout all the rules that regulate ideal Han life. They are also known for performing hard physical labor, symbolized in the "sun and moon" jackets that permit them to carry heavy loads (see figure 6.2).

One person told me in an interview that of all the minorities, Naxi were the least like the Han, while Hui were sinicized long ago. He claimed that Naxi were visible from their dress, their language, and their general demeanor. Others mentioned that the Naxi are advanced, very much like the Han, with a thousand-year tradition of bilingualism. It seems that while the Naxi are often invoked, there are in some cases conflicting ideas about what their nature is.

Finally, a statistical "portrait" of the Naxi, as guessed in the linguistic identification and evaluation test, appears in table 6.1.

Naxi were guessed to be speaking twenty-two times. This case is more complex than many of the others because there was a Naxi speaker among

Table 6.1: Naxi Statistical Portrait (Attributions of Persons Guessed "Naxi" in the Linguistic Identification and Evaluation Task)

N = 22

	Language pleasing?/ Easy to understand?		Person decent?		Potential friend?		Wealthy?	
Yes	6	27.3%	6	27.3%	6	27.3%	6	27.3%
Avg.	1	4.5	7	31.8	1	4.5	2	9.1
No	15	68.2	8	36.4	14	63.6	14	63.6
Blank/ Don't know	0	0	1	4.5	1	4.5	0	0

Profession (N = 44)	(number)	(%)	Mean educational level
Teacher	4	9	
Cadre	7	15.9	
Worker	7	15.9	6.0 years
Peasant	18	40.9	
Getihu	7	15.9	
Blank/Don't know	1	2.3	

the voices. She spoke twice, once in Naxi and once in the Yunnan dialect spoken in Lijiang. When she spoke in Yunnanhua, eleven (out of eighty-five) people guessed her identity as Naxi; when she spoke Naxihua, only four identified her as Naxi. The remaining seven guesses of "Naxi" are scattered among three other speakers (one Yi speaker, one a speaker of Kunminghua, two of Shanghai dialect, and three of Kucong).

The speaker was a high school graduate, with twelve years of education. Nonetheless, the mean level of education guessed for those believed to be Naxi was six years, the second-lowest of the six groups considered here. (Only the Yi were believed to have a lower level of education, at a mean of 5.47 years.) So it seems that when people in Kunming believe they hear a Naxi speaker, that speaker is likely to be rural and uneducated. They do not hear clues about education, only prompts of identity that remind them of the prototypes they already hold for those groups.

The Naxi are regarded as colorful, aloof, a bit mysterious, with primitive marriage practices (for example, the Mosuo, with "matriarchy") along with patriarchy that exceeds that of the Han. They are categorized as relatively advanced, with their own writing system, and yet they are associated with low levels of education. They contrast rather clearly, however, with the Yi, another of Yunnan's significant ethnic groups, especially in terms of attributed level of "civilization."

THE YI OF MANY COLORS

The Yi are the most numerous minority nationality group in Yunnan, with a population of 3.35 million (in 1982). They are the fourth largest group in China as a whole (6.6 million in 1990), following Zhuang, Hui, and Uygur (Uighur). They are also named most frequently in the linguistic identification and evaluation test (fifty-five times, the same figure as the "Bai") and the student essays (eighteen times). Yet the Yi are not a homogeneous group, just as the Miao are not, although their languages are all classified within the Burmese-Lolo or Burmese-Yipho branch of the Tibeto-Burman group. Prior to the official classification of the post-1949 period, they had been known by a vast number of different names (see Harrell 1990, 1995a). Many of these names are still used as those of subgroups (referred to as XX *ren* [person]) of the Yi: Sani *ren*, Aini *ren*, Ahi (Axi, Asi) *ren*, Nuosu *ren*, and others.

Stevan Harrell (1990) shows something of the range of Yi ethnicity and self-identity, from complete acceptance of the state definition to lukewarm acceptance to rejection. These correlate to some extent with the degree of distance from Han culture. As with most of the cases we have examined thus far, the state has been extremely instrumental in ethnogenesis in China (see also Gladney 1991:96–98, 299–300, 309–12), creating groups that would otherwise have little sense of shared identity. One of the forces behind such creation is the reification of groups through coining new names, names that are then reiterated in every context until there is simply no other way to speak of them (see Harrell 1995a, Swain 1995; but see also Harrell 1995b).[5]

But for Han in Kunming—no matter what the historical "facts" or the experience of "the Yi" themselves—the category seems real. Indeed, what linguists and philosophers of language call "presupposition" is the most powerful shaper of reality: by discussing "the social structure of the Yi" or "the population of the Yi," one presupposes their existence. By hearing these terms, one has confidence in others' knowledge.

In Kunming itself, the Sani—technically a branch of the Yi, many of whom live in a community in Lunan, not far from Kunming—are noteworthy, dressing flamboyantly in brightly embroidered clothing and selling crafts on the street. A side specialty is money changing. Many people feel that the Sani are crass and intrusive, not accepting refusals of their services and wanting only to get rich (see Swain 1991 for a nuanced view of the Sani and their use of tourism). Yet day trips to Stone Forest, a "compact community" of Yi (Sani), are considered mandatory for tourists to Kunming, and thus the Sani are quite salient for people in Kunming. In the following essay, we learn of the deeply held prejudice toward the Sani but also see that it is possible to fight this prejudice with other, more persuasive experience:

"Sani People of the Yi Nationality"

In Yunnan there are as many as 25 minority nationalities living in compact communities. And in the world-famous Stone Forest which lies within the boundaries of Lunan County, 126 kilometers to the southeast of Kunming, there is a branch of the Yi nationality, named Sani People. Those who can go to Stone Forest, will see them.

One day during the last winter holiday, I led a tourist group of Hongkong People to Stone Forest. When our bus was coming slowly into the Stone Forest Hotel, a crowd of Sani People, men and women, old and young, in their vari-colored dress dashed off towards the bus. After the bus stopped, they completely surrounded the entrance of the bus and waved their minority handicrafts, such as suits, bags, etc. and shouted, "look at this beautiful bag, just 30 *yuan*." "Look! Look at this gala attire of Sani people, just 100 F.E.C." ["F.E.C." stands for "foreign exchange currency," which was a special form of money that was exchangeable for foreign currency, unlike the domestic Chinese unit of Renminbi. It was also used for purchase of limited luxury goods and for exchange on the black market. It is no longer in use.] "Oh, it's too cheap, if you want it, you may bargain." . . . In fact, the tourists had already bought a lot of handicrafts of nationalities, so they were not interested in those handicrafts at all; they wanted nothing but to get off the bus and see the grand views of Stone Forest. But their exit was blocked by the Sani People. It seemed that if the tourists did not buy their handicrafts, the Sani People would not let them go. Inside and outside the bus, a hubbub was heard. At that moment, the security personnel in the Stone Forest Hotel came and drove the Sani People out. The startled tourists shouted angrily, "Oh, Sani People, such a wild nationality." "They aren't salesmen, they're just robbers."

That night, the tourists and I sauntered into a village which was very near the Stone Forest. Because there were a lot of young tourists, I suggested we invite some Sani People to teach us folk dances and decided we would give them money if Sani people taught us. It really seemed adventurous and risky. But we decided to do so. After a short time, more than ten Sani youth in their gala attire came to the playground in the village; all of them were willing to teach us. At the centre of the playground, we lit a haystack. At the very beginning, the young beautiful Sani girls were very shy; they lowered their heads, pinched each other gleefully and giggled. After a loud blare of gongs and drums, all the people formed a large circle and danced trippingly to the beats of gongs and drums. After a while, we excitedly found that we could dance, we could dance. . . . A happy and cheerful night was over, smiles showed on the faces of every person. To show our thanks to the Sani People, we suggested that we should give them some money. But to our surprise, they refused . . . angrily and said, "We wanted to teach you folk dances, and we wanted to make friends with you. Not every Sani person regards money as the most important thing!"

Oh, Sani People, I don't know how to show my feelings about you. Maybe some of you are very wild, but I believe that most of you are kind. Kindness, hospitality, . . . are your characteristics.

This person clearly began with the prevalent stereotypical assumption that the Sani were less than admirable, especially because of their desire for money. Contemporary Han show profound ambivalence toward money—or at least toward greed. Learning that some Sani were free from this greed, he granted them the sort of praise usually associated with minority nationalities: kindness and hospitality. (See figure 6.3.)

There is also some general feeling about a kind of generic "Yi," at least as understood by the relatively distant urban Han. The Torch Festival is commonly named, often as an event that the speaker/writer has personally experienced (compare this with the treatment of festivals among the Dai). When people mention this festival, comments are enthusiastic and favorable, as shown below.

"The Torch Festival"

I went to Chuxiong to see the Torch Festival of the Yi Minority nationality last summer vacation. It is about five hours' ride by bus from Kunming to Chuxiong.

The Torch Festival is on June 24 in the Lunar Calendar. I arrived at Chuxiong on June 25; the local people told me that the Torch Festival had already begun the day before. The streets were crowded with people. From their accent I knew they were from many provinces of our country. And there were many foreign friends. Because of the crowded state of traffic, riding bikes was forbidden during the Festival. Everybody was walking on the road. After supper, it gradually grew dark. I went to the street. I saw many minorities, men and women in their costumes. The street was bustling and full of life. Those minorities with torches raised in their hands were standing in a long line; I couldn't see the first and the last. Then they began to run frantically. They sang and shouted loudly. Their high spirits were infectious. Dissension had arisen among people who were looking on. We pushed each other and I almost fell on the ground. A long dragon of fire was dancing and twisting. With the throng, I walked on. In the center of the street, many Yi people in their costumes formed a ring in a circle. Someone told me that this was "Tiao Jiao" [dance feet]. "Tiao

Figure 6.3   Sani young lady
(Source: KMRB)

撒尼姑娘   菲菲   摄

Jiao" was a kind of dance that Yi people dance in their festivals. When dancing, many people formed a circle. In the center of the circle, there was a man playing an instrument somewhat like a Chinese lute [should be "flute"]. He was dancing when playing, and people around him were dancing and singing to his rhythm. This dance was regular and easy to learn. But what they sang I couldn't understand. They were singing in the local dialect. Everybody was in high spirits. And such public merry-making lasted about a week. I really had a good time during the Torch Festival in Chuxiong.

Some people wondered further about this festival, and especially about its origins. One student recounted an explanation that he got from a Yi (Asi) friend:

"The Huoba [Torch] Festival of the Asi People"

The 24th day of the 6th month of the lunar calendar is the Huoba Festival (Torch Festival) of the Yi nationality. It is the traditional festival of the Yi people. The Yi people are divided into several branches: Asi, Sani, Samei, Nasu, and Laluo. Every branch has their own story about the Huoba Festival.

I am lucky enough to have an Asi friend who knows the story:

Long, long ago, the forebears of the Asi lived by the Jinsha River (the Gold Sands River). They lived a comfortable life; there, far away from here, lived a slave owner named Zhaozhao. He owned countless slaves and livestock and vast areas. He was so proud of this that he wanted to make all his slaves form a line along the road to the Capital. His slaves were soon exhausted when the line came to Hunan Province. He decided to take more people by force as his slaves since Guizhou had a large population.

On the 5th day of the 5th lunar month, men and women, the old and children in the village by the Jinsha River in Guizhou were tied up by ropes to be taken away as slaves. So ever since then, on every 5th day of the 5th lunar month, men of the Asi people will put threads of black or various colors around their left hands and women around the right, then throw them into fire to remember their forebears' hard time.

But the Man Line was not long enough and it was still quite far away from the Capital.

Zhaozhao changed his mind and decided instead that he wanted to build a tower and put his name on it to let the world remember him forever.

Many people died in the building project. The slaves could bear no more and ran away. But many of them were captured back and a lot of them were killed. Azheng, one of the escaped slaves, called upon the others to fight back.

On the 23rd day of the 6th lunar month, the escaped slaves, led by Azheng, attacked Zhaozhao's castle but they failed.

Next day, Azheng got a good idea: he asked his men to tie two torches on each goat's horns. He had the goats go in the front of his troops and men followed with torches in their hands.

Zhaozhao's men did not know what was happening. They shot arrows. When Zhaozhao saw his goats had been killed, he told his men to stop shooting and opened the door to let the goats in. The slaves seized the opportunity and rushed in and killed Zhaozhao.

Ever since then, every 24th day of the 6th lunar month has been the Huoba Festival; on the night of the next day the Asi people will have a gigantic gathering.

Origin stories abound in discussions of minorities. In many ways the prototypical minority folktale is a just-so story, an origin-tale of some strange practice that requires justification by appeal to a timeless event in the past. The tales often contain the story of triumphant heroes doing improbable things. Thus we also learn about what counts as an explanation for cultural practices: a mythological event that has been recalled through a symbolic association. (None of these are exactly historical, though they are all single events rather than habitual associations.)

In the story above, the author mentions the misfortunes associated with the fifth day of the fifth lunar month. Interestingly, the Han also have an ominous reading of this day, which they call *"duanwujie,"* usually rendered "Dragon Boat Festival." It is seen as a time of danger, when bad vapors and dangerous insects abound. To ward off both, they wear embroidered sacks of fragrant herbs, especially out of concern for children's vulnerability. The day is further associated with the legend of Qu Yuan, the poet-official who drowned himself out of protest at being disregarded by his lord. To distract the fishes from eating his remains, boats shaped like dragons race and people throw triangular leaves stuffed with sticky rice into rivers. The many elements of this festival have not really been explained nor has their juxtaposition, though there have been many explanations of parts of the legend, especially Qu Yuan (Werner 1922:152, Eberhard 1968, Bodde 1975:314–16, Schneider 1980), as mentioned in chapter 4. It is especially fascinating that part of the Asi (Yi) legend includes a disaster that occurred on the fifth day of the fifth month. A materialist would explain this as the height of the heat (the lunar calendar begins in the second month of the solar calendar, so the fifth lunar month is the sixth solar month) and the zenith of climatic and hygienic dangers.

Another story contains an entirely different explanation of the origin of what this source calls "Torch Day." Here is an excerpt:

After dinner, I followed them to wander everywhere, visiting the decorations for the "Torch Day." I found there was a torch set before the doors of almost every family. At that time, as soon as the gong was struck, the old, young, men, and women were gathered at the playground, lifting rice wine, fried peas, and other foods, lighting the torch, and . . . at once, the sky was full of brilliance, and cheer sounded in every corner. All the people were dancing lightly surrounding the torch. It lasted three days or so. I also was pushed into the crowd dancing with them. My friend told me the origin of the "Torch Day" during this time. It was said that a woman named Anan was the wife of Man Ana chief, and then, the chief was killed by General Ge Shizhong of the Han people. When the general forced Anan to be his wife, she asked for three conditions: that there were three fires for her husband and his clothes and for her remarriage. After permission was granted, she lit all those things and killed herself in the fire.

I quote at length to show how the Han fascination with festivals and gender is almost a reflex, and that origins are very much connected with enjoyment of the celebrations (see also Harrell 1990 for discussion of these festivals, which are unknown among some remote "branches" of the Yi).[6] People told me on several occasions that by participating in such festivals, they get a sense of life in past years—in addition to having fun.

In contrast to the celebration of festivals, however, the fact that the Yi like to live in high, cold mountains provides a source of bewilderment and disdain. The Yi of Liangshan (Cold Mountain) in Sichuan, bordering Yunnan—known as the Nuosu—are often described in newspaper articles and are the prototypical Yi in the popular Yunnan imagination. *Shanqu* (mountain districts) are regarded as generally unpleasant places that no sane person would choose to live in: remote, chilly, rocky, without rice or entertainment or transportation, places of exile and horror.[7] One minority nationality student I interviewed admitted that there were extremely few people willing to go live and work in mountainous regions. When I pursued the matter and asked if anyone finds the mountains "romantic," she laughed and said, "Perhaps there is no one who thinks that," a polite way of dismissing this idea as ludicrous and impossible.

In traditional literati thought, mountains are places where Daoist hermits can reside. Mountains are also seen as powerful, both culturally and as loci of geomantic forces (see, for example, Lu 1997). Many official religious ceremonies took place on the tops of mountains, especially the state sacrifices performed by the lawful emperor on the Five Sacred Mountains (Shryock 1932, Naquin and Yu 1992). The fact that minority nationalities are able to inhabit such dangerous yet potent locations adds to the fear felt about them and the tendency to regard them as less advanced and closer to nature.

The Yi are not necessarily liked, even if they are often invoked when talking about ethnicity. Yi informants report a great deal of discrimination against themselves, particularly in a cosmopolitan setting like Kunming. Characterizations and judgments of ethnic others are by no means uniformly complimentary, as we have seen above. Conflicting reports about the sorts of relations that exist between nationalities suggests that this dimension of attitudes deserves exploration.

The Yi (the Nuosu in Liangshan) have also been taken as having possessed a slave society before Liberation, with the top layer of society consisting of slaveholders (Black Yi), the next layer of serfs (White Yi), and the lowest layer of Han slaves (Ramsey 1987:252–253, He 1988: 249–304, Ma Yin 1989:236–241, 245, Yang Yucai 1989:193–203). Given the diversity of the Yi, it is important to point out that only Nuosu had "castes"; other groups had feudal social organization. Still, the Yi nationality is often brought up to discuss the backward customs still in existence just on the eve of Liberation and now so mercifully rescued from that situation by the democratic socialist reforms.

A further complication is introduced by Yi possession of writing. Though not used as a medium for ordinary communication but rather as a tool of divination, its mere existence places the Yi, like the Naxi, in the small group of minorities that have their own traditional scripts.[8] Groups that have "primitive" production but also their own writing systems befuddle the classificatory schema a bit. But Yi writing, unlike Naxi writing, is not commonly mentioned. Only scholars seem to be aware of it, in contrast to Naxi writing, which has in some sense seized the popular imagination.

The Yi have no cities or towns of their own, as the Bai do. Given the overall valorization of urban life, groups that are exclusively rural would tend to be seen as more primitive. Yi are frequently regarded as poor peasants, uneducated, perhaps dirty and unsophisticated. Indeed, I witnessed a Han-Yi interaction in Kunming in 1997 that clearly revealed this instinctual Han judgment. My Yi friend Zhao Ling, who wryly observes Han reactions to her, has now married a Dutch man. One evening I was at their apartment, and as a favor to me they invited their neighbor, whom they hadn't really met, to chat with me about life in Kunming. This young woman, they felt, was a "typical" Kunming *xiaojie* (young miss): vain, proud, and capable of gentle talk that could erupt into anger and crudeness. The neighbor entered, clearly excited and honored to have a chance to represent Kunming to a foreigner. Zhao Ling was host. The neighbor asked at one point where Zhao Ling came from, and she gave the name of the prefecture. A scarcely concealed dismayed reaction followed: this place was known as poor, rural, minority, which meant that this neighbor of hers, married to a foreign man and having increased her status by this marriage, was nonetheless below her and not really worthy of curiosity. Zhao Ling observed this reaction clearly. After the snobbish neighbor left, we talked about this reaction, agreeing that it was far from unusual but also unfortunate.

There is certainly truth to the notion that Yi are commonly poor. Largely rural dwellers, in some places the Yi grow rice, but for the most part they cultivate what the Han consider the inferior staples: maize, buckwheat, oats, and potatoes (Ma Yin 1989:241). In contrast, the Bai are valley-dwelling rice growers (though there are "mountain Bai" as well, distinguished by the Bai themselves from the "valley Bai"). The mountain Bai are characterized by valley Bai much as city Han characterize peasants—dumber, naive, but more honest (Lucien Miller, personal communication). The Bai thus present a sort of exemplary minority group that others, such as the Yi, might do well to emulate. Here too, as with the Hui, food is seen to help draw the boundary between those who are civilized and eat like people and those who are not and eat like animals.

In the language identification and evaluation test, Yi were guessed to be speaking fifty-five times—quite a large number. Statistically, the Yi come out much less favorably than most groups and are comparable to the Hui, except in wealth, where the "Hui" were guessed to be wealthy ("yes" and "average") 44.4 percent of the total, compared to the Yi total of 17.2 percent (see table 6.2).

Here, some extremely interesting things may be observed. First, there was a Yi speaker among those recorded, and she spoke three times: once in Yi, once in the Yunnan dialect near her home of Honghe, and once in Putonghua. Though "Yi" did represent the greatest number of guesses of minorities, a total of fifty-five guesses is far lower than the number of times—3 x 85, or 255—that the Yi speaker was heard. One person guessed that six speakers were Yi, but he was correct only once—when the Yi speaker spoke in Yi. He was wrong when she spoke Putonghua. It turns out that this informant's mother is Yi, though he follows his father's Han identity.

The Yi were believed to have the lowest educational levels of the groups discussed here (5.47 years) and to have by far the lowest status jobs ("teacher" and "cadre" total only 13.4 percent, compared, to, for example, the 35.7 percent of the Dai and the 26.8 percent of the Bai). Disdain for Yi "civilization" accompanies the enthusiastic reception for their "colorful" festival and their tradition of strong independence.

CONCLUSION

Naxi are among the best-known ethnic groups in Yunnan. They are salient not because of their numbers but because they are regarded as retaining many aspects of "primitive" culture (especially matriarchy) along with a mys-

Table 6.2: Yi Statistical Portrait (Attributions of Persons Guessed "Yi" in the Linguistic Identification and Evaluation Task)

N = 55

	Language pleasing?/ Easy to understand?		Person decent?		Potential friend?		Wealthy?	
Yes	9	16.4%	11	20.0%	21	38.2%	6	10.9%
Avg.	1	1.8	10	18.2	0	0	5	9.1
No	42	76.4	32	58.2	33	60.0	41	74.5
Blank/ Don't know	3	5.4	2	3.6	1	1.8	3	5.4

Mean educational level   5.47 years

Profession (N = 75)

	(number)	(%)
Teacher	2	2.7
Cadre	8	10.7
Worker	20	26.7
Peasant	36	48.0
Getihu	7	9.3
Blank/Don't know	2	2.7

terious writing system that can be visually represented. Their current relatively disadvantaged status contrasts with their long history in Yunnan.

Yi are among the most numerous and most disdained of the minority
groups considered here. Known in Yunnan for their many branches, they are
nevertheless often lumped together as "Yi" and mentioned for their festivals
such as the Torch Festival. Pushed further, informants often talk about Yi as
mountain dwellers, a puzzling fact that nevertheless seems to result from Yi
naturalness in contrast to the Han civilized nature. (No one ever mentioned
the possibility that the Yi were forced to become mountain dwellers because
they were pushed upward by Han and other migrations.) The Yi are seen as
"primitive," poor, and generally remote from the city-dwelling Han. A significant contrast will be seen in the next chapter, which describes Han associations with the Bai, the minority group perhaps most embraced by Kunming Han.

ALMOST US:
THE BAI NEXT DOOR

Bai Nationality

The Bai are perhaps the greatest success story of Yunnan ethnicity. The locus of the Bai population is in Dali, now a favorite destination of Chinese and foreign tourists. Dali is renowned for three stone pagodas, which are highlighted as one of the wonders of the world (see figure 7.1). Whenever I told people I was interested in minorities, they told me I should go to Dali (and Lijiang and Xishuangbanna). One young woman brought her scrapbook of photographs from her trip to Dali the previous summer. Dali is one of the places firmly on the psychological map in Yunnan.

David Wu (1990, 1991) explains Bai success as based on the situational nature of Bai identity. He argues that Bai identity is illusory and has been taken on only recently so that people could benefit from the advantages conferred on ethnic minorities. Of course the Bai are educated, Han-speaking, and well adapted, this argument goes: they were Han all along! Wu bases his view in part on his own ethnographic experience in a Bai autonomous district in Yunnan and in part on the fact that Francis L. K. Hsu's classic ethnography of southwest China just before Liberation, *Under the Ancestors' Shadow* (1967 [1948]), was actually an ethnography of the Bai. For all these decades, Hsu and his readers have been content to consider the Bai exemplars of "Chineseness." Wu argues that this is because nothing *did* separate them from the Chinese.

Figure 7.1   Dali and its pagodas as icon of Yunnan's picturesqueness (Source: Yunnan's Web site, June 1996)

A different way of explaining Bai similarity to the Han is to suggest that, after denying their ethnicity in favor of assimilation to the Han during periods of cultural intolerance, people are now more willing to claim their identity as being of the Bai minority.

A third explanation takes Fredrik Barth's claim seriously and points out the relative unimportance of the cultural "stuff" contained within boundaries and the greater importance placed on recognition and maintenance of boundaries (Barth 1969). It takes contact and interaction, he argues, not isolation, to have ethnic groups. Though this view too has been disputed, it could help account for the somewhat paradoxical aspects of Bai identity that Wu discusses.

When the Mongols invaded Dali in 1253, the ancestors of what are now the Bai were already cultivating rice and were comparable agriculturally to the Han. The set phrase referring to the Bai of the time is *"Yuyan sui xiao chuan'e, dalue yu zhong Xia tong"* (Although there were slight linguistic errors, overall they were the same as the zhong Xia, the central plains Han.) (Baizu Jianshi Editorial Group 1988:85). This unique status makes them stand out from the other minority nationalities in the area, much as the Mongols, Manchus, and Koreans do in China in general (by having higher levels of education, status, and so on). Everyone concurs that the Bai are "advanced" and "civilized," showing the diversity of levels of development possible for the minority nationalities. They are consequently not given extra points in the provincial college entrance examinations.

The Bai have produced famous people as well as a form of architecture (pagodas with tightly fitted stones and no mortar) that has great permanence. They were rulers of the Nanzhao kingdom (seventh century to 902), followed by the kingdom of Dali (937–1253), making them appear quite nearly as "advanced" as the central plains Han. (The Yi, Naxi, and Dai also claim to have been rulers of the Nanzhao kingdom. See Backus 1981.)

The fact that they were not called Bai until 1956 does not cause any current lack of familiarity with them as Bai. In fact the old name of some of those now called Bai, Minjia, was virtually unknown in Kunming in 1991. In describing the Bai to me, one young man said that he thought they were also called Hakka ("Kejia" in Mandarin)! A few days later, he realized what his mistake was and corrected himself (see Fitzgerald 1941, Wu 1990).[1]

Of the young, educated Bai I met in Kunming, none could speak Bai, though they claimed their grandparents did. From such experience, one might conclude that there is no such thing as the Bai language. Though young intellectuals raised in Kunming do not speak it, it exists, but it is never heard in non-Bai settings. Wu reports widespread bilingualism among Bai even in remote areas, where most people can speak both Bai and the local variant of Mandarin (Hanhua).[2]

The Bai language, and the identification of the Bai, is scarcely straightforward, at least according to Ramsey (1987:290), Bradley (1987), and other Western sources. Though the Chinese sources classify the Bai language in the Yi branch of the Tibeto-Burman family, this classification assumes more than is justifiable. Bai has many Tibeto-Burman features, but it also has some that appear similar to Tai or Mon-Khmer and many that look like Chinese.

I need not judge matters of history here; whether the category "Bai" is "real" is not my concern, only that people in Kunming and Yunnan in general take it to be real. Whatever the "reality" of their identity, the Bai are quite salient. When one asks a Yunnan resident about minorities, in most cases the Bai of Dali will be in the first three named (with Dai and Yi). In my linguistic identification and evaluation task, fifty-five instances of Bai identity were guessed—and in reality there were no Bai speakers at all.

Contemporary Bai are said to retain their own festivals (March Fair [or Third-Month Street], Torch Festival) in addition to celebrating most Han festivals. (David Wu reports that Bai in outlying regions have not learned yet of these official new "Bai" festivals [1990:9].) These festivals are widely cited in the essays concerned with personal experience as well as those concerned with general minority characteristics.

People also mention customary Bai clothing, with women dressed modestly in long pants with vests and short aprons—quite different from the Wa or Miao, with their scandalous short skirts, or even the Dai, who often wore no top garments in earlier times (see figure 7.2).

Figure 7.2   A Bai "girl"

The stereotypical view of the Bai is of rural people; Bai were predominantly guessed as peasants in the linguistic identification and evaluation test (37.8 percent). The mean level of education guessed was 6.75 years, though one student clarified that he thought the speaker had a graduate school education. This mean level contrasts with the one of 5.47 years guessed for the Yi.

Comments in conversations about the Bai often involve their relatively "advanced" culture and their degree of assimilation, followed by their preservation of traditional festivals. People often express surprise that the Bai do not possess a writing system of their own but must use Chinese characters to write. This reaction reveals again the association commonly made between civilization and writing: ethnic groups that are more advanced are expected to have their own writing system.

Bai folklore has become famous in its own right. Lucien Miller has collected Bai folktales and has translated many in his collection of folktales from Yunnan, *South of the Clouds* (1994). Bai identity has become quite clear-cut for many people now, but it is permeable. Miller describes his *peitong* (official companion) as someone who had originally been Han but had married a Bai and then become Bai (see also Miller 1993). Recall my Han friend from the introduction, who is married to a Bai man. She told me many times that there was no real content to his "Bainess," that he and his family did things exactly as hers did; in fact she was puzzled about this identification in general. There was also a record of his family having come from Nanjing . . . "so how could they be indigenous?" she wondered.

Commonsense Han views of ethnicity are visible here: ethnic groups must have a kind of purity of practice, purity of descent, and cultural content. Without these features, the groups may be accused of being *jia* (false) or *kong* (empty).

One aspect of Bai character often mentioned is hospitality. Every essay written about them mentions this attribute and also mentions their festivals. The popular account of their festivals is very straightforward, but as one Bai student wrote, he cannot keep them straight because there are so many and because Bai in different places celebrate different festivals. Han writers, in contrast, have no trouble making sense of these festivals, at least as far as homogenizing them in a list, as the following essay does.

> I was born and grew up in Dali, a beautiful place where the Bai minority live. There are more Bai people than Han, so they are the "majority" in my hometown. We live in great harmony with each other.
>
> The Bai minority is hard-working, intelligent and hospitable. They have a long history and have had unforgettable influence on the development of Dali. First, they have flourishing culture and customs. They have their own spoken language. When they are talking with Han people, they speak the Han language,

but when they stay together, they talk with their own language that the Han people can hardly understand. They have many folk songs that are passed from generation to generation. Dancing and singing are their favorite activities. They are good at playing their own special musical instruments and dancing a kind of charming dance called "The Lord's Whip." Folk tales of the Bai people are very interesting and moving. The stories of the Butterfly Spring, the Three Pagodas, the Cloud Looking for Her Husband, etc., are great treasures of the Bai people. Changshan Mountain and Erhai Lake are resources of their legends, poetry, songs and traditions.

Bai people care very much about their dwellings. In Dali, Bai people used to live in stone houses. The stones are regular and as white as snow. Each stone is fitted so well that the house is built as perfect architecture. Some houses are built from marble because the Changshan Mountains are a marble-producing area. Flower blossoms and vegetables are green in the gardens. Streams from the mountains usually flow around the gardens. The furniture of the Bai people is elegant and comfortable, for there are many skillful carpenters among them. They like to make their own furniture according to their own choices.

The costumes of the Bai people are very beautiful. Young girls always wear colorful shirts and red vests, decorated aprons with embroidered flowers and other designs. Their trousers are also sewn, and so are their shoes. Bai girls are very beautiful and attractive. Their names are usually "Golden Flowers," because they are as beautiful as shining flowers. They are all experts in housekeeping, singing and dancing. Young men are brave and handsome. They go hunting, fish-catching and farming.

Bai people are very kind to each other. They love their neighbors and have good relationships with each other. They are willing to help those who are in difficulties. They are hospitable to all friends and guests.

As a minority with a long history, the Bai people have their own festivals and religious beliefs. In addition to the national festivals, they have the Third Month Market, the Grand Yutan (?) Gathering, the Butterfly Spring Gathering, the Gathering of the Goddess of Mercy, etc. Horse-racing is one of their favorite sports. Visitors to Dali may have the opportunity to watch it on these great days. Most of the Bai people are materialists [that is, atheists], though some of them are Buddhists and Catholics. In small villages, people worship their own ancestors, some famous men in history, folktales or in legends.

Bai people are very good people. I am so glad to be with them. We love each other and devote ourselves to the development of our hometown.

The notion of "being hospitable" requires comment. It is a translation of the Chinese term *haoke,* literally "to find guests pleasing" or "to love guests." It is said particularly often of the Miao, the Dai, and the Bai, though not of the Hui or Tibetans. Interestingly, I never heard it said of the Han Chinese in general, though I did hear individuals use it of other people they knew. Once it was used to explain a friend's mother's forcing of food on me when I was at their house. My friend explained, *"Wo mama zhen haoke"* (My mother is really a good host.). My claim that I was already full was disregarded.[3] The term as used to describe minorities seems to refer to the tendency to offer food and shelter to people without any prior claim on one's loyalty, such as relatives or old friends or even friends of friends. Han generally do not feel it necessary, advisable, or enjoyable to welcome strangers, and the Bai tendency to do so strikes the Han as noteworthy.

If one were to construct an idealized cognitive model of the Bai, it would include the following features:

1. The Bai have a long and illustrious history.
2. They are good at architecture.
3. They are hospitable.
4. They have unique festivals.
5. Bai "girls" are beautiful, as are their "costumes."

Many of these features are shared with other groups, but the constellation of them suffices to uniquely identify the Bai. The Dai, for instance, have festivals, beautiful women, and hospitality, but they are not mentioned as possessing a long history of civilization (which is ironic given the growing archaeological evidence of prehistoric Thai culture). Dai architecture is mentioned as "unique" and suited for the hot climate, but it is impermanent (made of bamboo) and far from monumental. On this count they are clearly "behind" the Han, and even behind the Bai.

The Bai are salient because of the combination of both picturesque and civilized characteristics. This makes them comfortable for the Han; they have no puzzling traits, such as violence, headhunting, or a desire for separatism, and they can serve as an example for the other minorities. In many ways they have long embraced assimilation while retaining just enough evident features to identify them as ethnically other. They typify the "good" and "advanced" nationalities, reflecting many characteristics the Han take pride in possessing themselves.

In the linguistic identification and evaluation test, Bai were guessed to be speaking fifty-five times, the same number as the Yi (see table 7.1). In this case there were no Bai speakers. Statistically, the Bai are regarded positively in many cases, though they are surpassed by the Dai in others.

Their hypothesized educational level was the highest of all groups. They were most likely to be cadres (18.3 percent) and most likely to hold the most prestigious positions (their total of "teacher" and "cadre" was the highest, at 26.8 percent).

Table 7.1: Bai Statistical Portrait (Attributions of Persons Guessed "Bai" in the Linguistic Identification and Evaluation Task)

N = 55

	Language pleasing?/ Easy to understand?		Person decent?		Potential friend?		Wealthy?	
Yes	5	9.1%	17	30.9%	19	34.5%	10	18.2%
Avg.	2	3.6	11	20.0	1	1.8	4	7.3
No	46	83.6	24	43.6	31	56.4	35	63.6
Blank/	2	3.6	5	9.1	4	7.3	6	10.9
Don't know								

Profession (N = 82)			Mean educational level
	(number)	(%)	
Teacher	7	8.5	
Cadre	15	18.3	
Worker	15	18.3	6.75 years
Peasant	31	37.8	
Getihu	12	14.6	
Blank/Don't know	2	2.4	

CONCLUSION

The Bai are the ethnic group most like the Han in Kunming. They are considered very comfortable, familiar, and known. Tension between Han and Bai was never mentioned to me (though it is rumored by Western experts to exist to some extent). The features that make the Bai so palatable and desirable include demonstrable physical constructions such as architecture as well as a history of sinicized agriculture and culture. Their clothing is purely ornamental and is not seen to hinder economic rationality or agricultural production. In short, their culture is moderate, modest, and unthreatening. If anything, they are seen as representing the recent history of the Han, just before modernization hit hard in the last century. The Bai, more than any of the other groups I have discussed, represent the Han curiosity about their own past, without having to look all the way back at "primitive" society.

TYPIFICATION AND IDENTITY IN A COMPLEX NATION-STATE

IDENTITY THROUGH CONTRAST

Something can be learned, ultimately, about Han self-characterization (cf. Crapanzano 1990) from the portraits of other groups. As mentioned in chapter 2, there is little explicit characterization of the Han because they in effect constitute the unmarked case; they are invisible because they are so pervasive. The minority nationalities help the Han to see themselves. The minority views of the Han are rarely reproduced for outside consideration, aside from periodic complaints in autonomous regions about *da Hanzuzhuyi* (Han chauvinism). A collection of Han views of ethnic minorities relies on the ability to make explicit models that are often only implicit or that are explicit only within an officially sanctioned vocabulary.

Minority nationalities are often assumed to be vastly different from the Han, but people classified as belonging to a single minority group are assumed to be quite similar. This is to say, differences between intergroup features are emphasized, while intragroup similarities are often assumed: "The Bai are . . ." Though the categories are stereotypical and essentialized, they have real consequences in the Chinese world. One of the unintended and ironic consequences of reifying categories of ethnic groups, making them all ontologically equivalent, as I have mentioned previously, is that of encouraging ethnogenesis (see Gladney 1991, Schein 1993, Harrell 1995a). As the categories of ethnic otherness are reified, the minorities themselves employ such categories and strengthen their ethnic identities.[1] It is much more difficult for Han to say anything concrete about the Han. Minority nationalities in general are often lumped together, in distinction to the Han, although it is clear upon inquiry that some are more distinct than others.

The seven groups portrayed here are among the most distinctive for Han in Kunming. "Han" as a category is slippery, yet it is not impossible to draw conclusions about the Han.

The characteristics attributed to other groups contrast fairly sharply with those attributed to the Han by themselves. The positive attributes mentioned for the ethnic minorities have to do with quaint, picturesque features. Both positive and negative attributes tell much about the Han self-conception. Where the minorities are considered almost uniformly "hospitable," one can surmise that the Han feel they themselves are not. Indeed, incredulity was expressed by one writer that in some minority regions total strangers would be invited into people's houses to share food (Zheng 1981:19). The Han indifference to people with whom they have no relationship is well documented (Bond 1991:52, M. Yang 1986:244).

Negative judgments attach to Hui, Zang, and Wa especially, because they are separate or "irrational." Their insistence on their own traditional ways of subsisting and practicing, which means refusing Han efforts to "modernize" or integrate them, shows the value placed on modernization. Minority groups' refusal of the welcoming hand of the Chinese state makes them appear especially irrational, ungrateful, and hostile.

Those groups regarded positively—Naxi, Bai, Dai—are also not seen uniformly by people living in the southwest. (In Beijing, people I asked had scarcely heard of any of them.) The most purely comprehensible are the Bai, seen as differing either not at all or just slightly from the Han. Naxi and Yi are less developed yet with possibilities for developing into more tractable participants in the nationalizing, modernizing, civilizing project. The Dai are loved as they are—beautiful, graceful, separate but not too separate, suggesting an image of the best of the simple folk who are not quite barbarian.

Difference is desired, on some level, for its suggestion that the human universe has multiple forms—but some differences are deplored. Some irreconcilable differences, such as adamant refusal to eat pork, insistence on spending time in worship, or "waste" of resources, are too near to Han activities to accept. Other differences—especially those that float on the surfaces of material life, such as clothing, secular festivals, or a writing system—are embraced.

This suggests that aspects of identity that reflect deeply valued practices and unconscious patterning—food, frugality, time use—are extremely important in constructing identity. Minorities who add foods to a basic repertoire—sour moss (Dai) or fatty pork (Naxi)—produce no animosity (just revulsion) on the part of Han observers. Rejection of central Han practices, by contrast, is a significant problem.

Different social groups occupy different psychological spaces, clinging to some identities more closely than to others. For Han in Kunming, the term "ethnic minorities" in general suggests poverty, backwardness, and primitivism, but subtle distinctions are also made among the various groups, especially those that are salient. (The less salient simply fall into an undifferentiated category of "ethnic minorities.")[2]

If the minorities love to sing and dance, according to the Han, can we conclude that the Han do not? If they have beautiful clothing and ornaments, do not the Han? If the minorities are simple and trusting, are the Han cynical and complex? Indeed, Han answers to the question of how they think the minorities view the Han—compiled in table 2.1—suggest just such conclusions. One use of prototypes of minority groups is to emphasize difference from the Han.

"We" are the Han: advanced, clean, urban, modern.[3] "They"—really a set of inanimate categories—are remote, backward, dirty, rural, closed up, inhabitants of mountains. "We Han" are crafty, but it is the craftiness of agency and action, while "they" are simple, passive, and easily manipulated. "We" speak; "they" understand. "We" watch them dance and sing; "they" oblige.[4]

Ethnic minorities are known by the Han for the ways they contrast with the Han, and the most celebrated differences can be viewed as emblems of difference, as badges of lives unlived, as ways the Han could never be but could dream of being. The desires of the Han for self-affirmation are satisfied in part by a glance at the backward nature of the ethnic minorities, and so too are the desires to imagine a greater spontaneity and freedom and simplicity. Aspects of minority life that are antithetical to urban Han values—unstructured "mating" practices, exuberant festivals with spontaneous singing and dancing, blurting out the truth without a thought for the consequences—are all things that Han can read about, see on television, and repeat in many-layered stories. Identities are made clearer once the boundaries are known, as is evident throughout the world. In this particular case, one can locate the identity within the boundaries as a contrast with what has been excluded, yet desires can reach outside the boundaries, for imagination can go beyond the everyday and the lived to include that which lies at the margins of the possible. For many Han, the minority nationalities live lives just scarcely believable and provide a source of longing along with contentment. These identifications are not the most salient for most urban Han Chinese, but they are very useful.

Identity in China does not occupy the same position as identity everywhere else. The anthropological question is: How does a concern with identity figure into the specifics of each society? Americans are preoccupied with identities of all sorts, and this concern is visible in academic studies carried out by Americans (in the works of anthropology, cultural studies, psychology, and sociology) as well as in ordinary people's conversations. One reason for this focus on identity, I believe, is that "identity" seems to be simultaneously the source of our greatest achievements—to be a real somebody, to know who you really are—and of our greatest distress and tragedy—as the world grapples with crises of ethnic and national identities at war. It puzzles us also because it seems to be simultaneously something we can choose or attain (an identity as an artist, a mother, a millionaire) and one we can't (an African American, a male, a forty-seven-year-old, a big-boned tall person with frizzy red hair). "Identity" gets at this ambiguity and ambivalence.

In this sense, this ordinary word of American English serves us well by pointing to our dilemmas about independence and belonging, about individuality and community. We "identify with" people who save the whales, or with the Christian Right, or with those who try to eat right and live better. We are more than the mere sum of our identities, but we need to include all these identities in any discussion of our selves (what I would argue is the American national pastime).

Even the U.S. legal system is struggling to figure out which identities to protect and which not to: People of color? Yes. Women? Yes. People of minority sexual orientation? Usually. The mentally ill? It depends. Psychopaths? Not exactly. Where we draw the line between acceptable identities and those that are considered medically or legally dangerous is what Foucault (1979, 1988, 1994) tried to document, showing the changing way this line was mapped in recent European history.

But there is even more to identities than these personal matters. We also have social identities that come in some way from our associating and being associated with people of a certain type: Chinese Americans or Jews, Latinos or Southerners, Bosnians or Serbs, Hindus or Muslims, Hutus or Tutsis, Anglophones or Francophones. . . . This too is not all there is to a person's being. No one would claim it is a complete characterization of a person to say something like, "he is a Serb." But these comments are often the sole characterizations made of others, as if sufficient to explain all that is relevant of an unknown person's life. These are often the characterizations that lead to exclusion from power or to automatic conferral of privilege.

It is easy to dismiss categorizing others. But categorization of social groups has exquisite vitality—excruciating viciousness—in our world. Rather than impose a technical term of my own making, I have used ordinary people's ordinary words to try to make sense of a certain kind of identity in a single part of a single place.

Things work differently in China. Though this book has not explored the details of Chinese personhood and selfhood (for various views of these, see Hsu 1971, Munro 1977, Chu 1985, Elvin 1985, Kipnis 1997), a preliminary sketch suggests that identity may not play as prominent a role as in the United States, at least for the majority group. "Prominence" is difficult to measure, but contrast and proximity would seem to figure into an equation. Groups that interact frequently, such as the Bai and the Naxi, might be more likely to think and act seriously about their differences. The Han are not usually threatened directly—economically or politically—by China's ethnic minorities. Yet the state is involved in establishing a standard viewpoint about them, and ordinary people have views of them. The position of ethnic minorities as "primitive" reinforces a contrasting view of Han as "modern" and "advanced," as well as reifying this group as solid, destined to occupy the center of the nation.

The relationship between ordinary people's views of ethnic minorities and various official positions is far from straightforward. In Kunming, where the *minzu* are prominently displayed, ethnic minorities are nonetheless shadowy, stereotypical categories. In other parts of central China, where only the Hui are to be found in any number, how much less important are these groups. Despite half a century of ideological "work" to promote tolerance and (in some periods) appreciation of the minorities at their edges, people in the new nation-state of the People's Republic of China have not learned much about these confrères. This conclusion suggests that the nation-building that takes place does not occur in a vacuum. There are important cognitive categories already in existence that have a ponderousness of their own. However tempting to treat all majorities as similar in their domination of minorities, I suggest that it is essential to bear the details in mind. "Whiteness" in the United States and "Hanness" in China share some characteristics, yet the differences are equally important. The relations among such categories differ when there are fifty-six compared to when there are five; the unmarked case also changes meaning when features involve subsistence rather than "color." There are also different kinds of forces operating to manipulate the categories. In the United States, this force is commerce, and in China it is political ideology. Human kinds are crucial ways of ordering the human world, and they cross-cut more personal ways of conceptualizing self and person. Yet there have been few ethnographic investigations of these matters in context.

The Chinese case as I have described it requires understanding of the political and historical context within which matters of identity are shaped, but the popular, cultural, and cognitive context in turn shapes those political and historic forces. Issues of identity are political, as well as personal and social. They are struggled over and accepted alongside concerns for many other aspects of life, rising to prominence only in certain moments. To return to the bus ride that began this book, ethnic difference is displayed casually in many contexts, such as when a Dai woman wound a towel around her hair for the spring day. Seekers of ethnic markers might record this towel as meaningful and important. It might come to play in debates about ethnic classification and ethnic authenticity. Or it might simply cover her hair. What a head covering means to the person using it might differ slightly from observers who wear similar coverings and considerably from observers who do not. It takes on meaning only in the context of a universe of ethnic categories within the larger whole that is the nation of China.

The task of unifying questions of identity and selfhood remains. Psychological anthropology is uniquely positioned to inquire into this relationship because of its twin foci on individuals and society. The relative importance of such factors as ethnic and national identity in different societies—both collectively and for the individuals concerned—is a matter for investigation, using the most subtle tools available to us. In this book I have made a preliminary sketch of some of the ways people construct portraits (prototypes) of the other people with whom they share a society (if not face-to-face interaction) in the hopes of contributing to the understanding of the role identity plays in such complex politically fraught societies as China. One would not expect things to work identically elsewhere, but I have suggested some of the ways tendencies in human cognition—tendencies to construct prototypes—might operate in domains of great human complexity.

NOTES

INTRODUCTION

1. Cf. Tomlinson (1991:90–94) on the problem of "cultural 'authenticity.'" Fredrik Barth's work on the construction of boundaries as critical in the situational identity of ethnic groups is informative as well (1969). See Clifford 1988:346 for a strikingly similar observation.

2. Note that I am not claiming a more "accurate" reading, just a productive one.

CHAPTER 1

1. For a more detailed account of the official positions on ethnicity, including their history, see Blum 1994, chapter 2. See also Wiens 1954, Moseley 1973, Dreyer 1976, Fei 1980, Eberhard 1982, Heberer 1989, Harrell 1990, 1993, 1995a, Gladney 1991, and Mackerras 1994, 1995.

2. A. Doak Barnett's book *China's Far West* (1993) makes much the same point from a perspective based on economics and politics but also incorporates Barnett's lifetime of personal involvement with China.

3. See his book *The Travels* (Polo 1958) for this account. A fascinating new book challenges the veracity of Marco Polo's claim to have visited the capital in China during the Yuan. See Wood 1996.

4. "Backward" is used in the spirit of Chinese usage, whereby there is an absolute scale from "backward" to "advanced" or "modern," measured by such things as new buildings, availability of indoor plumbing and electricity, types of conveyances, wide, paved streets, and so on.

5. Fruit is peripheral only ideologically, being a snack food and not part of meals. People often eat enormous amounts of it. I'm grateful to Stevan Harrell for refining my ideas on this point. See also Anderson 1988 on the components of a Chinese diet and how these have changed during the course of Chinese history.

6. Throughout the world there is a wide range of attitudes toward linguistic varieties. For some of the literature on language attitudes, see Fishman 1966, Fishman et al. 1968, Das Gupta 1975, Giles and Saint-Jacques 1979, Gumperz 1982b, Woolard 1983, 1989, Edwards 1984, Fabian 1986, Goldwin et al. 1989, Edwards 1994, Schiffman 1996, Urla 1996, and Ramaswamy 1997.

7. I focus here only on what people in China say about such varieties, rather than on the actual linguistic description of varieties of Chinese.

8. There is evidence of growing prestige of non-Mandarin varieties in China and "Greater China," as the economic standing of areas where such languages are spoken increases. Erbaugh (1995) has written of the increasing power of the southern dialects, as Hong Kong, Taiwan, and the adjacent mainland provinces have achieved global economic prominence. "Dialects" are not usually considered legitimate enough to have their own writing systems, but in Cantonese and Taiwanese this is changing. In the summer of 1996, a conference on "written Taiwanese" *(taibun)* was held at the University of British Columbia.

9. Ideas about Mapu are strikingly similar to attitudes toward non-standard Spanish in the United States. See Zentella 1997:81.

10. These terms are used quite imprecisely in Kunming by all but linguists. Just as English speakers use "accent" as the general term descriptive of linguistic differences, so do ordinary people tend to speak of, for example, *kouqiang* or Baoshan*qiang*, reserving *fangyan* for more technical discussions.

11. Glazer and Moynihan (1975:8) pointed out in the 1970s that in the United States, an increase in ethnic awareness was accompanied by a decrease in actual difference between ethnic groups. In the 1990s, ethnic awareness is accompanied by separatism and insistence on recovery of a putative "authentic" tradition, even if it must be (re)constructed. See the description in Clifford (1988) of the "predicament of culture" wherein identity is lost but claimed nonetheless. I am grateful to Lucien Miller for this point. See Hannerz 1992 for consideration of the evidence as to whether cultural differences are being eradicated. There is some evidence that these differences may be growing, despite widespread belief that the world is becoming more homogeneous.

12. See, for example, Thurston and Pasternak 1983, Wolf 1985, and Gold 1989 for very interesting treatment of the realities of anthropological fieldwork—post Mosher—in the PRC. For a discussion of the case of Steven Mosher, the Ph.D. candidate dismissed from Stanford University's anthropology program as a result of allegations that he engaged in illegal, immoral, or unprofessional activities, and the consequences of this event, see *New York Times* 1983a, 1983b, 1983c, 1985, and van Ness 1984.

13. See Agar 1991 for discussion of anthropological research "stretch[ed] . . . over part of a state." See Augé 1995 for a discussion of the limitations of a place-centered anthropology in the contemporary world. See also Friedrich 1986b:203–19 for discussion of sources of ethnographic understanding, and Agar 1996 on ethnographic research.

14. The title reveals the state's attempt to co-opt the resistance of the post-1989 democracy *(minzhu)* movement and use its terminology for its own purposes.

15. Stevan Harrell kindly sent me a copy of an unpublished honors thesis from the University of Washington, written by Cindy Adams (1986) using a matched-guise test in Taiwan under Harrell's supervision. Again it is a basically bilingual setting—though Hakka and other dialects are spoken in Taiwan, in addition to Mandarin and Taiwanese.

16. Gladney 1994 and Schein 1997 have written about the use of minorities as commodities in the state project Schein calls "internal orientalism," and I will not go into detail about it here. Oakes 1998 is a probing analysis of tourism and its relationship to modernity in southwestern China.

17. Here I use "Language" to mean something like Saussure's notion of *langue,* or some idealized Platonic notion of a language, in contrast to what people actually speak *(parole)*. See Saussure 1983.

18. According to Robert Ramsey (1987:230–91), languages spoken in South China and northern Southeast Asia (the two areas being ethnolinguistically connected), including those of the minority nationalities, belong to at least five different

language groups: Chinese, Tibeto-Burman (with over two hundred languages recorded so far [Ramsey 1987:248]), Tai (Zhuang-Dong, according to the Chinese), Hmong-Mien (Miao-Yao), and Mon-Khmer. There are additional groups whose languages have not been classified at all and may not belong to any of these families. The Chinese criteria for assigning languages to language families differ from Western ones and often result in grouping together languages that Western linguists would keep separate. See also Bradley 1987 and Keyes 1995.

CHAPTER 2

1. For some of the extensive literature on prototypes, see Labov 1972:314–317, Rosch 1975, McConnell-Ginet 1979, Miller 1982, Lakoff 1987, van Dijk 1987, Shibamoto 1987, MacLaury 1991.

2. This involved trying to reflect people's sense that sparrows were more prototypical birds than, say, eagles, and much more than ostriches or chickens, even though feature analysis could not easily specify the differences among them.

3. See Greenblatt 1991 for a similar view of medieval conceptions of the "New World," in which he details the "marvelous" as the precursor of judgment and appropriation.

4. Examples of the former include Freud 1921, Mead 1934, Eriksen 1950, Vygotsky 1962, Piaget 1978, Daniel 1984, Shweder and Levine 1984, Marsella, DeVos, and Hsn 1985, and Kondo 1990. These tend to be more focused on affective and cognitive matters. Examples of the latter include Friedlander 1975, Handler 1988, Bhabha 1990, Spivak 1990, Pemberton 1994, and Guha 1997. These tend to be studies of "complex" societies, with political matters placed in the foreground. While Daniel's *Fluid Signs* is one of my favorite books, one could not claim that it has much political content in it. The challenge is to discover the relationships among these factors.

5. The long history of discussing the self—or sometimes the individual—in Western thought usually universalizes its findings without including two enriching perspectives: selfhood in non-Western, non-elite settings and selfhood as part of a political collectivity. For a history of the self in Western thought, see Taylor 1989; see also Morris 1972 and Lukes 1973. For treatments in academic psychology, see Mead 1934, Eriksen 1950, and Piaget 1978. For anthropological treatments, see Fortes 1959, 1973, Carrithers et al. 1985, Mauss 1985, James 1988, Kondo 1990, Rosenberger 1992, and Cohen 1994. The self and the person are often distinguished clearly, though there are important reasons to bracket such a separation. "Self" is usually believed to be the "internal" part of an individual, while "person" is usually believed to be the social and moral function. The way these two are related, if all societies indeed separate them, is a matter for empirical investigation in each case. There are some fascinating treatments of "identity" as part of "self" in, for instance, writing by minority or "ethnic" American novelists, such as James Baldwin and Maxine Hong Kingston.

6. See Urla 1993 for a fascinating and relevant discussion of the use of statistics for the forging of modern Basque identity.

7. See Pye 1975 on incorporation of ethnic minorities, and Grunfeld 1985 for discussion of China's motives for emphasizing minority participation; see DeFrancis 1950, Lehmann 1975, Seybolt and Chiang 1979, Ramsey 1987, and Norman 1988 on language reform.

8. Although in this book I treat the construction of identity only in the PRC, areas of similarity might be pointed out in Taiwan. PRC policies are in many ways a result of the Guomindang legacy (see Pye 1975, Deal 1979), but the situation the Guomindang faced in Taiwan was quite different from that on the mainland. In Taiwan the principal tension was between Han who migrated before the twentieth century, known (in Mandarin) as *benshengren* (natives) and those who arrived in 1949, the *waishengren* (outsiders). See Lai, Myers, and Wou 1991 for a history of the February 28 [1947] incident (Er Er-ba), the most violent confrontation between the two groups.

9. As noted in Chapter 1, excerpts from student essays will be used throughout this text.

10. See Slugoski and Ginsburg 1989 for discussion of the relationship between development of the two terms "self" and "identity" in Western thought and the equation of self with substance in, for example, Descartes.

11. In the late 1990s, one can see evidence of a new wave of anti-Western sentiment, epitomized in the recent best-selling book, *Zhongguo keyi shuo "bu"* [China Can Say "No"] (Song et al. 1996); see Lam 2000 on the use of this book in ethnic nationalism.

12. I borrow the notion of "modal" persons from Cora DuBois (1961), who attempted to represent a sense of frequency or likelihood of encountering a particular personality type without claiming a false average or an absolute inevitability. Her aim was to represent "others" for anthropology. But it seems clear that some tendency like this occurs in many settings, not only professional academic ones.

13. This is not to say that the American view is entirely homogeneous; we have tension between ideals of community and individuality. See Riesman et al. 1961, Hsu 1983, and Bellah et al. 1985.

14. Similar observations have been made about the nature of stereotypes when social psychologists observed that there is often a "kernel of truth" that may have been contained in such generalizations (Miller 1982:1–31).

15. Jane Hill (1995:137) presents a challenge to the widespread belief that a more authentic self may be identified through contrasts in fluidity and hesitation.

CHAPTER 3

1. They are never referred to as "sisters," only as "brothers," even by women and even though the vast majority of all pictorial representations are of minority women.

2. The fact that Western social scientists have largely discarded such cultural evolutionary vocabulary (but see Diamond 1981 for a defense of the term "primitive") means that Western readers are sensitive to it. But in China the paradigm is still very much a nineteenth-century one, and these terms are not questioned at all.

3. Norma Diamond (personal communication) points out that "the Han Chinese model of ordered society excludes people without a fixed abode, a settlement with at least several generations of historical depth." Anyone—such as itinerant artisans—who moved around and was difficult to find was not trustworthy. See also Kuhn 1962, Ward 1965, and Scott 1999.

4. Strongly held beliefs are undoubtedly overdetermined, in Freud's sense of the term. There can be a variety of associations and causes, which makes them harder to give up than those held more loosely.

5. Classen (1992) chronicles the worldwide use of olfactory symbolism to differentiate self and other. The metaphor of dirt and smell serves to justify prejudices in many, if not most, societies.

6. It is often difficult to separate the degree to which change has permeated people's thought. Analyses range from saying that everything is different from the past to those claiming utter continuity, despite a veneer of changed vocabulary. This points to a long-standing question in anthropology about the relationship between language and thought (see Sapir 1921, Whorf 1956, Vygotsky 1962, Mertz and Parmentier 1985, Friedrich 1986a, Hill and Mannheim 1992, Lucy 1985, 1992a, 1992b, 1996, and Gumperz and Levinson 1996). But despite inconclusiveness about this, it is impossible to disregard the importance of vocabulary.

7. On a recent trip to Beijing (1997), I was shocked to find corn something of an expensive delicacy. I'd become accustomed to its role in Yunnan as an inferior "grain."

8. There are many fascinating and technical debates about the nature of Chinese writing. It was very much mystified by the Imagist poets, such as Ezra Pound and Ernest Fenollosa, who nevertheless increased Western awareness of Chinese literature through their efforts. Though Pound took many liberties with the form of ancient Chinese poetry, his translations often grasp the essence of the poems quite well. Such sinologists as George Kennedy and John DeFrancis have labored to dispel the "monosyllabic myth" of the nature of Chinese writing. Most "words"—and the definition of "word" plagues linguistic discussions about Indo-European and other languages as well—in Chinese are polysyllabic even though they are based on monosyllabic morphemes. Linguists in China can use the more technical distinction between ci (word) and zi (ideograph) to emphasize the difference, but ordinary people often disregard such nuances. The category of zi has preeminence psychologically. See Fenollosa 1936, Pound 1949, Kennedy 1964, and DeFrancis 1984, 1989.

9. Chiang 1995 also points out nuances in the way various scripts are regarded. The more phonetic, the less regard they command. *Nüshu* (women's script) has several versions; the most ideographic has the most prestige.

10. See Bernhardt 1999 for a discussion of changing laws regarding the status of widows.

11. These attitudes are held predominantly by Han but may also be held by people of other nationalities.

12. See van Dijk for a distinction between "high-contact" and "low-contact" neighborhoods—contact between different ethnic groups—and the attitudinal consequences of this difference (1987:18, 349, 352–355).

CHAPTER 4

1. Keyes 1995 argues that the category "Tai" is quite instructive because of the way it intersects with the nation-building activities of the various states whose borders include "Tai" people: Thailand, Laos, China, and Vitenam. The Chinese divide Tai-speaking peoples among Dai and Zhuang. See also Hsieh 1995.

2. See Oakes 1998 for comparable festivals in the neighboring province of Guizhou.

3. This is not to say that Chinese society is in fact as prudish as the official culture maintains. Premarital and extramarital sexual relations exist, and there is evidence that they are increasing (see, for example, Honig and Hershatter 1988, Link 1992:101, Liu et al. 1997). But most marriages are still arranged to some degree, and the idea of "love at first sight" followed by immediate intimacy strikes many Han as incredible—but fascinating!

4. A strong argument can be made that many of the most lionized aspects of high Chinese culture are originally Thai in origin (Eberhard 1968, Tong Enzheng 1983, Sage 1992), such as rice, bronze, and silk. Archaeological research in China has focused most intensively on the traditional center of "Chinese" culture, around the Yellow River, though in recent years there has been more excavation in the damper areas of Sichuan and Yunnan. This work demonstrates clearly that an advanced civilization existed in China's southwest at a period nearly as early as that in the north, though with strikingly different imagery (see Cook and Major 1999). There are theories that at least one significant "cradle of civilization" was here, with the influence going toward the north. Ongoing archaeological research in the eastern Soviet Union and central Asia may produce new explanations. Bai folktales tell of a civilized kingdom to the "west" that predates the Nanzhao kingdom (Lucien Miller, personal communication).

5. The Chinese media are not alone in their fluctuating representation of other groups. *Newsweek* showed China as "Friend or Foe?" in 1996, when China was "conducting war games" with Taiwan. In 1994, the message about China conveyed in *National Geographic* was one of modernization and social change, though in 1980 (July) an edition on Shanghai, despite its claims that the city was a "born-again giant," depicted China's colorless multitudes.

CHAPTER 5

1. In the 1930s and 1940s, ethnologist Ruey Yifu went to do research on the Wa, along with a set of helpers. Thanks to Stevan Harrell for pointing this out.

2. The Swedish anthropologist Magnus Fiskejø is now conducting research among the Wa.

3. See Martin 1986 for a discussion of Boas's original invocation of Eskimo terminology for snow and its successive incarnations. Boas was trying to point out the way grammatical categories operated unconsciously and productively, but his point has been altered to conform more easily to North American linguistic ideology, where our focus is on words rather than grammatical processes, which are much harder to call up to consciousness.

4. In one case the chapter on marriage is combined with material on funerals and material life. In the other case it is combined only with that on funerals.

5. Opium is rarely mentioned in the Chinese sources, though it was in widespread cultivation—and use—by both the Wa and the Dai. The Yi, Miao, and Lahu also cultivated and sold it, without necessarily using it themselves. Some Han are now convinced that the Hui are the masterminds behind the current revival of the opium trade in Yunnan, which fits the characterization of the Hui as lawless and dangerous. Thanks to Norma Diamond for this point.

6. The use of history to justify occupation or annexation of territory—for example, Taiwan, Tibet—is itself a fascinating move. Discussions on the Internet listserv H-ASIA of Taiwan and its proper relationship to mainland China (or, as the PRC prefers, the Chinese mainland) have pointed out some of the ways these relations have varied and been rationalized.

7. Lest we immediately invoke the image of a Shangri-la where all prospered, I refer the reader to Thomas Grunfeld, who in his book *The Making of Modern Tibet* points out that there are "two sharply differing views" of the changes Tibet has undergone since China began to exert its influence in 1959 (1987:1–3, 7), and that one's predisposition leads directly to one's conclusions about Tibet's pre-1949 state: hell or paradise. The information available about Tibet's irretrievable past is perhaps all equally tainted by the brush of ideology. See also Bishop 1989.

8. Stevan Harrell (personal communication) reports that in Sichuan "there are pictures of Tibetans all over the place." This contrast with Yunnan is suggestive; clearly my results are not generalizable to all of China.

9. The Miao, who are extremely different from one another in various places, are often glossed over by people in Kunming, much as the Wa are, even though there are many more Miao than Wa (over 7 million compared to just over 300,000 [Ma Yin 1989:431]). Treatment of the Miao makes a fascinating study in its own right. See Schein 1993, 2000, Diamond 1995, and Oakes 1998.

10. Yunnan figures are from the 1982 census (Yang Yucai 1989:27). Figures for China are from the 1990 census.

11. Craig Janes reports (personal communication) a figure of approximately twenty thousand Han relocated in Tibet each month. The Han are either desperately seeking any sort of livelihood, having failed in China proper, or they go forcibly. The Tibetans do not want them there, and many Han resent being forced to be there as well.

12. At the same time there are reports of extremely brutal reactions to all expressions of desire for independence or even of resentment at Han unfairness. The entire province is periodically closed to foreign journalists. One might be suspicious of the fanfare surrounding restoration of a few very visible temples in central Lhasa and ask further questions about permission to return to a religiously nuanced life. Craig Janes (personal communication) reports having witnessed daily occurrences of violence between Han and Tibetans during the spring of 1993.

13. Gladney 1998a discusses the creation of the category "Hui" and the anomalous use of religion alone to categorize them as an ethnic minority.

14. Lucien Miller (personal communication) reports a Han friend who had been a soldier in the Vietnam War saying the same thing: Chinese were "unafraid to die," unlike American soldiers. Perhaps it is a conventional statement of awe and dread.

15. *Fengsu xiguan* (customs and habits) carries with it an implication of quaintness; Han are not really said to have *fengsu xiguan*. I propose a translation of "folkways."

16. Some of the literature on food in China includes Ahern 1974, Chang (ed.) 1977, Anderson 1988, Thompson 1988, and Yue 1999. See also Brownell 1995 for an insightful formulation of the porosity of the body and of the role of nurturer played by either parents or the state (in the case of athletes). See Sutton 1995 for a discussion of cannibalism in the context of Chinese views of food and the body. Notice too the portrayal of eating in recent Chinese films from both the PRC and Taiwan: *Yellow Earth* (Chen 1984), *Red Sorghum* (Zhang 1988), and *The Blue Kite* (Tian 1993) all begin with wedding scenes and show much eating. *Eat Drink Man Woman* (Ang Lee 1995) and *The Wedding Banquet* (Ang Lee 1993) of course center around food as symbol. (I suspect that the Taiwan and PRC versions of the role of food differ considerably.) Eating provides the backdrop to almost all everyday behavior.

17. Features very similar to these were used to discriminate against Hakka during the nineteenth century, with the important difference that Hakka women had a much more public role than did Han women, while Hui women were confined more. Ultimately, the Hakka are not recognized as an official ethnic group, though they have one characteristic that the Hui do not: a distinctive language—though a Chinese language (Erbaugh 1990). The political and capricious nature of *minzu shibie* (differentiation of nationalities) has been remarked upon by many writers. See, for example, Harrell 1990, Wu 1990, and McKhann 1995.

18. If the current loosening up of policies toward minority nationalities continues, Hui men and women may begin to wear distinctive headgear in Kunming as they do elsewhere in China, such as Ningxia and Gansu, as ethnic markers. But there is much

contemporary evidence to suggest a tightening of policies toward other Muslim groups, especially in Xinjiang.

CHAPTER 6

1. Only one "branch" of the Naxi is believed to "practice matriarchy"—the Mosuo. Whether they are to be classified with other Naxi depends on one's classificatory schema.

2. See McKhann 1992 to clarify the facts with regard to lovers' suicides around Lijiang. The practices of *ahzu* concern the Lugu Lake people. Much of the popular understanding is vague and confused, but my concern is not so much to set the facts straight as to explain the popular interest in this material.

3. Stevan Harrell says that there are similar groups in Sichuan who are classified as Mongolians.

4. See Watson 1994 for discussion of this model and the reliance of socialist states on it for legitimation.

5. Stevan Harrell points out (personal communication) that "the majority of the Naze (which is what they call themselves in their own language) live in Sichuan and are officially Mongols."

6. Harrell adds that "in Liangshan, only 3 of the 4 dialect groups within Nuosu celebrate what they call Fire Festival."

7. See Waley-Cohen 1991 on exile in late imperial China. Though mostly concerned with Xinjiang, she makes the point that places on the periphery were regarded as punishing destinations. See also Oakes 1998:8–9.

8. See Ramsey 1987:258–61 about this form of writing; Bradley 1987 about Yi dialects and language planning, including romanization, and Harrell 1993 on the use of linguistics in discussions of ethnicity in China.

CHAPTER 7

1. *Minjia* means something like "ordinary citizen" or "civilian"—as does *min* in Zhongguo Minhang "Chinese Civil Aviation"—in opposition to the Han who were present in a military capacity. The Bai terms for themselves were a set of variants of /Pɛ² tsi¹/, meaning "white people" (Ramsey 1987:289). The official terminological change to Baizu in 1956 was intended to capture both the sound and the meaning of the native term in the Han equivalent.

2. In fact the same thing should probably be stated with regard to nearly all minority languages. People rarely recognize the sound of any minority language nor the accents of minorities speaking other varieties—mostly Hanhua—but, rather, make judgments about speakers' ethnicity by a sort of free association, in which salience rather than likelihood is the primary criterion.

3. Kipnis (1997:1) mentions that it was said that citizens of Fengjia village, Zouping County in north China (Shandong province) were also *haoke* (hospitable).

CONCLUSION

1. Norma Diamond (personal communication) says that the Bai are now no longer willing to admit to being completely sinicized but instead hold up their old Bai books, written in characters, and show that they are in fact subversive, talking of Bai (not Han) matters.

2. See Blum 1998 for evidence that undifferentiated minorities are often referred to by the singular third-person pronoun *ta,* indicating a group entity, while those attributed more agency are referred to with the plural *tamen.*

3. This view of themselves is somewhat belied by the constant campaigns exhorting people to be "civilized," to stop spitting, littering, shouting, relieving themselves in public, shoving, and so forth. They are being reminded constantly that they are not entirely advanced, clean, urban, or modern. But the minorities are even worse (Norma Diamond, personal communication).

4. See also Blum (1998) for discussion of the way pronouns are used to index self and other, through close analysis of discourse about identity.

GLOSSARY OF SELECTED CHINESE CHARACTERS

I. PROPER NAMES AND EXPRESSIONS

Bai	白	Bai
Chuncheng	春城	Spring City (i.e., Kunming)
Chuncheng Wanbao	春城晚報	*Spring City [Kunming] Evening News*
Dai	傣	Dai
Dou si, pi xiu	斗私批修。	Fight self(-ishness), repudiate revisionism.
Duanwujie	端午節	Dragon Boat Festival
Er Er-ba	二二八	February 28 (massacre in 1947 in Taiwan)

Gege minzu dou you yuyan, wenzi de ziyou.

各個民族都有語言，文字的自由。

		Every nationality has freedom of spoken language and script.
Guangming Ribao	光明日報	*Illustrious Daily*
Guoyu	國語	National Language
Han	漢	Han
Hanhua	漢話	Han language (non-standard term, used in Yunnan)
Hanhua	漢化	Sinified, Hanified
Hanyu	漢語	Han language
Hanzu zhuyi	漢族主義	Han chauvinism
Hui	回	Hui
I Ching	易經	*The Book of Changes*

Kejia	客家	Hakka
Kunming	昆明	Kunming
Kunming Ribao	昆明日報	*Kunming Daily*
Lianda	聯大	Southwest Associated University
Majie Putonghua	馬街普通話	Street Putonghua, non-standard Putonghua
MaPu	馬普	nonstandard Putonghua
Minjia	民家	"civilian," Bai
Minzhu yu Fazhi	民主譽法制	*Democracy and Law*
Mosuo	摩梭	Mosuo (branch of Naxi)
Musilin	穆斯林	Muslim
Naxi	納西	Naxi
Putonghua	普通話	"Common Speech," Standard Mandarin
Renmin Ribao	人民日報	*People's Daily*
Shi Ji	史紀	*Historian's Records*
Sige xiandaihua	四個現代化	Four modernizations
Sihua	四化	Four modernizations (abbreviation)
Siji ru chun	四季如春	Four seasons (i.e. year-round) like springtime.
Sichuan haozi	四川耗子	Sichuan rats
Tiao Jiao	跳腳	Dance Festival
Wa	佤	Wa
Xinan Lianhe Daxue	西南聯合大學	Southwest Associated University
Yi	彝	Yi
Yi Jing	易經	*Book of Changes*

Yifu, yinyue, fuzhuang tamenxihuan, dan tamen bu xihuan ren.

衣服音樂服裝他們喜歡但他們不喜歡人。

They like our clothes and our music, but they don't like *us*.

Yunnan Ribao	雲南日報	*Yunnan Daily*
Zang	藏	Zang, Tibetan
Zhongguo Qingnian Bao	中國青年報	*China Youth News*
Zhongguoren	中國人	Chinese person, person of China
Zhonghua renmin	中華人民	people of Chinese culture
Zhong Xia	中夏	central plains Han
Zhou Yi	周易	*Book of Changes*
Zongjiao qifen hen nong.	宗教氣氛很濃。	The religious atmosphere is thick.

II. OTHER TERMS

baozao	暴躁	violent, fierce
benshengren	本省人	native to Taiwan
benxing	本性	itself
benzhi	本質	its own quality
biaozhun	標準	standard
bieren	別人	other people
bu fada	不發達	not advanced, backward
butong	不同	different
butongwu	不同物	difference, otherness

chengken	誠懇	sincere
chi	尺	(Chinese) foot (measure)
chunpuxing	純樸性	honesty, purity
ci	詞，辭	word, compound
congming	聰明	clever
cun	寸	Chinese inch
da Hanzuzhuyi	大漢族主義	Han chauvinism
daoyou	導遊	tour guide
diaocha	調查	investigation, fieldwork
difangfangyan	地方方言	local form of speech
difangqiang	地方腔	local accent
dongba (wen)	東巴文	dongba hieroglyphic script (Naxi)
dushi	篤實	honest and sincere, solid
fada	發達	advanced, modern
fangyan	方言	dialect, topolect
fen	份	allotment
fenbie	分別	differentiate
fengjian	封建	feudal, old-fashioned
fengsu	風俗	custom, folklore
fengsuxiguan	風俗習慣	customs and habits
fuquanzhi	夫權制	patriarchy
gerende zhengchang qingkuang		
	個人的正常情況	an individual's normal situation (personality?)
getihu	個體戶	independent entrepreneur
gu	蠱	a kind of poison (said of Miao)

guanhua	官話	administrative vernacular, "Mandarin"
guocui	國粹	national essence
haoke	好客	hospitable
haoting	好聽	pleasant to listen to; comprehensible
hen xin	很信	really believe
huoshi	活石	"living fossil"
jia	假	false
jiaotong	交通	transportation and communication
jirou	雞肉	chicken (meat)
juju	聚居	live [collected] in compact communities
kang	炕	(heated) platform beds
kong	空	empty
kouqiang	口腔	accent
kouyin	口音	accent
laoshi	老實	honest, simple
lihai	厲害	fierce
lingwaide ren	另外的人	other people
lingyiwu	另議物	otherness
luohou	落後	primitive, backward
mafan	麻煩	bother
man	蠻	"barbarian"
mianbaoche	麵包車	bread loaf car, van
minjian chuanshuo	民間傳說	folklore, popular legends
minzhu	民主	democracy
minzu	民族	nation, nationality, ethnic group

minzu shibie	民族識別	ethnic differentiation
muquanzhi	母權制	matriarchy
muxishizuzhi	母系氏族制	matriliny
nüshu	女書	women's script
niurou	牛肉	beef
peitong	陪同	official companion
pian	騙	cheat, deceive
pinyin	拼音	romanization, writing/spelling system
pohuai shengchanli	破壞生產力	destroy production
pusu	樸素	ingenuous, simple
qin	琴	Chinese lute
qingzhen	清眞	"pure and clean", following Hui (Muslim) dietary rules
qitade ren	其他的人	other people
qiyi	起義	righteous uprisings
qu	區	region
qubie	區別	differentiate
ren	人	person; often used of subethnic categories (a person of XX ethnic group)
rou	肉	meat (pork)
sahuang	撒謊	spreading untruths, gossip
sha	傻	dumb
shanqu	山區	mountain area
shaoshuminzu	少數民族	minority nationality, ethnic minority
shenfen	身份	identity, role, allotment

shenfenzheng	身份證	identification card
shengchanli	生產力	productivity
shi	實	actual, full
shuijiu	水酒	alcohol
si	私	selfishness
sili	私利	selfish
sixin	私心	selfishness
taren	他人	others
teshu	特殊	special, odd
waishengren	外省人	people in Taiwan of recent mainland ancestry
wenhua	文化	culture
wenming	文明	"culture," civilization
wenzi	文字	writing system, script
xia qu	下去	"go down", go to the countryside
xian	縣	county
xiancheng	縣城	county seat
xiandaihua	現代化	modernization
xianjin	先進	advanced, progressive
xiao huozi	小伙子	"guy," boyfriend
xiaojie	小姐	"miss," young lady
xiaomi	小米	millet ("birdseed")
xungen	尋根	seek roots
yanyu	言語	spoken language
yao nuli	要努力	be diligent
yeman	野蠻	wild

youdai	優待	special treatment, affirmative action
yuan	圓	unit of Chinese currency
yuanshi	原始	primitive, primeval
yuyan	語言	language, a language
zang	髒	dirty
zhaogu	照顧	special treatment, affirmative action
zhen	眞	real, true
zhenzhengde Huizu	眞正的回族	a real Hui
zhiyin	知音	one who hears (understands) one's music; the ideal friend
zhou	州	prefecture
zhushi	主食	staple food
zi	字	Chinese character, ideograph; word
zi	自	self-
ziji	自己	self
zisi	自私	selfish
ziwo	自我	self, "I"
ziyou ai	自由愛	"free love," free choice in marriage
zizhi	自治	autonomy, self rule
zizhiqu	自治區	autonomous region
zizhixian	自治縣	autonomous county
zizhizhou	自治州	autonomous prefecture
zu	族	ethnic group (as in XX-zu)

BIBLIOGRAPHY

ABBREVIATIONS USED FOR PERIODICALS

BR   *Beijing Review*
CCWB   *Chuncheng Wanbao* (Spring City [Kunming] Evening News)
CD   *China Daily*
FBIS   Foreign Broadcast Information Service
GMRB   *Guangming Ribao* (Illustrious Daily)
KMRB   *Kunming Ribao* (Kunming Daily)
MZFZ   *Minzhu yu Fazhi* (Democracy and Law)
MZYW   *Minzu Yuwen* (Nationalities Language and Literature)
NYT   *New York Times*
QNB   *Zhongguo Qingnian Bao* (Chinese Youth News)
RMRB   *Renmin Ribao* (People's Daily)
WZZK   *Wenzhai Zhoukan* (Weekly Readers' Digest [weekly supplement to YNRB])
YNRB   *Yunnan Ribao* (Yunnan Daily)

Adams, C. L. 1986. "Language Attitudes and Language Use in Taiwan (R. O. C.)." Master's thesis, University of Washington (Seattle).

Agar, Michael. 1991. "Stretching Linguistic Ethnography over Part of a State." *Journal of Linguistic Anthropology* 1 (December):131–42.

———. 1996. *The Professional Stranger: An Informal Introduction to Ethnography.* 2d ed. San Diego: Academic Press.

Ahern [Martin], Emily M. 1974. "Affines and the Rituals of Kinship." In *Religion and Ritual in Chinese Society,* edited by Arthur P. Wolf, 279–307. Stanford, Calif.: Stanford University Press.

Anagnost, Ann Stasia, 1987. "Politics and Magic in Contemporary China." *Modern China* 13 (1) (January).

Anderson, Benedict. 1991 [1983]. *Imagined Communities: Reflections on the Origin and Spread of Nationalism.* Rev. ed. London: Verso.

Anderson, E. N. 1988. *The Food of China.* New Haven: Yale University Press.

Ang Lee, director. 1993. *The Wedding Banquet* (film).

———. 1995. *Eat Drink Man Woman* (film).

Appadurai, Arjun. 1996. *Modernity at Large: Cultural Dimensions of Globalization.* Minneapolis: University of Minnesota Press.

Augé, Marc. 1995. *Non-places: Introduction to an Anthropology of Supermodernity.* Translated by John Howe. London: Verso.

Avedon, John F. 1984. *In Exile from the Land of Snows.* New York: Vintage.

Backus, Charles. 1981. *The Nan-chao Kingdom and T'ang China's Southwest Frontier.* Cambridge: Cambridge University Press.

Bai Hua. 1994 [1988]. *The Remote Country of Women.* Translated by Qingyun Wu and Thomas O. Beebee. Honolulu: University of Hawaii Press.

Baizu Jianshi Editorial Group. 1988. *Baizu Jianshi* (A brief history of the Bai). Kunming: Yunnan renmin chubanshe.

Bakhtin, Mikhail. 1984 [1965]. *Rabelais and His World*. Translated by Hélène Iswolsky. Bloomington: Indiana University Press.

Banister, Judith. 1987. *China's Changing Population*. Stanford, Calif.: Stanford University Press.

Barfield, Thomas J. 1989. *The Perilous Frontier: Nomadic Empires and China, 221 BC to AD 1757*. Cambridge, Mass.: Blackwell.

Barnett, A. Doak. 1993. *China's Far West: Four Decades of Change*. Boulder, Colo.: Westview Press.

Barth, Fredrik, ed. 1969. *Ethnic Groups and Boundaries: The Social Organization of Culture Difference*. Boston: Little, Brown.

Basso, Keith H. 1979. *Portraits of "the Whiteman": Linguistic Play and Cultural Symbols among the Western Apache*. Cambridge: Cambridge University Press.

Becker, Alton L. 1984. "Biography of a Sentence: A Burmese Proverb." In *Text, Play, and Story: The Construction and Reconstruction of Self and Society*, edited by Edward M. Bruner, 135–55. Prospect Heights, Ill.: Waveland Press.

Bellah, Robert N., Richard Madsen, William M. Sullivan, Ann Swidler, and Steven M. Tipton. 1985. *Habits of the Heart: Individualism and Commitment in American Life*. Berkeley and Los Angeles: University of California Press.

Berger, Maurice. 1999. *White Lies: Race and the Myths of Whiteness*. New York: Farrar, Straus, Giroux.

Berlin, Brent, and Paul Kay. 1969. *Basic Color Terms: Their Universality and Evolution*. Berkeley and Los Angeles: University of California Press.

Bernard, H. Russell. 1995. *Research Methods in Anthropology: Qualitative and Quantitative Approaches*. 2d ed. Walnut Creek, Calif.: Alta Mira Press.

Bernhardt, Kathryn. 1999. *Women and Property in China, 960–1949*. Stanford, Calif.: Stanford University Press.

Berreman, Gerald. 1982. "Bazar Behavior: Social Identity and Social Interaction in Urban India." In *Ethnic Identity: Cultural Continuities and Change*, edited by George De Vos and Lola Romanucci-Ross, 71–105. Chicago: University of Chicago Press.

Bhabha, Homi K., ed. 1990. *Nation and Narration*. London: Routledge.

Bishop, Peter B. 1989. *The Myth of Shangri-La: Tibet, Travel Writing, and the Western Creation of Sacred Landscape*. Berkeley and Los Angeles: University of California Press.

Blum, Susan D. 1992. "Ethnic Diversity in Southwest China: Perceptions of Self and Other." *Ethnic Groups* 9:267–79.

———. 1994. "Han and the Chinese Other: The Language of Identity and Difference in Southwest China." Ph.D. diss., University of Michigan, Ann Arbor.

———. 1998. "Pearls on the String of the Chinese Nation: Pronouns, Plurals, and Prototypes in Talk about Identities." *Michigan Discussions in Anthropology* 13 (special issue on "Linguistic Form and Social Action"): 207–37.

———. Forthcoming. "Prestige, Pride, and Polyvocality: The Matched-Guise Test and Perceptions of the Other in Southwest China." In *The 1991 Mid-America Linguistics Conference Papers.*

———. n.d.(a) *Deception and Truth in China.*

———. n.d.(b) "A Matched-Guise Test in a Multilingual Society: Identifications and Evaluations of Speakers in Kunming, Yunnan, Southwest China."

———. n.d.(c) "Metalinguistic and Folk Linguistic Practice in Southwest China."

———. n.d.(d) "Toward an Anthropology of Self and Identity."

Bockman, Harald. 1989. "The Typology of the Naxi Tomba Script." In *Ethnicity and Ethnic Groups in China,* edited by Chien Chiao and Nicholas Tapp, 149–56. *New Asia Academic Bulletin* 8.

Bodde, Derk. 1975. *Festivals in Classical China: New Year and Other Annual Observances during the Han Dynasty 206 B.C.–A.D. 220.* Princeton: Princeton University Press.

Bond, Michael Harris. 1991. *Beyond the Chinese Face: Insights from Psychology.* Oxford: Oxford University Press.

Booz, Patrick R. 1987. *Yunnan.* Lincolnwood, Ill.: Passport Books.

Bourdieu, Pierre, and Jean-Claude Passeron. 1990 [1970]. *Reproduction in Education, Society and Culture.* Translated by Richard Nice. London: Sage.

Bowen, Elenore Smith [Laura Bohannan]. 1954. *Return to Laughter: An Anthropological Novel.* New York: Doubleday.

Bradley, David. 1987. "Language Planning for China's Minorities: The Yi Branch." In *Pacific Linguistics, C-100, A World of Language: Papers Presented to Professor S.A. Wurm on His 65th Birthday,* edited by Donald C. Laycock and Werner Winter, 81–89. Canberra: Australian National University.

Briggs, Charles L. 1986. *Learning How to Ask: A Sociolinguistic Appraisal of the Role of the Interview in Social Science Research.* Cambridge: Cambridge University Press.

Brilliant, Richard. 1991. *Portraiture.* Cambridge: Harvard University Press.

Brodkin, Karen. 1998. *How Jews Became White Folks and What That Says about Race in America.* New Brunswick, N.J.: Rutgers University Press.

Brown, Melissa, ed. 1996. *Negotiating Ethnicity in China.* Berkeley: Institute of East Asian Studies.

Brownell, Susan. 1995. *Training the Body for China: Sports in the Moral Order of the People's Republic.* Chicago: University of Chicago Press.

Bruner, Jerome. 1990. *Acts of Meaning.* Cambridge: Harvard University Press.

Carrithers, Michael, Steven Collins, and Steven Lukes, eds. 1985. *The Category of the Person: Anthropology, Philosophy, and History.* Cambridge: Cambridge University Press.

Cassell, Joan, ed. 1987. *Children in the Field: Anthropological Experiences.* Philadelphia: Temple University Press.

Cen Kailun. 1988. *Xingfu Hua* (Flower of happiness). Wuhan: Changjiang wenyi chubanshe.

Chambers, Ross. 1997. "The Unexamined." In *Whiteness: A Critical Reader*, edited by Mike Hill, 187–203. New York: New York University Press.

Chang, K. C. 1977. "Introduction." In *Food in Chinese Culture: Anthropological and Historical Perspectives*, edited by K. C. Chang, 3–21. New Haven: Yale University Press.

Chang, K.C., ed. 1977. *Food in Chinese Culture: Anthropological and Historical Perspectives*. New Haven: Yale University Press.

Chao, Emily, and Sydney White. 1990. "Saving Sisterhoods: Naxi 'Huo Cuo'." Paper presented at the American Anthropological Association annual meeting, December 1990, New Orleans.

Chen Kaige, director. 1984. *Yellow Earth* (film).

Cheng Deqi. 1986. "Notable Case Studies of Matriarchal Societies." Translated by Deng Shiwu. *Social Sciences in China* (Spring): 219–30. Originally published in *Zhongguo Shehui Kexue* 4 (1985).

Chiang, William Wei. 1995. *"We Two Know the Script; We Have Become Good Friends": Linguistic and Social Aspects of the Women's Script Literacy in Southern Hunan, China*. Lanham, Md.: University Press of America.

Chow Tse-tsung. 1978. "The Childbirth Myth and Ancient Chinese Medicine: A Study of Aspects of the *Wu* Tradition." In *Ancient China: Studies in Early Civilization*, edited by David T. Roy and Tsuen-hsuen Tsien, 43–89. Hong Kong: Chinese University Press.

Chu, Godwin C. 1985. "The Changing Concept of Self in Contemporary China." In *Culture and Self: Asian and Western Perspectives*, edited by Anthony J. Marsella, George DeVos, and Francis L. K. Hsu, 252–77. New York: Tavistock.

Classen, Constance. 1992. "The Odor of the Other: Olfactory Symbolism and Cultural Categories." *Ethos* 20 (2) (June): 133–66.

Clifford, James. 1988. *The Predicament of Culture: Twentieth-Century Ethnography, Literature, and Art*. Cambridge: Harvard University Press.

Cohen, Anthony P. 1994. *Self Consciousness: An Alternative Anthropology of Identity*. London: Routledge.

Coleman, Linda, and Paul Kay. 1981. "Prototype Semantics: The English Word 'Lie'." *Language* 57: 26–44.

Cook, Constance A., and John S. Major, eds. 1999. *Defining Chu: Image and Reality in Ancient China*. Honolulu: University of Hawaii Press.

Crapanzano, Vincent. 1980. *Tuhami: Portrait of a Moroccan*. Chicago: University of Chicago Press.

———. 1990. "On self characterization." In *Cultural Psychology: Essays on Comparative Human Development*, edited by James W. Stigler, Richard A. Shweder, and Gilbert Herdt, 401–23. Cambridge: Cambridge University Press.

Daizu Jianshi Editorial Board. 1985. *Daizu Jianshi* (A brief history of the Dai). Kunming: Yunnan renmin chubanshe.

D'Andrade, Roy, and Claudia Strauss, eds. 1992. *Human Motives and Cultural Models*. Cambridge: Cambridge University Press.

Daniel, E. Valentine. 1984. *Fluid Signs: Being a Person the Tamil Way.* Berkeley and Los Angeles: University of California Press.

Das Gupta, Jyotirindra. 1975. "Ethnicity, Language Demands, and National Development in India." In *Ethnicity: Theory and Experience,* edited by Nathan Glazer and Daniel P. Moynihan, with the assistance of Corinne Saposs Schelling, 466–88. Cambridge: Harvard University Press.

Davis, Sara. 1999. "Singers of Sipsongbanna: Folklore and Authenticity in Contemporary China." Ph.D. diss., University of Pennsylvania.

Deal, David M. 1979. "Policy toward Ethnic Minorities in Southwest China, 1927–1965." In *Nationalism and the Crises of Ethnic Minorities in Asia,* edited by Tai S. Kang, 33–40. Contributions in Sociology, no. 34. Westport, Conn.: Greenwood Press.

DeFrancis, John. 1950. *Nationalism and Language Reform in China.* Princeton: Princeton University Press.

———. 1984. *The Chinese Language: Fact and Fantasy.* Honolulu: University of Hawaii Press.

———. 1989. *Visible Speech: The Diverse Oneness of Writing Systems.* Honolulu: University of Hawaii Press.

De Man, Paul. 1971. *Blindness and Insight: Essays in the Rhetoric of Contemporary Criticism.* New York: Oxford University Press.

Diamond, Norma. 1988. "The Miao and Poison: Interactions on China's Southwest Frontier." *Ethnology* 27: 1–25.

———. 1995. "Defining the Miao: Ming, Qing, and Contemporary Views." In *Cultural Encounters on China's Ethnic Frontiers,* edited by Stevan Harrell, 92–116. Seattle: University of Washington Press.

Diamond, Stanley. 1981 [1974]. *In Search of the Primitive: A Critique of Civilization.* New Brunswick: Transaction Books.

Dikötter, Frank. 1992. *The Discourse of Race in Modern China.* London: Hurst.

Dreyer, June. 1976. *China's Forty Millions: Minority Nationalities and National Integration in the People's Republic of China.* Cambridge: Harvard University Press.

Duara, Prasenjit. 1995. *Rescuing History from the Nation.* Chicago: University of Chicago Press.

DuBois, Cora. 1961 [1944]. *The People of Alor.* 2 vols. New York: Harper & Row.

Duranti, Alessandro. 1997. *Linguistic Anthropology.* Cambridge: Cambridge University Press.

Dwyer, Arienne. 1993. "Altaic Elements in the Linxia Dialect." *Journal of Chinese Linguistics* 20 (1): 160–79.

Dyer, Richard. 1997. *White.* London: Routledge.

Eberhard, Wolfram. 1968. *The Local Cultures of South and East China.* Translated by Alide Eberhard. Leiden: Brill.

———. 1982. *China's Minorities: Yesterday and Today.* Belmont, Calif.: Wadsworth.

Edwards, John R. 1994. *Multilingualism.* London: Routledge.

Edwards, John, ed. 1984. *Linguistic Minorities, Policies and Pluralism*. London: Academic Press.

Elvin, Mark. 1985. "Between the Earth and Heaven: Conceptions of the Self in China." In *The Category of the Person: Anthropology, Philosophy, History*, edited by Michael Carrithers, Steven Collins, and Steven Lukes, 156–89. Cambridge: Cambridge University Press.

Erbaugh, Mary S. 1990. "The Chinese Revolution as a Hakka Enterprise: Language, Ethnicity, and Post-Revolutionary Alliances." Paper presented at the Center for Chinese Studies, University of California, Berkeley.

———. 1995. "Southern Chinese Dialects as a Medium for Reconciliation within Greater China." *Language in Society* 23 (1) (Spring): 79–94.

Eriksen, Erik H. 1950. *Childhood and Society*. New York: Norton.

Fabian, Johannes. 1986. *Language and Colonial Power: The Appropriation of Swahili in the Former Belgian Congo 1880–1938*. Berkeley and Los Angeles: University of California Press.

Fairbank, John K. 1968. "The Early Treaty System in the Chinese World Order." In *The Chinese World Order: Traditional China's Foreign Relations*, edited by John K. Fairbank, 257–75. Cambridge: Harvard University Press.

FBIS (Foreign Broadcast Information Service). 1990. "State Issues 1990 Census Communique No 3." *FBIS*-CHI-90-223 (19 November 1990), 29.

Fei Xiaotong. 1980. "Ethnic Identification in China." *Social Science in China* 1: 94–107.

Feng Jicai. 1994 [1986]. *The Three-Inch Golden Lotus: A Novel on Foot Binding*. Translated by David Wakefield. Honolulu: University of Hawaii Press.

Fenollosa, Ernest Francisco. 1936. *The Chinese Character as a Medium for Poetry*. Edited by Ezra Pound. San Francisco: City Lights.

Ferguson, Charles. 1964. "Diglossia." In *Language in Culture and Society: A Reader in Linguistics and Society*, edited by Dell Hymes. New York: Harper & Row.

Fillmore, Charles. 1975. "An Alternative to Checklist Theories of Meaning." In *Proceedings of the First Annual Meeting of the Berkeley Linguistics Society*, 123–31. Berkeley: Berkeley Linguistics Society.

———. 1976. "Topics in Lexical Semantics." In *Current Issues in Linguistic Theory*, edited by Peter Cole, 76–138. Bloomington: Indiana University Press.

Fishman, Joshua. 1966. *Language Loyalty in the United States: The Maintenance and Perpetuation of Non-English Mother Tongues by American Ethnic and Religious Groups*. The Hague: Mouton.

Fishman, Joshua A., Charles A. Ferguson, and Jyotirindra Das Gupta, eds. 1968. *Language Problems of Developing Nations*. New York: John Wiley and Sons.

Fitzgerald, C. P. 1941. *The Tower of Five Glories: A Study of the Min Chia of Ta Li, Yunnan*. London: Cresset Press.

Fortes, M. Meyer. 1959. *Oedipus and Job in West African Religion*. Cambridge: Cambridge University Press.

——. 1973. "On the concept of the person among the Tallensi." In *La notion de personne en Afrique Noire,* edited by G. Dieterlen. Paris: Editions du Centre National de la Recherche Scientifique.

Foster, George M. 1967. "Peasant Society and the Image of the Limited Good." In *Peasant Society: A Reader,* edited by Jack M. Potter, May N. Diaz, and George M. Foster, 300–323. Boston: Little, Brown.

Foster, Robert J. 1991. "Making National Cultures in the Global Ecumene." *Annual Review of Anthropology* 20: 235–60.

Foucault, Michel. 1979 [1975]. *Discipline and Punish: The Birth of the Prison.* Translated by Alan Sheridan. New York: Vintage.

——. 1988 [1961]. *Madness and Civilization: A History of Insanity in the Age of Reason.* Translated by Richard Howard. New York: Vintage.

——. 1994 [1973]. *The Birth of the Clinic: An Archaeology of Medical Perception.* Translated by A. M. Sheridan Smith. New York: Vintage.

Fowler, Edward. 1993. "Minorities in a 'Homogeneous' State: The Case of Japan." In *What Is In a Rim?,* edited by Arif Dirlik, 211–33. Boulder, Colo.: Westview Press.

Frankenberg, Ruth. 1993. *White Women, Race Matters: The Social Construction of Whiteness.* Minneapolis: University of Minnesota Press.

Freud, Sigmund. 1921. *Group Psychology and the Analysis of the Ego.* Standard ed. New York: Norton.

Friedlander, Judith. 1975. *Being Indian in Hueyapan: A Study of Forced Identity in Contemporary Mexico.* New York: St. Martin's Press.

Friedman, Edward. 1994. "Reconstructing China's National Identity: A Southern Alternative to Mao-Era Anti-Imperialist Nationalism." *Journal of Asian Studies* 53 (1) (February): 67–91.

Friedrich, Paul. 1986a. *The Language Parallax: Linguistic Relativism and Poetic Indeterminacy.* Austin: University of Texas Press.

——. 1986b. *The Princes of Naranja: An Essay in Anthrohistorical Method.* Austin: University of Texas Press.

Gao Fayuan, ed. 1990. *Zhongguo Xinan Shaoshuminzu Daode Yanjiu* (Research on morality among China's southwest minorities). Kunming: Yunnan minzu chubanshe.

Geertz, Clifford. 1983. "Common Sense as a Cultural System." In *Local Knowledge: Further Essays in Interpretive Anthropology,* 73–93. New York: Basic Books.

Giles, Howard, and Bernard Saint-Jacques, eds. 1979. *Language and Ethnic Relations.* Oxford: Pergamon Press.

Gladney, Dru C. 1991. *Muslim Chinese: Ethnic Nationalism in the People's Republic.* Cambridge: Council on East Asian Studies, Harvard University (Harvard East Asian Monographs 149).

——. 1994. "Representing Nationality in China: Refiguring Majoritiy/Minority Identities." *Journal of Asian Studies* 53 (1): 92–123.

——. 1998a. "Clashed Civilizations? Muslim and Chinese Identities in the PRC." In *Making Majorities: Constituting the Nation in Japan, Korea, China, Malaysia, Fiji, Turkey, and the United States,* edited by Dru C. Gladney, 106–31. Stanford, Calif.: Stanford University Press.

———. 1998b. "Introduction: Making and Marking Majorities." In *Making Majorities: Constituting the Nation in Japan, Korea, China, Malaysia, Fiji, Turkey, and the United States,* edited by Dru C. Gladney, 1–9. Stanford, Calif.: Stanford University Press.

———, ed. 1998c. *Making Majorities: Constituting the Nation in Japan, Korea, China, Malaysia, Fiji, Turkey, and the United States.* Stanford, Calif.: Stanford University Press.

Glazer, Nathan, and Daniel P[atrick] Moynihan. 1975. "Introduction." In *Ethnicity: Theory and Experience,* edited by Nathan Glazer and Daniel P. Moynihan, with the assistance of Corinne Saposs Schelling, 1–26. Cambridge: Harvard University Press.

Gold, Thomas B. 1989. "Guerrilla Interviewing among the *Getihu.*" In *Unofficial China: Popular Culture and Thought in the People's Republic,* edited by Perry Link, Richard Madsen, and Paul G. Pickowicz, 175–92. Boulder, Colo.: Westview Press.

Goldstein, Melvyn. 1989. *A History of Modern Tibet, 1913–1951: The Demise of the Lamaist State.* Berkeley and Los Angeles: University of California Press.

Goldwin, Robert A., Art Kaufman, and William A. Schambra, eds. 1989. *Forging Unity out of Diversity: The Approaches of Eight Nations.* Washington, D.C.: American Enterprise Institute for Public Policy Research.

Gordon, Richard, and Carma Hinton, producers and directors. 1995. *The Gate of Heavenly Peace,* a production of Long Bow Group, produced in association with WGBH/Frontline and the Independent Television Service.

Goullart, Peter. 1955. *Forgotten Kingdom.* London: John Murray.

Gramsci, Antonio. 1957. *The Modern Prince and Other Writings.* New York: International Publishers.

Granet, Marcel. 1926. *Danses et légendes de la Chine ancienne.* Paris: Alcan.

———. 1932. *Festivals and Songs of Ancient China.* London: Routledge.

Greenblatt, Stephen. 1991. *Marvelous Possessions: The Wonder of the New World.* Chicago: University of Chicago Press.

Greenhalgh, Susan. 1993. "The Peasantization of the One-Child Policy in Shaanxi." In *Chinese Families in the Post-Mao Era,* edited by Deborah Davis and Stevan Harrell, 219–50. Berkeley and Los Angeles: University of California Press.

———. 1994. "Controlling Births and Bodies in Village China." *American Ethnologist* 21 (1): 3–30.

Grunfeld, A. Tom. 1985. "In Search of Equality: Relations Between China's Ethnic Minorities and the Majority Han." *Bulletin of Concerned Asian Scholars* 17 (1): 54–67.

———. 1987. *The Making of Modern Tibet.* London: Zed.

Guha, Ranajit, ed. 1997. *A Subaltern Studies Reader, 1986–1995.* Minneapolis: University of Minnesota Press.

Gumperz, John J. 1982a. *Discourse Strategies.* Cambridge: Cambridge University Press.

———, ed. 1982b. *Language and Social Identity.* Cambridge: Cambridge University Press.

Gumperz, John J., and Stephen C. Levinson, eds. 1996. *Rethinking Linguistic Relativity.* Cambridge: Cambridge University Press.

Hacking, Ian. 1997. "An Aristotelian Glance at Race and the Mind." *Ethos* 25 (1) (March): 107–12.

Handler, Richard. 1988. *Nationalism and the Politics of Culture in Quebec.* Madison: University of Wisconsin Press.

Haney-López, Ian. 1996. *White by Law: The Legal Construction of Race.* New York: New York University Press.

Hannerz, Ulf. 1992. *Cultural Complexity: Studies in the Social Organization of Meaning.* New York: Columbia University Press.

Haraway, Donna. 1988. "Situated Knowledges: The Science Question in Feminism and the Privilege of Partial Perspective." *Feminist Studies* 14 (3) (Fall): 575–99.

Harrell, Stevan. 1990. "Ethnicity, Local Interests, and the State: Yi Communities in Southwest China." *Comparative Studies in Society and History* 32 (3) (July): 515–48.

———. 1993. "Linguistics and Hegemony in China." *International Journal of the Sociology of Language* 103: 97–114.

———. 1995a. "Civilizing Projects and the Reaction to Them." In *Cultural Encounters on China's Ethnic Frontiers,* edited by Stevan Harrell, 3–36. Seattle: University of Washington Press.

———. 1995b. "The Prmi and Naze, Peoples of a Triple Periphery." Paper presented at the Association for Asian Studies annual meeting, April 9, 1995, Washington, D.C.

———, ed. 1995c. *Cultural Encounters on China's Ethnic Frontiers.* Seattle: University of Washington Press.

Harvey, G. E. 1957. "The Wa People of the Burma-China Border." *St. Antony's Papers* (London), no. 2: 126–35.

He Liyi, with Claire Anne Chik. 1993. *Mr. China's Son: A Villager's Life.* Boulder, Colo.: Westview Press.

He Yaohua. 1988. *Zhongguo Xinan Lishi Minzuxue Lunji* (Collected essays on historical and ethnographic studies of China's southwest). Kunming: Yunnan renmin chubanshe.

Heberer, Thomas. 1989. *China and Its National Minorities: Autonomy or Assimilation?* Translated by Michel Vale. Armonk, N.Y.: Sharpe.

Hevia, James. 1995. *Cherishing Men from Afar: Qing Guest Ritual and the Macartney Embassy of 1793.* Durham, N.C.: Duke University Press.

Highlights of Minority Nationalities in Yunnan. N.d. The Foreign Affairs Office of Yunnan Provincial People's Government. N.p.

Hill, Jane H. 1995. "The Voices of Don Gabriel: Responsibility and Self in a Modern Mexicano Narrative." In *The Dialogic Emergence of Culture,* edited by Dennis Tedlock and Bruce Mannheim, 97–147. Urbana: University of Illinois Press.

Hill, Jane, and Bruce Mannheim. 1992. "Language and World View." *Annual Review of Anthropology* 21: 381–406.

Hill, Mike, ed. 1997. *Whiteness: A Critical Reader.* New York: New York University Press.

Hirschfeld, Lawrence. 1994. "Is the Acquisition of Social Categories Based on Do-
main-Specific Competence or on Knowledge Transfer?" In *Mapping the Mind: Domain Specificity in Cognition and Culture,* edited by Lawrence A. Hirschfeld and
Susan A. Gelman, 201–33. Cambridge: Cambridge University Press.

———. 1997. "The Conceptual Politics of Race: Lessons from Our Children." *Ethos*
25 (1) (March): 63–92.

Hirschfeld, Lawrence A., and Susan A. Gelman, eds. 1994. *Mapping the Mind: Domain
Specificity in Cognition and Culture.* Cambridge: Cambridge University Press.

Hobsbawm, E. J. 1990. *Nations and Nationalism since 1780: Programme, Myth, Reality.* Cambridge: Cambridge University Press.

Holland, Dorothy, and Naomi Quinn, eds. 1987. *Cultural Models in Language and
Thought.* Cambridge: Cambridge University Press.

Honig, Emily. 1992. *Creating Chinese Ethnicity: Subei People in Shanghai,
1850–1980.* New Haven: Yale University Press.

Honig, Emily, and Gail Hershatter. 1988. *Personal Voices: Chinese Women in the
1980's.* Stanford, Calif.: Stanford University Press.

Hsieh Shih-chung. 1995. "On the Dynamics of Tai/Dai-Lue Ethnicity: An Ethno-
historical Analysis." In *Cultural Encounters on China's Ethnic Frontiers,* edited by
Stevan Harrell, 301–28. Seattle: University of Washington Press.

———. 1998. "On Three Definitions of Han Ren: Images of the Majority People in
Taiwan." In *Making Majorities: Constituting the Nation in Japan, Korea, China,
Malaysia, Fiji, Turkey, and the United States,* edited by Dru C. Gladney, 95–105.
Stanford, Calif.: Stanford University Press.

Hsu, Francis L. K. 1967 [1948]. *Under the Ancestors' Shadow: Kinship, Personality,
and Social Mobility in China.* Stanford, Calif.: Stanford University Press.

———. 1971. "Psychosocial Homeostasis and *Jen:* Conceptual Tools for Advancing
Psychological Anthropology." *American Anthropologist* 73: 23–44.

———. 1983. *Rugged Individualism Reconsidered: Essays in Psychological Anthropology.* Knoxville: University of Tennessee Press.

Hyde, Sandra Teresa. 1998. "The Chinese State and Everyday AIDS Practices in the Borderlands." *Bad Subjects* (published at the University of California, Berkeley): 12–14.

———. 1999. "Sex, Drugs and Karaoke: Making AIDS in Southwest China." Ph.D.
diss., University of California, Berkeley.

Institute of Literature, Chinese Academy of Social Sciences, comp. 1979. *Stories
about Not Being Afraid of Ghosts.* Translated by Yang Hsien-yi [Yang Xianyi] and
Gladys Yang. Beijing: Foreign Languages Press.

Irvine, Judith. 1996. "Sound Politics: Speaking, Writing, and Printing in Early Colonial Africa." Paper presented at the Ethnohistory Workshop, University of Pennsylvania, April 18, 1996.

Israel, John. 1998. *Lianda: A Chinese University in War and Revolution.* Stanford,
Calif.: Stanford University Press.

Jackson, Anthony. 1989. "Naxi Studies: Past, Present, and Future." In *Ethnicity and
Ethnic Groups in China,* edited by Chien Chiao and Nicholas Tapp, 133–47. *New
Asia Academic Bulletin* 8.

Jacobson, Matthew Frye. 1998. *Whiteness of a Different Color: European Immigrants and the Alchemy of Race.* Cambridge: Harvard University Press.

James, Wendy. 1987. *The Listening Ebony: Moral Knowledge, Religion, and Power among the Uduk of Sudan.* Oxford: Clarendon Press.

Jankowiak, William R. 1993. *Sex, Death, and Hierarchy in a Chinese City: An Anthropological Account.* New York: Columbia University Press.

Jing Dexin, ed. 1986. *Yunnan Huizu Qiyi Shiliao* (Historical materials on the Hui uprisings in Yunnan). Kunming: Yunnan minzu chubanshe.

Johnson, Parker C. 1999. "Reflections on Critical White(ness) Studies." In *Whiteness: The Communication of Social Identity,* edited by Thomas K. Nakayama and Judith N. Martin, 1–9. Thousand Oaks, Calif.: Sage.

Jones, Russell A. 1982. "Perceiving Other People: Stereotyping as a Process of Social Cognition." In *In the Eye of the Beholder: Contemporary Issues in Stereotyping,* edited by Arthur G. Miller, 41–91. New York: Praeger.

Kennedy, George A. 1964. *Selected Works.* Edited by Tien-yi Li. New Haven: Yale University Far Eastern Publications.

Keyes, Charles F. 1995. "Who Are the Tai? Reflections on the Invention of Identities." In *Ethnic Identity: Creation, Conflict, and Accommodation* (3d ed.), edited by Lola Romanucci-Ross and George DeVos, 136–60. Walnut Creek, Calif.: Alta Mira Press.

Kincheloe, Joe L., Shirley R. Steinberg, Nelson M. Rodriguez, and Ronald E. Chennault, eds. 1998. *White Reign: Deploying Whiteness in America.* New York: St. Martin's Press.

Kipnis, Andrew B. 1997. *Producing Guanxi: Sentiment, Self, and Subculture in a North China Village.* Durham, N.C.: Duke University Press.

Kondo, Dorinne K. 1990. *Crafting Selves: Power, Gender, and Discourses of Identity in a Japanese Workplace.* Chicago: University of Chicago Press.

Kuhn, Philip A. 1990. *Soulstealers: The Chinese Sorcery Scare of 1768.* Cambridge: Harvard University Press.

Kuhn, Thomas. 1962. *The Structure of Scientific Revolutions.* Chicago: University of Chicago Press.

Labov, William. 1972. *Sociolinguistic Patterns.* Philadelphia: University of Pennsylvania Press.

Lacan, Jacques. 1977 [1966]. *Ecrits: A Selection.* Translated by Alan Sheridan. New York: Norton.

Lai, Tse-han, Ramon H. Myers, and Wei Wou. 1991. *A Tragic Beginning: The Taiwan Uprising of February 28, 1947.* Stanford, Calif.: Stanford University Press.

Lakoff, George. 1987. *Women, Fire, and Dangerous Things: What Categories Reveal about the Mind.* Chicago: University of Chicago Press.

Lakoff, George, and Mark Johnson. 1980. *Metaphors We Live By.* Chicago: University of Chicago Press.

Lam, Tong. 2000. "Identity and Diversity: The Complexities and Contradictions of Chinese Nationalism." In *China Beyond the Headlines,* edited by Timothy B. Weston and Lionel M. Jensen, 147–70. Lanham, Md.: Rowman & Littlefield.

Lambert, Wallace, R. C. Hodgson, R. C. Gardner, and S. Fillenbaum. 1972 [1960]. "Evaluational Reactions to Spoken Languages." In *Language, Psychology, and Culture: Essays by Wallace E. Lambert*, 80–96. Stanford, Calif.: Stanford University Press. Originally published in *Journal of Abnormal and Social Psychology* 60: 1.44–51.

Lattimore, Owen. 1951 [1940]. *Inner Asian Frontiers of China*. Boston: Beacon Press.

Leach, E. R. 1954. *Political Systems of Highland Burma: A Study of Kachin Social Structure*. Boston: Beacon Press.

Lehmann, Winfred P., ed. 1975. *Language and Linguistics in the People's Republic of China*. Austin: University of Texas Press.

Levenson, Joseph R. 1958 [1964, 1965]. *Confucian China and Its Modern Fate: A Trilogy*. Berkeley and Los Angeles: University of California Press.

Li Zhisui. 1994. *The Private Life of Chairman Mao: The Memoirs of Mao's Personal Physician*. Translated by Tai Hung-chao, with editorial assistance by Anne F. Thurston. New York: Random House.

Lin Yue-hwa [Yaohua]. 1961. *The Lolo of Liang Shan*. Translated by Liu Su-chi and Pan Ju-shu. New Haven: HRAF Press.

Linde, Charlotte. 1987. "Explanatory Systems in Oral Life Stories." In *Cultural Models in Language and Thought*, edited by Dorothy Holland and Naomi Quinn, 343–66. Cambridge: Cambridge University Press.

———. 1993. *Life Stories: The Creation of Coherence*. New York: Oxford University Press.

Lindzey, Gardner. 1961. *Projective Techniques and Cross-Cultural Research*. New York: Appleton-Century-Crofts.

Link, Perry. 1992. *Evening Chats in Beijing: Probing China's Predicament*. New York: Norton.

Lipman, Jonathan N. 1990. "Ethnic Violence in Modern China: Hans and Huis in Gansu, 1781–1929." In *Violence in China: Essays in Culture and Counterculture*, edited by Jonathan N. Lipman and Stevan Harrell, 65–86. Albany: State University of New York Press.

Liu Dalin, Man Lun Ng, Li Ping Zhou, and Erwin J. Haeberle. 1997. *Sexual Behavior in Modern China: Report on the Nationwide Survey of 20,000 Men and Women*. English-language edition by Man Lun Ng and Erwin J. Haeberle. New York: Continuum.

Liu Xiaobin. 1991. *Dian Wenhua Shi* (A history of Dian culture). Kunming: Yunnan renmin chubanshe.

Liu Yan. 1988. "Dui Xishuangbanna Daizu Jiaoyu de Sikao" (Thoughts on the education of Dai in Xishuangbanna). *Minzu Gongzuo* 97 (11): 28–31.

Lonner, Walter J., and John W. Berry, eds. 1986. *Field Methods in Cross-Cultural Research*. Beverly Hills: Sage.

Lu, Huei-min. 1997. "The Compass and the Ruler: Theory and Practice in Taiwanese Geomancy." Ph.D. diss., University of Pennsylvania.

Lucy, John A. 1985. "Whorf's View of the Linguistic Mediation of Thought." In *Semiotic Mediation: Sociocultural and Psychological Perspectives,* edited by Elizabeth Mertz and Richard J. Parmentier, 73–97. Orlando: Academic Press.

———. 1992a. *Grammatical Categories and Cognition: A Case Study of the Linguistic Relativity Hypothesis.* Cambridge: Cambridge University Press.

———. 1992b. *Language Diversity and Thought: A Reformulation of the Linguistic Relativity Hypothesis.* Cambridge: Cambridge University Press.

———. 1996. "The Scope of Linguistic Relativity: An Analysis and Review of Empirical Research." In *Rethinking Linguistic Relativity,* edited by John J. Gumperz and Stephen C. Levinson, 37–69. Cambridge: Cambridge University Press.

Lukes, Steven. 1973. *Individualism.* Oxford: Blackwell.

Lutz, Catherine. 1985. "Ethnopsychology Compared to What? Explaining Behavior and Consciousness among the Ifaluk." In *Person, Self, and Experience: Exploring Pacific Ethnopsychologies,* edited by Geoffrey M. White and John Kirkpatrick, 35–79. Berkeley and Los Angeles: University of California Press.

Lutz, Catherine A., and Jane L. Collins. 1993. *Reading National Geographic.* Chicago: University of Chicago Press.

Ma Yin, ed. 1989. *China's Minority Nationalities.* Beijing: Foreign Languages Press.

Mackerras, Colin. 1994. *China's Minorities: Integration and Modernization in the Twentieth Century.* Hong Kong: Oxford University Press.

———. 1995. *China's Minority Cultures: Identities and Integration since 1912.* New York: St. Martin's Press.

MacLaury, Robert. 1991. "Prototypes Revisited." *Annual Review of Anthropology* 20: 55–74.

Mair, Victor H. 1991. "What Is a Chinese 'Dialect/Topolect'? Reflections on Some Key Sino-English Linguistic Terms." *Sino-Platonic Papers* 29 (September).

Marsella, Anthony J., George DeVos, and Francis L. K. Hsu, eds. 1985. *Culture and Self: Asian and Western Perspectives.* New York: Tavistock.

Martin, Emily. 1988. "Gender and Ideological Differences in Representations of Life and Death." In *Death Ritual in Late Imperial and Modern China,* edited by James L. Watson and Evelyn S. Rawski, 164–79. Berkeley and Los Angeles: University of California Press.

Martin, Laura. 1986. "Eskimo Words for Snow: A Case Study in the Genesis and Decay of an Anthropological Example." *American Anthropologist* 88 (2): 418–23.

Mauss, Marcel. 1985 [1938]. "A Category of the Human Mind: The Notion of the Person; the Notion of Self." In *The Category of the Person: Anthropology, Philosophy, and History,* edited by Michael Carrithers, Steven Collins, and Steven Lukes, and translated by W. D. Halls, 1–25. Cambridge: Cambridge University Press.

McBride, James. 1996. *The Color of Water: A Black Man's Tribute to His White Mother.* New York: Riverhead.

McConnell-Ginet, Sally. 1979. "Prototypes, Pronouns, and Persons." In *Ethnolinguistics: Boas, Sapir, and Whorf Revisited,* edited by Madeleine Mathiot, 63–83. The Hague: Mouton.

McFarlane, Graham. 1981. "Shetlanders and Incomers: Change, Conflict and Emphasis in Social Perspectives." In *The Structure of Folk Models*, edited by Ladislav Holy and Milan Stuchlik, 119–36. London: Academic Press.

McKhann, Charles F. 1992. "Fleshing Out the Bones: Kinship and Cosmology in Naxi Religion." Ph.D. diss., University of Chicago.

———. 1995. "The Naxi and the Nationalities Question." In *Cultural Encounters on China's Ethnic Frontiers*, edited by Stevan Harrell, 39–62. Seattle: University of Washington Press.

Mead, George Herbert. 1934. *Mind, Self, and Society from the Standpoint of a Social Behaviorist*. Chicago: University of Chicago Press.

Mei Lichong, Wei Huailuan, and Yang Junxuan. 1993. *Zhongguo Wenhua Mianmianguan* (The ins and outs of Chinese culture). Beijing: Huayu jiaoxue chubanshe.

Mertz, Elizabeth, and Richard J. Parmentier, eds. 1985. *Semiotic Mediation: Sociocultural and Psychological Perspectives*. Orlando: Academic Press.

Miller, Arthur G., ed. 1982. *In the Eye of the Beholder: Contemporary Issues in Stereotyping*. New York: Praeger.

Miller, Lucien. 1993. "The Ethnic Chameleon: Bakhtin and the Bai." Paper presented at the annual meeting of the International Society for the Comparative Study of Civilizations, Scranton, Pennsylvania.

Miller, Lucien, ed. 1994. *South of the Clouds: Tales from Yunnan*. Translated by Guo Xu, Lucien Miller, and Xu Kun. Seattle: University of Washington Press.

Moerman, Michael. 1965. "Ethnic Identification in a Complex Civilization: Who Are the Lue?" *American Anthropologist* 76: 1215–30.

Morris, Colin. 1972. *The Discovery of the Individual, 1050–1200*. London: S.P.C.K. for the Church Historical Society.

Moseley, George V. H., III. 1973. *The Consolidation of the South China Frontier*. Berkeley and Los Angeles: University of California Press.

Munro, Donald J. 1977. *The Concept of Man in Contemporary China*. Ann Arbor: University of Michigan Press.

———. 1985. "The Family Network, the Stream of Water, and the Plant: Picturing Persons in Sung Confucianism." In *Individualism and Holism: Studies in Confucian and Taoist Values*, edited by Donald Munro, 259–91. Ann Arbor: University of Michigan Center for Chinese Studies.

Nakayama, Thomas K., and Judith N. Martin, eds. 1999. *Whiteness: The Communication of Social Identity*. Thousand Oaks, Calif.: Sage.

Naquin, Susan, and Chun-fang Yu, eds. 1992. *Pilgrims and Sacred Sites in China*. Berkeley and Los Angeles: University of California Press.

Nash, Manning. 1989. *The Cauldron of Ethnicity in the Modern World*. Chicago: University of Chicago Press.

National Geographic. 1980. "Shanghai: Muscle and Smoke. Born-Again Giant" (July).

———. 1994. "Shanghai: Where China's Past and Future Meet," by William S. Ellis, photographs by Stuart Franklin. Vol. 185, no. 3 (March): 2–35.

New York Times. 1983a. February 26, sec. 1, p. 7.
———. 1983b. June 7, sec. 1, p. 1.
———. 1983c. July 8, sec. 1, p. 7.
———. 1985. October 5, sec. 1, p. 6.
Newsweek. 1996. "China: Friend or Foe? China on the Move." (April 1): 24–53.
Norman, Jerry. 1988. *Chinese.* Cambridge: Cambridge University Press.
Oakes, Tim. 1998. *Tourism and Modernity in China.* London: Routledge.
Ohnuki-Tierney, Emiko. 1993. *Rice as Self: Japanese Identites through Time.* Princeton: Princeton University Press.
Ortega y Gasset, José. 1957. *Man and People.* New York: Norton.
Ortner, Sherry B. 1973. "On Key Symbols." *American Anthropologist* 75: 1338–46.
Oxford English Dictionary. 1971. *The Compact Edition of the Oxford English Dictionary.* Oxford: Oxford University Press.
Pemberton, John. 1994. *On the Subject of "Java."* Ithaca: Cornell University Press.
People's Republic of China Year Book 1986. 1986. Beijing: Xinhua.
Pepper, Stephen C. 1942. *World Hypotheses: A Study in Evidence.* Berkeley and Los Angeles: University of California Press.
Piaget, Jean. 1978. *The Development of Thought.* Oxford: Blackwell.
Pietz, William. 1985. "The Problem of the Fetish, I." *Res* 9 (Spring): 5–17.
———. 1987. "The Problem of the Fetish, II: The Origin of the Fetish." *Res* 13 (Spring): 23–45.
———. 1988. "The Problem of the Fetish, IIIa: Bosman's Guinea and the Enlightenment Theory of Fetishism." *Res* 16 (Autumn): 105–23.
Pollard, Samuel. 1921. *In Unknown China.* Philadelphia: Lippincott.
Polo, Marco. 1958 [14th century]. *The Travels.* Translated and with an introduction by Ronald Latham. Harmondsworth: Penguin.
Pound, Ezra. 1949. *Confucius: The Unwobbling Pivot and the Great Digest.* Translated by Ezra Pound. Bombay: Orient Longmans.
Pruitt, Ida. 1967 [1945]. *A Daughter of Han: The Autobiography of a Chinese Working Woman.* Stanford, Calif.: Stanford University Press.
Pu Songling. 1989. *Strange Tales from Make-Do Studio.* Translated by Denis C. and Victor H. Mair. Beijing: Foreign Languages Press.
Pye, Lucian W. 1975. "China: Ethnic Minorities and National Security." In *Ethnicity: Theory and Experience,* edited by Nathan Glazer and Daniel P. Moynihan, with the assistance of Corinne Saposs Schelling, 489–512. Cambridge: Harvard University Press.
Quine, Willard Van Orman. 1960. *Word and Object.* Cambridge: MIT Press.
Quinn, Naomi. 1982. "'Commitment' in American Marriage: A Cultural Analysis." *American Ethnologist* 9: 775–98.
Ramaswamy, Sumathi. 1997. *Passions of the Tongue: Language Devotion in Tamil India, 1891–1970.* Berkeley and Los Angeles: University of California Press.
Ramsey, S. Robert. 1987. *The Languages of China.* Princeton: Princeton University Press.

Riesman, David, with Nathan Glazer and Reuel Denney. 1961 [1950]. *The Lonely Crowd*. New Haven: Yale University Press.

Rock, Joseph. 1947. *The Ancient Na-khi Kingdom of Southwest China*. 2 vols. Cambridge: Harvard University Press.

———. 1963. *The Life and Culture of the Na-khi Tribe of the China-Tibet Borderland*. Wiesbaden: Franz Steiner Verlag.

Roediger, David R. 1999. *The Wages of Whiteness: Race and the Making of the American Working Class*. London: Verso.

Rosaldo, Michelle Z. 1980. *Knowledge and Passion: Ilongot Notions of Self and Social Life*. Cambridge: Cambridge University Press.

Rosch, Eleanor. 1975. "Cognitive Representations of Semantic Categories." *Journal of Experimental Psychology: General* 104: 192–233.

Rosenberger, Nancy R., ed. 1992. *Japanese Sense of Self*. Cambridge: Cambridge University Press.

Rossabi, Morris. 1981. "The Muslims in the Early Yuan Dynasty." In *China under Mongol Rule*, edited by John D. Langlois, Jr., 257–95. Princeton: Princeton University Press.

Rothstein, Stanley W. 1993. *The Voice of the Other: Language as Illusion in the Formation of the Self*. Westport, Conn.: Praeger.

Sage, Steven F. 1992. *Ancient Sichuan and the Unification of China*. Albany: State University of New York Press.

Sanjek, Roger. 1990. "A Vocabulary for Fieldnotes." In *Fieldnotes: The Makings of Anthropology*, edited by Roger Sanjek, 92–121. Ithaca: Cornell University Press.

Sapir, Edward. 1921. *Language: An Introduction to the Study of Speech*. New York: Harcourt Brace Jovanovich.

Saussure, Ferdinand de. 1983 [1915]. *Course in General Linguistics*. Edited by Charles Bally and Albert Sechehaye, with Albert Riedlinger, and translated by Roy Harris. La Salle, Ill.: Open Court.

Schein, Louisa. 1987. "'A Colorful Element in the National Community': Miao Women, The State and Difference." Paper presented at the annual meeting of the American Anthropogical Association, New Orleans.

———. 1993. "Popular Culture and the Production of Difference: The Miao and China." Ph.D. diss., University of California, Berkeley.

———. 1996. "The Other Goes to Market: The State, the Nation, and Unruliness in Contemporary China." *Identities* 2 (3): 197–222.

———. 1997. "Gender and Internal Orientalism in China." *Modern China* 23 (1) (January 1997): 69–98.

———. 2000. *Minority Rules: The Miao and the Feminine in China's Cultural Politics*. Durham, N.C.: Duke University Press.

Schiffman, Harold. 1996. *Linguistic Culture and Language Policy*. London: Routledge.

Schneider, Laurence G. 1980. *A Madman of Ch'u: The Chinese Myth of Loyalty and Dissent*. Berkeley and Los Angeles: University of California Press.

Scott, James C. 1999. *Seeing like a State: How Certain Schemes to Improve the Human Condition Have Failed*. New Haven: Yale University Press.

Seybolt, Peter J., and Gregory Kuei-ke Chiang. 1979. *Language Reform in China: Documents and Commentary*. White Plains, N.Y.: Sharpe.

Shen Congwen. 1982a. "Fenghuang." In *Recollections of West Hunan*, translated by Gladys Yang, 105–28. Beijing: Panda.

———. 1982b. "Qiaoxiu and Dongsheng." In *Recollections of West Hunan*, translated by Gladys Yang, 139–64. Beijing: Panda.

Shibamoto, Janet S. 1987. "The Womanly Woman: Manipulation of Stereotypical and Nonstereotypical Features of Japanese Female Speech." In *Language, Gender and Sex in Comparative Perspective*, edited by Susan U. Philips, Susan Steele, and Christine Tanz, 26–49. Cambridge: Cambridge University Press.

Shih, Chuan-kang. 1985. "A Challenge to the Concept of Universal Male Authority: The Moso Case and Comparative Studies." Ph.D. qualifying paper, Stanford University.

———. 1993. "The Moso: Sexual Union, Household Organization, Ethnicity and Gender in a Matrilineal Duolocal Society in Southwest China." Ph.D. diss., Stanford University.

Shryock, John Knight. 1932. *The Origin and Development of the State Cult of Confucius: An Introductory Study*. New York: Century.

Shue, Vivienne. 1988. *The Reach of the State: Sketches of the Chinese Body Politic*. Stanford, Calif.: Stanford University Press.

Shweder, Richard A. 1984. "Anthropology's Romantic Rebellion against the Enlightenment, or There's More to Thinking Than Reason and Evidence." In *Culture Theory: Essays on Mind, Self, and Emotion*, edited by Richard A. Shweder and Robert A. LeVine, 27–66. Cambridge: Cambridge University Press.

Shweder, Richard A., and Robert A. Levine, eds. 1984. *Culture Theory: Essays on Mind, Self, and Emotion*. Cambridge: Cambridge University Press.

Silverstein, Michael. 1987. "Monoglot 'Standard' in America: Standardization and Metaphors of Linguistic Hegemony." Working Papers and Proceedings of the Center for Psychosocial Studies, Chicago.

———. 1996. "Monoglot 'Standard' in America: Standardization and Metaphors of Linguistic Hegemony." In *The Matrix of Language: Contemporary Linguistic Anthropology*, edited by Donald Brenneis and Ronald H. S. Macaulay, 284–306. Boulder, Colo.: Westview Press.

Slugoski, B. R., and G. P. Ginsburg. 1989. "Ego Identity and Explanatory Speech." In *Texts of Identity*, edited by John Shotter and Kenneth J. Gergen, 36–55. London: Sage.

Song Qiang, Zhang Zangzang, and Qiao Bian. 1996. *Zhongguo Keyi Shuo "Bu"* (China can say "no"). Beijing: Zhonghua gongshang lianhe chubanshe.

Song Sichang. 1985. "Kunming ji qi Shijiao Zongjiao Chubu Diaocha" (Preliminary research on religion in Kunming and environs). In *Kunming Minzu Minsu he Zongjiao Diaocha* (Research on Kunming nationalities, customs, and religion), edited by Yunnan Editorial Group, 122–48. Kunming: Yunnan minzu chubanshe.

Spain, David. 1972. "On the Use of Projective Tests for Research in Psychological Anthropology." In *Psychological Anthropology,* edited by Francis L. K. Hsu, 267–308. Cambridge, Mass.: Schenkman.

Spence, Jonathan D. 1990. *The Search for Modern China.* New York: Norton.

Spivak, Gayatri Chakravorty. 1990. *The Post-Colonial Critic: Interviews, Strategies, Dialogues.* Edited by Sarah Harasym. New York: Routledge.

Stalin, Joseph. 1975 [1934]. *Marxism and the National-Colonial Question.* San Francisco: Proletarian.

Stocking, George W., Jr. 1982. "The Dark-Skinned Savage: The Image of Primitive Man in Evolutionary Anthropology." In *Race, Culture, and Evolution: Essays in the History of Anthropology,* 110–32. Chicago: University of Chicago Press.

—— 1983. "The Ethnographer's Magic: Fieldwork in British Anthropology from Tylor to Malinowski." In *Observers Observed: Essays on Ethnographic Fieldwork,* edited by George M. Stocking, Jr., 70–120. Madison: University of Wisconsin Press.

Strauss, Claudia, and Naomi Quinn. 1997. *A Cognitive Theory of Cultural Meaning.* Cambridge: Cambridge University Press.

Sutton, Donald S. 1995. "Consuming Counterrevolution: The Ritual and Culture of Cannibalism in Wuxuan, Guangxi, China, May to July 1968." *Comparative Studies in Society and History* 37 (1) (January 1995): 136–72.

Swain, Margaret Byrne. 1991. "Being Ashima: Living a Legend of Resistance." Paper presented at the annual meeting of the American Anthropological Association, Chicago, Illinois.

——. 1995. "Père Vial and the Gni-P'a: Orientalist Scholarship and the Christian Project." In *Cultural Encounters on China's Ethnic Frontiers,* edited by Stevan Harrell, 140–85. Seattle: University of Washington Press.

Tannen, Deborah. 1981. "New York Jewish Conversational Style." *International Journal of the Sociology of Language* 30: 133–49.

Taussig, Michael. 1980. *The Devil and Commodity Fetishism in South America.* Chapel Hill: University of North Carolina Press.

Taylor, Charles. 1989. *Sources of the Self: The Making of the Modern Identity.* Cambridge: Harvard University Press.

Terray, Emmanuel. 1972 [1968]. *Marxism and "Primitive" Societies.* Translated by Mary Klopper. New York: Monthly Review Press.

Thompson, Stuart E. 1988. "Death, Food, and Fertility." In *Death Ritual in Late Imperial and Modern China,* edited by James L. Watson and Evelyn S. Rawski, 71–108. Berkeley and Los Angeles: University of California Press.

Thongchai Winichakul. 1994. *Siam Mapped: A History of the Geo-Body of a Nation.* Honolulu: University of Hawaii Press.

Thrasher, Alan R. 1990. *La-Li-Luo Dance-Songs of the Chuxiong Yi, Yunnan Province, China.* Danbury, Conn.: World Music Press.

Thurston, Ann F., and Burton Pasternak, eds. 1983. *The Social Sciences and Fieldwork in China: Views from the Field.* AAAS Selected Symposium 86. Boulder, Colo.: Westview Press.

Tian Jizhou and Luo Zhiji. 1985. *Wazu (Minzu zhishi congshu)* (The Wa [Nationalities Information Series]). Beijing: Minzu chubanshe.

Tian Zhuangzhuang, director. 1993. *The Blue Kite* (film).

Time Magazine. 1988. "Lost Tribes, Lost Knowledge," by Eugene Linden. September 12, vol. 139, no. 12.

Todorov, Tzvetan. 1984 [1982]. *The Conquest of America: The Question of the Other.* Translated by Richard Howard. New York: Harper & Row.

Tofani, Loretta. 1996. "Ruili." *Philadelphia Inquirer,* May 6–10, A1.

Tomlinson, John. 1991. *Cultural Imperialism: A Critical Introduction.* Baltimore: Johns Hopkins University Press.

Tong Enzheng. 1983. "Shi tan gudai Sichuan yu Dongnanya wenming de guanxi." (Tentative inquiry into the ancient relations between Sichuan and Southeast Asian civilization.) *Wenwu* 9: 73–81.

Torgovnick, Marianna. 1990. *Gone Primitive: Savage Intellects, Modern Lives.* Chicago: University of Chicago Press.

Triandis, H. C., and J. W. Berry, eds. 1980. *Handbook of Cross-Cultural Psychology.* Boston: Allyn and Bacon.

Urla, Jacqueline. 1993. "Cultural Politics in an Age of Statistics: Numbers, Nations, and the Making of Basque Identity." *American Ethnologist* 20 (4): 818–43.

———. 1996. "Basque Hip-Hop?: Language, Popular Music, and Cultural Identity." Paper presented at the Ethnohistory Workshop, University of Pennsylvania, March 28, 1996.

van Dijk, Teun A. 1987. *Communicating Racism: Ethnic Prejudice in Thought and Talk.* Newbury Park, Calif.: Sage.

van Gulik, Robert Hans. 1974. *Sexual Life in Ancient China: A Preliminary Survey of Chinese Sex and Society from ca. 1500 B.C. till 1644 A.D.* Leiden: Brill.

van Ness, Peter. 1984. "The Mosher Affair." *The Wilson Quarterly* 8 (1): 160–72.

Vygotsky, Lev Semanovich. 1962 [1934]. *Thought and Language.* Translated by Eugenia Haufmann and Gertrude Vakar. Cambridge: MIT Press.

Vogel, Ezra F. 1989. *One Step Ahead in China: Guangdong under Reform.* Cambridge: Harvard University Press.

Wales, Nym [Helen Foster Snow]. 1939. *Inside Red China.* New York: Doubleday, Doran & Company.

Waley-Cohen, Joanna. 1991. *Exile in Mid-Qing China: Banishment to Xinjiang, 1758–1820.* New Haven: Yale University Press.

Walker, John. 1983. *Portraits: 5,000 Years.* New York: Abrams.

Ward, Barbara E. 1965. "Varieties of the Conscious Model: The Fishing People of South China." In *The Relevance of Models for Social Anthropology,* edited by Michael Banton, 113–37. London: Tavistock.

Watson, Rubie S. 1994. "Memory, History, and Opposition under State Socialism: An Introduction." In *Memory, History, and Opposition under State Socialism,* edited by Rubie S. Watson, 1–20. Santa Fe: School of American Research Press.

Wazu Jianshi Editorial Group. 1986. *Wazu Jianshi* (A brief history of the Wa). Kunming: Yunnan jiaoyu chubanshe.

Werner, E. T. C. 1982 [1922]. *Myths and Legends of China.* Reprint, Taibei: Dunhuang shuju.

Wetherell, Margaret, and Jonathan Potter. 1992. *Mapping the Language of Racism: Discourse and the Legitimation of Exploitation.* New York: Columbia University Press.

White, Sydney Davant. 1993. "Medical Discourses, Naxi Identities, and the State: Transformations in Socialist China." Ph.D. diss., University of California, Berkeley and San Francisco.

Whorf, Benjamin Lee. 1956. "The Relation of Habitual Thought and Behavior to Language." In *Language, Thought,and Reality: Selected Writings of Benjamin Lee Whorf,* edited by John B. Carroll, 134–59. Cambridge: MIT Press.

Wiens, Herold J. 1954. *China's March toward the Tropics.* Hamden, Conn.: Shoe String Press.

Williams, Dee Mack. 1996. "The Barbed Walls of China: A Contemporary Grassland Drama." *Journal of Asian Studies* 55 (3) (August 1996): 665–91.

Wolcott, Harry F. 1995. *The Art of Fieldwork.* Walnut Creek, Calif.: Alta Mira Press.

Wolf, Margery. 1985. *Revolution Postponed: Women in Contemporary China.* Stanford, Calif.: Stanford University Press.

Wood, Frances. 1996. *Did Marco Polo Go to China?* Boulder, Colo.: Westview Press.

Woolard, Kathryn A. 1983. "The Politics of Language and Ethnicity in Barcelona, Spain." Ph.D. diss., University of California, Berkeley.

———. 1989. *Double Talk: Bilingualism and the Politics of Ethnicity in Catalonia.* Stanford, Calif.: Stanford University Press.

Wu, David Y[en]-h[o]. 1990. "Chinese Minority Policy and the Meaning of Minority Culture: The Example of Bai in Yunnan, China." *Human Organization* 49 (1): 1–13.

———. 1991. "The Construction of Chinese and Non-Chinese Identities." *Daedalus* 120 (2) (Spring): 159–79.

Xu Ye, Wang Qinghua, and Duan Dingzhou. 1987. *Nanfang Lushang Sichou Lu* (The southern silk route). Kunming: Yunnan minzu chubanshe.

Yan Ruxian. N.d. "A Living Fossil of the Family—A Study of the Family Structure of the Naxi Nationality in the Lugu Lake Region." *Social Sciences in China,* translated by Xing Wenjun, 60–83.

Yang Guocai and Gong Youde, eds. 1990. *Shaoshuminzu Shenghuo Fangshi* (Lifestyles of the ethnic minorities). Lanzhou: Gansu kexue jishu chubanshe.

Yang Jingchu. 1989. "Han Minzu Xingcheng wei Shijie Diyida Minzu Qianxi" (How the Han became the world's greatest [most numerous] nationality). In *Han Minzu Yanjiu* (Research on the Han), edited by Yuan Shaofen and Xu Jiewu, 148–61. Nanning: Guangxi renmin chubanshe.

Yang, Mayfair Mei-hui. 1986. "The Art of Social Relationships and Exchange in China." Ph.D. diss., University of California, Berkeley.

———. 1994. *Gifts, Favors, and Banquets: The Art of Social Relationships in China.* Ithaca: Cornell University Press.

Yang Yucai, ed. 1989. *Yunnan Geminzu Jingji Fazhanshi* (A history of the economic development of Yunnan's ethnic groups). Kunming: Yunnan minzu chubanshe.

Yang Zhaojun, ed. 1989. *Yunnan Huizu Shi* (A history of Yunnan's Hui nationality). Kunming: Yunnan minzu chubanshe.

Yu Jiahua et al., eds. 1986. *Yunnan Fengwu Zhi* (Introduction to the sights of Yunnan). Kunming: Yunnan renmin chubanshe.

Yuan Shaofen and Xu Jiewu, eds. 1989. *Han Minzu Yanjiu* (On the Han nationality). Nanning: Guangxi renmin chubanshe.

Yue, Gang. 1999. *The Mouth That Begs: Hunger, Cannibalism, and the Politics of Eating in Modern China*. Durham, N.C.: Duke University Press.

Zentella, Ana Celia. 1997. *Growing Up Bilingual*. Malden, Mass.: Blackwell.

Zhan Chengxu. N.d. "Matriarchal/Patriarchal Families of the Naxi Nationality in Yongning, Yunnan Province." *Social Sciences in China*, translated by Xing Wenjun, 140–55.

Zhang Yimou, director. 1988. *Red Sorghum* (film).

Zheng Lan. 1981. *Travels through Xishuangbanna: China's Subtropical Home of Many Nationalities*. Beijing: Foreign Languages Press.

Zhong Xiu. 1983. *Yunnan Travelogue: 100 Days in Southwest China*. Translated by the staff of *Women in China*. Beijing: New World Press.

INDEX

ABOUT THE AUTHOR

Susan Blum is a cultural and linguistic anthropologist whose research in southwest China (Kunming) has focused on questions of identity, selfhood and personhood, naming practices, language as social action, and ethnicity and nationalism. In addition to her articles, she is the author of a co-edited book (with Lionel M. Jensen), *China Off Center: Readings on the Margins of the Middle Kingdom,* and is currently finishing *Deception and Truth in China.* Currently associate professor of anthropology at the University of Notre Dame, she has also taught at the University of Colorado at Denver, the University of Pennsylvania, the University of Denver, and Oklahoma State University.

DEMCO